A VIEWER'S GUIDE TO FILM THEORY AND CRITICISM

by

ROBERT T. EBERWEIN

The Scarecrow Press, Inc.
Metuchen, N.J., & London
1979

Library of Congress Cataloging in Publication Data

Eberwein, Robert T   1940-
    A viewer's guide to film theory and criticism.

    Bibliography: p.
    Includes index.
    1. Moving-pictures--Philosophy. 2. Moving-picture
plays--History and criticism. I. Title.
PN1995.E33   791.43'01'5   79-9380
ISBN 0-8108-1237-1

*PN
1995
.E33*

For my mother and in memory of my father,
who made film part of my life

ACKNOWLEDGMENTS

Publishers and individuals who gave permission to quote from their works are acknowledged within the text. I would also like to thank Oakland University for granting a sabbatical leave, 1975-76, which provided needed time for writing. Reuben Torch, Dean of the College of Arts and Sciences, and Joseph DeMent, Chairman of the Department of English, have been most supportive of my activities in connection with *Viewer's Guide*.

Two other persons deserve special credit. Marian Wilson aided immensely by typing, preparing and supervising the progress of the manuscript. I am grateful for her wisdom, discipline and understanding. My wife, Jane Donahue Eberwein, consistently encouraged the "cut stems struggling to put down feet," while she herself was writing a book and bringing order and calm to our home.

CONTENTS

INTRODUCTION

This book is designed for all moviegoers—general viewers and students of cinema—who would like to understand what the major film theorists and critics have said about film. My aim is to explain the views of the leading writers on film, point out relevant connections between them, and, most important, indicate their usefulness for today's audiences.

I have organized *A Viewer's Guide to Film Theory and Criticism* in two sections. The first, called "Pioneers," examines in detail the work of nine men acknowledged as the seminal theorists of modern film criticism: Vachel Lindsay, Hugo Münsterberg, Lev Kuleshov, V. I. Pudovkin, S. M. Eisenstein, Béla Balázs, Rudolf Arnheim, André Bazin and Siegfried Kracauer. Some are film makers themselves, some teachers, some psychologists. But they are all men of film whose insights, no matter how primitive, provide basic articulations of the major issues in film theory.

The second section, "Criticism Today," discusses the development and refinement of issues introduced by these pioneers and devotes specific attention to matters of current critical interest. I have divided this section into the following parts: examination of major voices in the American journalistic tradition, with consideration of the earlier writers James Agee and Robert Warshow, and emphasis on the contemporary critics Pauline Kael, Stanley Kauffmann and Andrew Sarris; commentary on the feminist criticism of Molly Haskell, Joan Mellen and Marjorie Rosen; and explanation of structuralism and semiotics, with extensive analysis of Noël Burch, Christian Metz and Peter Wollen.

I have limited the discussion to writers readily available in English, and thus omit analysis of such works as Jean Mitry's *Esthétique et psychologie du cinéma*. Besides restricting the *Guide* in this manner, I have also excluded excellent studies of particular genres, such as Gerald Mast's *The Comic Mind;* examinations of film's relations to other genres, such as George Bluestone's *Novels into Film;* historical works such as Lewis Jacobs' *The Rise of the American Film;* and various introductions to film appreciation. The bibliography at the end of the *Guide* directs readers to criticism which I do not discuss directly. The twenty writers considered here have been chosen on the basis of their importance and influence in relation to the entire critical spectrum. My hope is that readers will conclude these explications with a sense of what each critic thinks; what kind of method each employs; and what each offers a contemporary viewer by way of practical application of theory.

André Bazin, the great French film theorist, observes that "five years in cinema is the equivalent of an entire literary generation." Thus the eighty or so years in cinema's history would be equivalent to approximately twenty-four hundred years of literary history. To a significant extent, Bazin's insight applies equally to film theory and criticism insofar as we are constantly confronted with issues which have intrigued and challenged literary criticism from the time of ancient Greece to the present: defining the status of the work of art in relation to reality; determining the role of the artist in its creation; attempting to describe it; considering the effect of it on the audience.

The earliest major critics, Plato and Aristotle, disagree on the ontological location of the work of art. Plato argues that it is simply a copy of an existing model in nature, which itself is only a copy of divine forms or ideas in the mind of God; as such, it is inferior and can never give us a true approximation of the ultimate reality. In addition, the work of art appeals to our emotions rather than to our rational faculty, thus preventing us from employing reason in our attempt to contemplate reality. In contrast, Aristotle holds that the work of art, by organizing the chaotic material around us into an organic whole, improves on reality, and leads us to a more complete perception of existence. The particulars in a given work become the means for guiding the audience to the universals embodied in them.

In its turn, film has been the subject of a corresponding kind of debate. Critics have defended film against charges that it is an inferior form of copying reality, and have argued that it offers us much more than simply moving photographs. Even among its champions, there exists disagreement about film as an art in relation to reality; should it be strictly a visual medium, or should it embrace all the means which might make it more realistic, and employ sound, color, and three-dimensional effects? Again, where does the "art" lie in this mechanical reproduction of images and sounds, and what is the nature of the artistic contribution to the creation of a film? Some critics argue that there is only one true superintending force: the director who oversees the structuring of reality through his selection and organization of the strips of film. Granting that actors, technicians and writers contribute in some ways, these critics hold that the film be viewed as a piece of literature created or "written" by the director alone; thus we can investigate and identify his artistic personality and techniques in much the same way that some literary critics focus attention on the character of the artist. Even here, when critics agree that the director has the chief role in creation of the film, we encounter disagreement about the means for ordering the elements of reality. Does the director allow the camera to record external events with a minimum amount of interference, or does the artistic process demand a radical reorganization of that reality by staging the scene with an eye toward graphic design, by shifting the camera's angle of vision, and by assembling the strips of film into a form which goes beyond any normal perception of reality?

In addition to the issues of the status of the film in relation to reality and the nature of the creative process, we will also want to consider the problem of describing the work. We will find critics adopting methods of literary analysis to explain the structure of films, and, following the model of romantic literary theory, considering the organic unity and internal logic of films. The newest developments in literary criticism, the study of signs and deep structures, and the examination of literary language all have their counterparts in film theory. Critics have passed from early attempts to equate the cinematic "shot" with the literary "word," to complex models in which they search for the equivalents of language systems in film. Similarly, some modern critics have employed extremely sophisticated cross-disciplinary methods of structural analysis incorporating anthropological and linguistic aspects in an attempt to isolate the inherent principles of structure in given films and genres. Finally, the interest of literary criticism in the effect of art on the mind and emotion of the audience can be seen to figure prominently in film theory, particularly as critics discuss the different aesthetic experiences offered by the various arts.

PART I

PIONEERS

VACHEL LINDSAY*

Vachel Lindsay (1879–1931), the popular American poet, probably best known for "General William Booth Enters into Heaven," is also notable for his early discussion of film, *The Art of the Moving Picture* (1915). In this work, remarkable for its range of interests and for its curious blend of bizarre recommendations and significant insights, Lindsay, admittedly working as a beginning aesthetician, maps out several areas for analysis that remain of vital interest to us today. He divides films into various categories on the basis of their inner structural logic, thus anticipating in a very primitive form certain aspects of structural analysis; he proposes a theory of what he calls hieroglyphics, adumbrating modern semiological studies; and he enunciates, many years in advance of André Bazin, a rudimentary theory of the film director as an author.

Types of Photoplays

For Lindsay, the "photoplay" or narrative work of film is included in the total concept "motion picture." Although he mentions some possibilities for the non-photoplay, such as documentaries, he devotes most of his work to the narrative film and distinguishes three major divisions, each with its respective inner principle of coherence: gesture, affiliation to genre and correlation with specific plastic art.

The "Photoplay of Action," his first category, is based on the principle of the chase out of doors, whether down the highway, as in some comedies, or across deserts, as in westerns. The type distinguishes itself immediately from anything in the theatre, since such an activity cannot be presented on the stage. In an

---

*All quotations are from *The Art of the Moving Picture* (rev. ed., 1922; rpt. New York: Liveright, 1970). Reprinted by permission.

attempt to explain the particular development of this type in the United States, Lindsay attributes its appeal to the "speed-mania" of Americans (p. 41). Its features, besides the chase, include de-emphasis of characterization, since there is—given the basic situation—little opportunity to develop character. The gestures appropriate to the action photoplay are those of pantomime, i.e., conventionalized motions in line with a lack of any subtlety in drawing characters. Lindsay suggests such photoplays are analogous in form to the drama. But he is more interested in explaining the relation of the type to the plastic art of sculpture and has here some significant things to say. The action film is "sculpture-in-motion" (p. 108), in the sense that the director presents the figures, the "dumb giants" of the photoplay, in "high sculptural relief" (p. 112). The director surveys the scene with the eye of a carver and considers the characters in terms of their rhythmic potential visually. Lindsay specifically points out as helpful models the equestrian statues by Donatello and Verrochio as well as the frieze on the Parthenon, and also comments on the sculptural effects visible in magazine photographs of scenes from current films. His concern for the relation of the parts of the given image in this sense looks forward to more intense study of what the director does with spatial arrangements. A good example of his thinking occurs as he describes a scene depicting confusion in an office. He asks, "Is this . . . sculpture? Yes. The figures are in high relief. Even the surfaces of the chairs and the littered table are massive, and the eye travels without weariness, as it should do in sculpture. . . . The eye makes this journey, not from space to space, or fabric to fabric, but first of all from mass to mass. It is sculpture, but it is the sort that can be done in no medium but the moving picture itself" (pp. 119–120).

The "Intimate Photoplay," his second category, features more concern for mood; the camera purposely limits itself to a smaller area as the subject, unlike that in the action photoplay, is one of character and personality, such as D. W. Griffith's *Enoch Arden*. This category also includes the non-chase comedy as well as drama. Notice the articulation of Lindsay's main point here: that the central activity of the camera will necessarily be suited to and limited by the subject of a particular type of film.

The intimate class corresponds to the lyric form in literature

and also has its appropriate gestures, in this case "more elusive
personal gestures," ones which distinguish characters from each
other, such as "the difference between the table manners of two
preachers in the same restaurant, or two policemen" (p. 107). Instead of the sculptural qualities we encounter in the action
photoplay, intimate photoplays are characterized by low relief
such as we would find in paintings. We now watch for tableaus,
the interrelationship and shifting pattern and motion of planes in
a confined area, rather as in a kaleidoscope. Part of our pleasure
in viewing this "painting-in-motion" comes from the fact that we
"feel a certain thrill when the pieces of kaleidoscope glass slide
into new places," for "they progress in strange curves that are
part of the very shapes into which they fall" (p. 135). As Eisenstein would do shortly in his discussion of *Potemkin*, Lindsay
demonstrates how to "read" the painterly lines of a film in the
sense that he discovers a principle of visual coherence and explains how it dominates the shot. In one case, he points out the
"least common multiple" in visual terms whereby a series of interrelated *narrative* units are connected formally because they all
display the same pattern of movement: a sinuousness linking
waves, the motion of a boat, the bending of a tree, the curling of
smoke and the actions of humans (p. 138).

Given the relationship of the intimate photoplay to the lyric,
it is not surprising that Lindsay points to the significant development of Imagist poetry by such writers as Amy Lowell and Ezra
Pound appearing in Harriet Monroe's *Poetry* magazine. Both Imagist poetry and the intimate photoplay present "*space measured
without sound plus time measured without sound*" (p. 267). In
other words, the silent kaleidoscope of the screen and the mute
poem both give us various shifting relations, temporal and spatial.
Also, as Stanley Kauffmann has observed in his introduction,
Lindsay, like Eisenstein, sees a relationship between the filmed
image and the Japanese style of pictorial print; Imagist or intimate photoplays "would be Japanese prints taking on life, animated Japanese paintings, Pompeian mosaics in the kaleidoscopic
but logical succession, Beardsley drawings made into actors and
scenery, Greek vase-paintings in motion" (p. 268).

Lindsay's third category, the "Splendor Film" is analogous to
the literary epic, and has as its basic structural principle the activ-

ities of crowds of humanity. Four sub-categories exist. The film of Fairy Splendor has as its subject the world of imagination. Works of Crowd Splendor specifically display the sea of humanity. Lindsay observes the same thing noted by both George Bernard Shaw and Eisenstein: John Milton's *Paradise Lost* has tremendous cinematic potential because of its crowd scenes. Patriotic Splendor, the third sub-category, Lindsay views with Whitmanesque fervor as a means for showing the American people its own nature reflected on the screen. The last sub-category, Religious Splendor, contains clear ritualistic patterns of birth, life and death. Significantly, Lindsay praises film in general for its ability to take us, when controlled by poetic prophet wizards, back toward primitive forms of life, and, he hopes, to a democratic impulse. Films of Splendor have large crowd movements and gestures, not the individualized or pantomimed gestures of the first two.

This type relates to the plastic art of architecture and gives us "architecture-in-motion." In films of Fairy Splendor, in which directors utilize the camera's potential for trick photography, we find furniture assuming an active life. Rather like Jean Cocteau's later achievement in *Beauty and the Beast*, furniture has "vital individuality" given to it; similarly, Lindsay asks buildings in this category to "emanate conscious life" on the order of Nathaniel Hawthorne's *House of the Seven Gables* or Edgar Allan Poe's *The Fall of the House of Usher*, and singles out the trappings of *The Cabinet of Dr. Caligari* for praise in this regard (p. 144). In pictures of Crowd, Patriotic and Religious Splendor, the architectural impulse manifests itself in mural paintings; as the wall painting becomes an integral part of the structure containing it, so too will the human element become part of the vast landscape in which it is presented. In this way directors will be able to show the connection between humanity and the world itself by developing relations between visual structures.

Hieroglyphics

Lindsay's discussion of hieroglyphics is of particular relevance, not only because it indicates the extent to which various visual signs and cues were automatically acknowledged in the silent era, but, more importantly, because it is perhaps the first major commentary on the nature of cinematic signs. In a section

anticipating Eisenstein's theory of intellectual montage and Erwin
Panofsky's and Christian Metz's later analysis of signs, Lindsay
discusses Griffith's use of "apt hieroglyphics" in *The Avenging
Conscience*. A troubled youth who is contemplating murder
watches a spider kill a fly, which is in turn killed by ants. Lindsay
approves Griffith's interruption of the direct narrative action to
present images which provide visual equivalents for states of
mind as well as a symbolic commentary on the action.

In a more developed discussion of hieroglyphics, Lindsay
displays his own knowledge of ancient hieroglyphics, while enthusiastically welcoming film as "the new universal alphabet" (p.
203); he refers to film in fact as "Esperanto" (p. 205). Briefly, the
director's use of signs can be compared to the most primitive
form of writing or drawing on stone. Each sign has a commonly
accepted meaning as well as a symbolic potential. The various
signs we encounter in film have two sides to them—an obvious
literal meaning and a suggestive "spiritual" meaning. For example, when seeing a throne, "you know instantly you are dealing
with royalty or its implications"; its spiritual or symbolic extension
might be wisdom or liberty (pp. 201–202). He thinks that an
image of the duck, " a somewhat Z-shaped animal, suggests the
finality of Arcadian peace" (p. 202). Those familiar with Jan
Troell's *The Immigrants* may want to consider this comment in
connection with the conclusion of the film. A bowl can suggest
domestic and homely fare but also wine and godlike imbibing.
The lion "creeps through the photoplay jungle to give the primary picture-word of terror in this new universal alphabet" while
symbolically suggesting persecution or courage (p. 203). And a
lasso immediately conveys the imageword of trouble while the
"other side of the symbol" takes us to the meaning of "solemn
judgment and the hangman . . . the snare of the fowler, tempta-
tion" (p. 208). Whether or not we accept his examples, it is important to see that he recognizes images as picture-words, having
a double thrust of meaning. He cautions directors against the
overuse of signs such as these which have clear symbolic potential, but also sees audiences of the future becoming more and
more adept in the analysis of film as they acquire greater sophis-
tication in their ability to recognize them.

The issue of hieroglyphics figures in Lindsay's concept of film
criticism. Kauffmann notes how Lindsay anticipates the theory of

the director as an author in his description of the film as "not a
factory-made staple article, but the creative force of one soul, the
flowering of a spirit that has the habit of perpetually renewing
itself" (p. 195). But there is more to be said. Precisely because
the individual director's presence will be felt in the hieroglyphics
he chooses to offer on the screen, critics will have the ability to
distinguish directors from each other: "Let us hope that our new
picture-alphabets can take on richness and significance. . . . They
may develop into something more all-pervading, yet more highly
wrought, than any written speech. Languages when they evolve
produce stylists, and we will some day distinguish the different
photoplay masters as we now delight in the separate tang of O.
Henry and Mark Twain and Howells" (p. 211). Obviously that day
has come, for *auteur* critics discuss various directors' favorite
image complexes and isolate certain repeated techniques which
characterize the individual styles. Lindsay, whose prophetic voice
thrilled Americans decades ago, stands here equally as a prophet
of one path that would be taken by film criticism: "When these
are ancient times, we will have scholars and critics learned in the
flavors of early moving picture traditions with their histories of
movements and schools, their grammars, and anthologies" (p.
211).

Lindsay makes some other suggestions which seem less useful, it should be noted. In our own age, when television has
spawned a generation of annoying viewers who talk about the film
they are watching in the theatre in the same way they chatter on
in their living rooms, we tend to react negatively to Lindsay's idea
that there be no orchestral accompaniment for the silent film,
only "the hum of the conversing audience" (p. 217). Were pictures to develop sound techniques, it would be a different form,
the phonoplay. But as things stand now, the "buzzing commentary of the audience" seems to him like the murmur of "a pleas-
ant brook" (p. 224).

It is also difficult not to smile as Lindsay, himself a member
of the Anti-Saloon League, praises film for having edged out the
saloon in popularity and for drawing the family back together.
Still, there is a poignant quality in his observation that the only
art available to the ordinary saloon crowd consists of cheesecake
and of boxers and goats advertising beer. Since "man's dreams are

rearranged and glorified memories," how can people like this in the saloon "reconstruct the torn carpets and tin cans and waste-paper of their lives into mythology" (p. 237)? He believes that film will provide these unfortunates with a mythology which will remove them from this habitual squalor. This hope is very much in keeping with the prophetic tone with which he ends his work, as he calls on the poets of cinema, as opposed to the scientists like Thomas Alva Edison, to reveal the America of the future.

HUGO MÜNSTERBERG*

Of all the theorists and critics examined in the *Guide*, surely Hugo Münsterberg (1863–1916), a German psychologist and professor at Harvard, has been the most neglected, at least until the present time. In an introduction to Münsterberg's *The Film: A Psychological Study* (originally titled, *The Photoplay: A Psychological Study*, 1916), Richard Griffith explains the probable reasons for this unfortunate occurrence and also provides a useful commentary on his academic background and significance. For our purposes, Münsterberg deserves attention for his seminal contributions to film aesthetics, particularly in regard to the viewer's imaginative contribution while perceiving a film. Also noteworthy are his discussions of the differences between stage and screen, and of the nature of filmic art in relation to reality.

Creative Viewing

Essentially Münsterberg holds that the viewer of a film is creative not only insofar as the theory of the persistence of vision obtains, but also, and more important, as the viewer truly completes in his response the vision on the screen. A commonly accepted explanation of our ability to experience movement in films is that the retina of the eye retains the image flashed on the screen during the one twenty-fourth of a second period of darkness which occurs between projected frames. Consequently the succeeding projected frame is connected to an afterimage of the preceding frame, thus giving the viewer an illusion of movement within the image. Münsterberg considers this phenomenon as only one part of the reason for our sense of movement. In addi-

---

*All quotations are from *The Film: A Psychological Study* (1916; rpt. New York: Dover, 1970). Reprinted by permission.

tion to this *passive* process, he argues that the mind takes a much more *active* part in the viewing experience. He cites as examples ways in which the mind, having been excited by a stimulus, will then itself project this effect on an object. Thus, one seeing a white spiral with black lines rotated in a clockwise or coun- terclockwise direction will, when turning away to perceive a face, impose on the new object of visual attention the pattern of mo- tion absorbed in viewing the spiral. Consequently, the face viewed after looking at the spiral would appear to be smaller or larger, depending on the direction of the spiral. Münsterberg also cites the experiences in viewing moving lights and encountering word substitutions to support his argument that "the apparent movement is in no way the mere result of an afterimage," and "surely more than the mere perception of successive phases of movement." He concludes that movement "is superadded, by the action of the mind, to the motionless pictures" (p. 29).

This is a crucial point in his thesis, clearly based on Gestalt psychological theory which holds that the mind tends, in percep- tion, to complete the configuration of the various elements in a given form or structure. With this tenet about creative perception established, Münsterberg proceeds to consider the perception of movement in more detail, as well as the viewer's consciousness of depth. In both cases we are involved in a paradox somewhat akin to what the English literary critic Samuel Taylor Coleridge calls "the willing suspension of disbelief." We *know* that we watch a succession of individual frames projected at intervals on a screen. Nonetheless, we invest these individual images with depth and movement in the process of perceiving them.

The key to this paradox lies in the difference between our rational knowledge of the process and our impressions, both of what we see and what we in turn create. Münsterberg refers to the complex mental state induced by the viewing process where "*we certainly see the depth, and yet we cannot accept it*" because we know that our minds have created the motion (p. 24). The nature of the perceptual experience itself creates a situation whereby the depth and movement possess supercharged qualities—in effect, something akin to a symbolic realm beyond the mundane: "*Depth and movement alike come to us in the mov-*

ing picture world, not as hard facts but as a mixture of fact and symbol. They are present and yet they are not in the things. We invest the impressions with them" (p. 30).

The Camera and the Mind

For Münsterberg, the active primacy of the mind in perception thus stands as the condition of our experience in viewing film. The camera itself responds to the needs of the mind and acts as the imagination to realize the world of phenomena. For example, obviously the close-up as a filmic device exists to focus the viewer's attention on a significant detail. In the real world, when we devote our attention to a particular object or feature of an object, we tend to exclude or disregard other things around it, or, as he says, "The chaos of the surrounding impressions is organized into a real cosmos of experience by our selection of that which is significant and of consequence" (p. 31). Similarly, the close-up provides the same organizing function along the lines of the mind's activity. While watching a tense situation on the screen when a gun becomes important and is presented in a close-up: "The act of attention which goes on in our mind has remodeled the surrounding itself. The detail which is being watched has suddenly become the whole content of the performance, and everything which our mind wants to disregard has been suddenly banished from our sight and has disappeared. The events without have become obedient to our consciousness. . . . *The close-up has objectified in our world of perception our mental act of attention"* (pp. 37–38).

In addition to the close-up, filmic art also presents flashbacks or flashforwards as well as equivalents of feelings, all of which indicate the triumph of our perception and the objectification of our attention. Thus a shot of a missionary in the wilds intercut with his memory of home could not be presented in the theatre. But since this image could occur to us, if we had remembered this earlier image from the beginning of the narrative, the camera, by providing this memory image, objectifies our mental acts of attention: *"It is as if reality has lost its own continuous connection and become shaped by the demands of our soul"* (p. 41). In other words, by providing us with specific images which fulfill our perceptual needs, insofar as these complete the viewing experience, film "can act as our imagination acts" (p. 41). Also, the ability of film to range between the past, present and future itself meets a need of the soul, for we naturally wish to consider any event causationally in its total context. A film director can even duplicate our imagined sense of erratic or irregular movements, as in scenes reproducing the subjective impressions of trembling or whirling effected by editing and moving the camera. In short, filmic art adjusts the phenomena of the outside world to our perception of that world in such a way that our perceptual and imaginative impulses are objectified in the forms of depth, movement, close-up, flashbacks, etc.

Film and the Stage

To distinguish the means of filmic art from that of others, Münsterberg presents various arguments pointing out the differences between film and the stage, while establishing the nature of filmic and artistic reality in general. He does not elevate film at the expense of the stage; instead he sees them as two different but equally valid forms of art. They differ insofar as film can use actual settings, change backgrounds rapidly, present actions simultaneously, alter normal movements through slow and fast motion and employ special effects. In addition, he points to the physical nature of the viewing situation in the auditorium and the acting styles. Although both film and the stage show us imitations of real life, the stage is more realistic, since we *really* perceive motion, depth, color, sound and human beings—all merely illusions on the screen. It is the fact that film's illusions are so pronounced that stimulates Münsterberg to emphasize not only that the film *cannot* duplicate the realistic elements on the stage, but that it *should not* try to provide the same imitation of reality.

In a discussion which takes us back to the disagreement between Plato and Aristotle on the nature of the reality captured by the artist, Münsterberg argues that we value art not as it gives us a detailed reproduction of reality, but rather as it goes beyond our mundane world to generate a world of its own, the self-contained aesthetic object. Art thrives on isolating elements from the chaos of experience. We do not want reality, but instead want something better than reality in the aesthetic object. It *"becomes art just in so far as it overcomes reality, stops imitating and leaves the imitated reality behind it"*; it "changes the world, selects from it special features for new purposes. . . . To imitate the world is a mechanical process; to transform the world so that it becomes a thing of beauty is the purpose of art. The highest art may be furthest removed from reality" (p. 62). Thus, precisely *because* film lacks the inevitably realistic aspects of the stage, it is by definition in a position to approach the highest reaches of art, unhampered by those features which pull us back to reality.

Film and Reality

The film artist must work as all artists do; unlike the scholar and scientist who try to provide connections between their objects of interest and the world, artists isolate the work of art and give to it a system of internal harmony and coherence, making it complete in itself. Münsterberg relies heavily on the aesthetics of Immanuel Kant as he conceives of the work of art presenting *"things and events perfectly complete in themselves, freed from all connections which lead beyond their own limits, . . . in perfect isolation"* (p. 64).

To effect this perfect isolation, the film artist, as much as the poet, painter or sculptor, draws attention to his craft and artifice, thus drawing the work away from the merely practical everyday world. We will want to remember this assertion by Münsterberg when discussing the aesthetics of Noël Burch later, for both acknowledge the importance of identifying the presence of the transforming agent, the camera. Münsterberg notes that poems have meter, unlike speech; statues present whiteness that is unlike that of humans; paintings announce their lack of reality with frames, and so on. Specifically, the means unique to the film maker are those devices which give him mastery over the world through the ability of the camera to alter reality: *"the photoplay tells us the human story by overcoming the forms of the outer world, namely space, time, and causality, and by adjusting the events to the forms of the inner world, namely attention, memory, imagination, and emotion"* (p. 74). The camera tells a story in a unique way, because only in the filmic experience does the human mind work by penetrating and completing a world perceived and recognized as unreal although felt as real. The aim, then, of narrative film is to isolate experience and transform it into art by giving to it an inner unity: "*The photoplay shows us a significant conflict of human actions in moving pictures which, freed from the physical forms of space, time, and causality, are adjusted to the free play of our mental experiences and which reach complete isolation from the practical world through the perfect unity of plot and pictorial appearance*" (p. 82).

As for the pleasure offered to us by film, Münsterberg, again arguing along Kantian lines, attributes this to the uniqueness of the medium. The mind "*has triumphed over matter*"; the world now "*has been clothed in the forms of our own consciousness. . . . It is a superb enjoyment which no other art can furnish us*" (p. 95).

Like Lindsay, whom he quotes approvingly on the sculptural sense conveyed in film, Münsterberg attaches great importance to the director. The scenario for a given film can only be realized as a work of art through the efforts of the director who "must show himself a creative artist, inasmuch as he is the one who actually transforms the plays into pictures. . . . In the photoplay the whole emphasis lies on the picture and its composition is left entirely to the producing artist" (p. 83).

Like Arnheim, Münsterberg does not welcome sound to the film, since it would, he argues, destroy its visual purity. As might be expected from his acceptance of film as a means of escaping the realistic aspects of the stage, Münsterberg is also unenthusiastic about the addition of color, since this too brings us back to the world of reality.

THE RUSSIAN CONTRIBUTION

We turn now to three famous Russian critics and film makers in order to understand the most important concept in the creation of film: montage, the editing process whereby the pieces of film taken by the camera are assembled to produce the work of art. Lev Kuleshov, V. I. Pudovkin, and, towering above them, S. M. Eisenstein contribute in both theory and practice to the establishment, codification and dominance of the montage method for some years in their own cinema. All are worth studying for other theoretical aspects, as I shall indicate; but it is their seminal thinking about the shot as the basis of film language composed of words and sentences, and the effects created by juxtaposing shots, that remains most significant. It will become apparent that the three contemporaries and acquaintances by no means agree completely with each other; for example, we can detect diverse opinions on acting, and, more important, different underlying rationales for montage thinking. Their personal involvements have been treated elsewhere, especially in Yon Barna's biography, *Eisenstein*, and in Jay Leyda's definitive history of Soviet film, *Kino*. But it is helpful to conceive of all three as having a substantial degree of interaction: Kuleshov as instructor of both Pudovkin and Eisenstein; Pudovkin as actor in some of Eisenstein's films, and as designer for Kuleshov; in short, each is in a position to know the opinions of the others on the nature and practice of film.

LEV KULESHOV*

Many of the theories of Lev Kuleshov (1899–1970) are now available to those interested in film criticism, thanks to the recent translation of some of the writings by Ronald Levaco who has collected various works spanning the years from 1922 to 1968. Of particular significance are Kuleshov's discussions of montage and the dynamics of screen space; I also want to comment on his view of screen acting and some of his practical criticism.

Montage

Like Pudovkin and Eisenstein, Kuleshov responds to the films of D. W. Griffith enthusiastically, for in them he discovers a method of filming and composing which is qualitatively different from the Russian practice. Instead of long takes from a single fixed position, Griffith employs many more short takes, assembling these in such a way as to create greater tension and to generate more excitement in his audience. We are all familiar with the famous last-minute rescues which rely on constant but rhythmical cutting back and forth from the potential disaster, such as the execution of the innocent husband in *Intolerance*, to that force which can prevent it, the wife's attempt to reach the governor in time. Kuleshov remarks in several places on the different reactions he noticed in Russian audiences to this "American" method, so dependent on intercutting, as opposed to the Russian method of film making. Like Lindsay, who attributes the cause of the action photoplay to the American mania for speed, Kuleshov suggests that something in the make-up of the American character

*All quotations are from *Kuleshov on Film*, trans. and ed. Ronald Levaco (Berkeley: University of California Press, 1974). Quoted by permission of the University of California Press.

explains American film practice, specifically the demand of
Americans for the "maximum impressions"; "the American demands a full show for his dollar" (p. 46). The very tempo of life in
the United States could explain the fast-paced rhythm in the pictures produced there. Later Kuleshov criticizes the American
method for its pernicious and bourgeois impact on Russian film
making, for its negative influence on the spirit of the proletariat,
and for its debilitating effect on his own work. But in "Amer-
icanitis" and *Art of the Cinema* he demonstrates clearly what he
and other film makers learned: "We became convinced that the
fundamental source of the film's impact on the viewer... was not
simply to show the content of certain shots, but the organization
of those shots among themselves... the interrelationship of shots,
the replacement of one shot by another" (p. 46).

Kuleshov sees the relationship of shots in the American
cinema determined in the following way. Since movement seems
extremely important to the directors, they appear to solve "the
complexity of the scenes by shooting only that element of movement without which at any given moment a necessary vital action
could not occur" (p. 128). In other words, the only justification
for a particular shot is that it presents a particular movement.
Kuleshov refers to this as "the first postulate derived from American films... the concretion of a necessary movement into a separate shot and the assemblage into one scene of these concretely
expressed pieces" (pp. 129–130). Related to this is his suggestion
that Americans film each scene with an eye to its connection with
the larger structure: "They divided each separate scene into
montage sequences, into a series of shots that made up each sequence; in addition, they shot each separate movement in such a
way that only its action was visible, only that which was categori-
cally essential" (p. 49). As early as 1916, Kuleshov announces his
interest in following "the American method of shooting, that is,
employing scenes in which every given sequence shows what is
essential for the viewer to perceive, and shoots them in the
closest and clearest shots possible" (p. 50).

The effect of adopting the American method on Kuleshov is
vitally important, for with the notion of the shot as an entity or
kernel of meaning which contains its particular action and movement, Kuleshov proceeds to posit a theory of montage, or, in his

words, "the joining of shots into a predetermined order from
which a film is made" (p. 47). In the organization of the filmic
material lies meaning. In fact, not until shots have been related
through montage does the desired effect of creating meaning become possible. The creator of the film makes statements out of
his material, rather as a poet makes verses. Kuleshov pursues the
literary analogy between shot and word more completely than any
critics previously; Lindsay, for example, identifies his hieroglyphics as "picture-words," but leaves the issue at that. The effects of the word-shot analogy are still with us today as critics like
Christian Metz adapt linguistic methods of analysis to film.
Somewhat reminiscent of Lindsay, Kuleshov conceives of the
self-contained nature of the individual shot in terms of oriental
writing. The shot is like a particularly complex letter in the director's alphabet, a letter which, like a Chinese ideogram, stands as
a word: "The shot should act as a sign, as a letter of the alphabet,
so that you can instantly read it, and so that for the viewer what
is expressed in the given shot will be utterly clear"; "each separate shot must act as each letter in a word—but a complex type of
letter, say, a Chinese ideogram. The shot is a complete conception, and it must be read instantly" (pp. 62–63).

Kuleshov also discusses the shot as a sign or unit of meaning
in its manner of presentation as well as in its content. It is not
merely a picture because the form is part of the content: "The
film shot is not a still photograph. The shot is a sign, a letter for
montage." Consequently, the angle with which a shot is taken
will contribute to the meaning of the sign: "Any change from a
normal point of view ought to be used by the director with an
awareness of the work of the shot as a *sign*. A proud person may
be shot from a low angle—the foreshortening will stress, will help
to highlight the emphasis on pride. An oppressed or dispirited
person may be shot from a high angle—the dispiritedness will be
emphasized by the point of view of the camera" (p. 80).

Thus the individual shot and the form which it takes when
photographed combine to form a sign or complex letter. In montage, the director assembles these signs into larger structures of
meaning. Kuleshov conceives of the director presenting ideas
with two analogies. The first, rejected by Eisenstein, pictures the
director working like a bricklayer: "If one has an idea-phrase, a

fragment of the story, a link in the entire dramatic chain, then this idea is expressed, laid out in shot-signs, like bricks" (p. 91). The second analogy, clearly visible in Pudovkin's writings, combines the verbal element with the bricks: "A poet places one word after another, in a definite rhythm, as one brick after another. Cemented by him, the word-images produce a complex conception as a result. So it is that shots, like conventionalized meanings, like the ideograms in Chinese writings, produce images and concepts. The *montage* of shots is the construction of whole phrases. Content is derived from shots" (p. 91).

Kuleshov's discussions of various experiments with the montage process are worth noting. He does not acknowledge or develop clearly a point that seems apparent to us today—namely that the experiments themselves, by proving the essential neutrality of the shot, tend to weaken his assertions about the shot as a self-contained complex letter. In any event, students of film should know about them. In the most famous one, Kuleshov, working with Pudovkin, intercut shots of an actor's face having the same expression on it with shots of a bowl of soup, a little girl and a coffin. When the sequence was shown to viewers, the "performance" of the actor was praised for its sensitivity, even though he had not actually acted at all; that is, the actor was thought to be displaying *different* emotions because Kuleshov had juxtaposed the face with different objects. For Kuleshov this proves the fact that cinematic meaning derives from the assemblage of shots.

Several other experiments demonstrate his enthusiasm for the ability of montage "to create a new earthly terrain" (p. 52). In one, he wants to shoot a father and daughter supposedly looking at a pole, even though it is hard to film because of technical difficulties; instead, he takes separate shots of the family and the pole, and then joins them, thus giving the impression that the shots were originally taken in the same area—a technique used commonly by directors throughout the world. But the principle it illustrates is significant—the assemblage of two shots can indeed create the illusion of proximity in space when none in fact exists. In another experiment, he shoots an actor and actress in different locations, but juxtaposes the shots in such a way that they appear

to be walking toward one another in the same area; they seem to
meet, and then observe and enter a building which in reality is
nowhere near them; thus the impossible meeting "happens"
through the magic of montage. At one point Kuleshov even
"creates" a woman putting on makeup before a mirror: "in actuality she did not exist, because we shot the lips of one woman, the
legs of another, the back of a third, and the eyes of a fourth" (p.
53). The experiments prove "that the basic strength of cinema lies
in montage, because with montage it becomes possible both to
break down and to reconstruct, and ultimately to remake the material" (p. 52). Thus in the interrelationships of the film pieces
lies the potential utterance of the director. He makes phrases by
organizing reality through his choice of juxtapositions.

Acting

The principle of montage extends also to acting. In his early
writings, Kuleshov, like Eisenstein, argues that it is desirable to
use actors who are the essences they portray, thus lending more
of a sense of realism to the work, the theory of typage: "If we
simply choose a person, having no relationship to the theatre, and
make him do what we need, we shall see that his work on the
screen appears better than the work of a theatre actor" (p. 57).
For example, a real stevedore will move and perform his work
more realistically than an actor impersonating the laborer. Also,
by virtue of his experiments with montage wherein the actor is
merely a tool in the composition, as with the soup experiment,
Kuleshov seems to consider the actor of minimal importance.

But he later argues that in the actual performance of an actor
one can talk about a complex "montage curve." In any given
montage phrase of juxtaposed images, the performance itself becomes part of the composition and continuity; the actor's work
"has its own montage curve, particularly in montage interactions
and alternations. It is these very alternations, in meaning as in
rhythm, which are inextricably connected with the alternation of
the segments themselves—that is, the internal montage of the
construction of the shot cannot be separated from the entire
montage construction, from the montage of the shots" (p. 193).

The Nature of Space on the Screen

It is in connection with acting that Kuleshov introduces his discussion of the "metrical spatial web," a concept which foreshadows later studies of screen space by such critics as Manny Farber and Noël Burch. Briefly, Kuleshov conceives of the rectangular screen as the base of a triangle whose apex is the camera. The actor's motions within the screen space itself will be more easily "read" by viewers if they occur parallel to one pair of sides of the screen and perpendicular to the other pair. The actor's movements in relation to the apex of the triangle, the camera, must be so organized within space as to proceed in an orderly pattern. A crooked path, for example, is a perfectly acceptable line of motion as long as it fits formally into the "grid" established by the rectangle, parallels and perpendiculars. Even bodily actions in place should be conducted with the metric web in mind, by moving with a sense of the various axes of bodily parts and their relationship to screen space: "On the screen an imaginary web somehow results, and it is along it that one must move during the elementary action, while during the complex action, crooked movements must be situated into the fundamental parallel and perpendicular divisions" (p. 110). Again, "if a person works along clearly expressed axes of his mechanism, and movement along these axes is distributed within the space allocated on the screen—in the 'spatial grid'—you will get the maximum clarity, maximum purity in the work of an actor. You will read everything he does on the screen as clearly as in a mirror" (p. 67). To put this in other terms, Kuleshov here suggests that the dynamics of screen space are qualitatively different than those of the stage, where there are always numerous points of view—those of the individuals in the audience. On the screen, the actor appears in a point of view common to all: "the point of view of the lens. . . . The filmmaker takes the viewer as if by the scruff of his neck" (p. 59). Thus acting and the given volumes of space into which the actors move or put parts of their bodies all must be considered in relation to the apex of the triangle, the camera, and, ultimately, the eyes of the viewers.

As much as possible, directors should attempt to avoid confusing viewers with disorienting movements in space by the ac-

tors. One reason for Kuleshov's coolness to the "Kino-Eye"
theory of Dziga Vertov, who stresses the value of the random
views of life captured by documentary means, is that movement
in such circumstances is necessarily chaotic and disorganized because it has not been planned by a director in accordance with a
sense of the spatial grid; thus viewers have trouble reading the
screen. Even so, Kuleshov observes that "the foundation of
cinematography is the montage of real material" (p. 121). He
praises the contribution of non-fiction films and suggests that narrative films can benefit by trying to approach the sense of reality
conveyed by these.

Practical Criticism

As a practical critic, Kuleshov has comments on Eisenstein
worth noting. He challenges Eisenstein's emphasis on the shot
over montage; that is, Kuleshov detects an imbalance in the relationship of part to whole. Although the famous montage sequence
of the rising lions in *Potemkin* works very well, too often Eisenstein fails to utilize montage effectively, as in *Strike*: "Eisensteinian shots always overpower the rest. . . . The montage of *Strike*
is significantly weaker. It is overdone; it betrays a preoccupation
with an unnecessarily rapid editing tempo"; in particular,
Kuleshov complains about the "absence of a single line of movement in the juxtaposition of images and of a single thematic line"
(pp. 138–139).

Kuleshov also makes a perceptive distinction between the directing styles of Griffith and Charlie Chaplin. Actors for Griffith
emote out of themselves, for the director has "them portray their
psychological states by means of complex movements of their
whole bodies. . . . Lip biting, fidgeting, wringing of hands, touching of objects, etc., are the characteristic signs of Griffithian acting." In contrast, Chaplin deemphasizes this personal element of
emotion, and shifts the emphasis to the actors' relationship to
things. Kuleshov's insight should be considered in connection
with the astute observations of both Eisenstein and André Bazin
on this point: Chaplin "virtually reduced to nought the elementary ways of showing emotions in the face. He demonstrated the

behavior of a person through various events in his life by means of his relationship to things, to objects. The way in which the hero relates to his environment and to the people around him changes because of his state of being, and alters his behavior" (p. 94).

V. I. PUDOVKIN*

V. I. Pudovkin (1893–1953), another important pioneering film maker and critic, attributes his entrance into film specifically to Kuleshov. Having begun life as a chemical engineer, Pudovkin admits that he felt only contempt for film prior to his meeting with Kuleshov. As far as he was concerned, it was not even an art. But Kuleshov introduced Pudovkin to the concept of montage; as I indicated earlier, Pudovkin was involved with the experiment of the actor and the soup. As a result of their meeting, Pudovkin enters actively into the world of film as actor, director (*Mother* is perhaps his best-known work), and critic. I want here to examine his formulation and categorization of the montage processes; his theory of acting; and his conception of sound.

Montage

Pudovkin calls editing "the basic creative force, by power of which the soulless photographs (the separate shots) are engineered into living, cinematographic form" (p. 25). The director as editor functions in several ways. He coordinates and structures the pieces of film, providing "compulsory and deliberate guidance of the thoughts and associations of the spectator" (p. 73). In so doing, he allows the spectator to experience what the director wishes him to see and feel. The principle obtaining here is that the various rhythms and tempos of editing are bound up with the psychology of the spectator. The latter's process of perception will proceed along the lines of the editing process as he changes his objects of attention, looks carefully or quickly at details, or turns

---

*All quotations are from *Film Technique and Film Acting*, trans. and ed. Ivor Montagu (New York: Grove Press, 1970). Quoted by permission of Grove Press, Inc. and of Vision Press, Ltd.

away from objects. Citing a basic tenet of associationalist psychology, Pudovkin describes the fact that since emotions call forth certain movements, if a movement is presented, the corresponding emotion will be produced. The director's task is to guide thoughts and associations by choosing and structuring images in ways which will call up the desired emotions and associations. For example, the tempo of editing ought to parallel the attention span: "The more deeply [the spectator] is excited by the scene before him, the more rapidly and suddenly (staccato) his attention springs from one point to another. . . . The more disinterestedly and phlegmatically he observes the action, the calmer and slower will be the changes of his points of attention, and consequently the changes of set-up of the camera" (p. 114).

The editing process begins even before the camera begins to roll, since the director must make careful selections of the filmic material with which he will ultimately work. First he finds suitable material, then chooses the most expressive images to film. Using an analogy from mathematics, Pudovkin calls this procedure "differentiation," or the separation of the profilmic material into parts. For example, he reconstructs what must have been the process of differentiation used by Griffith when filming the courtroom scene in *Intolerance;* the director had to decide that a close-up of the hands belonging to the suffering wife would be included. Similarly, he mentions Eisenstein's decision to focus attention on the perambulator during the massacre in the Odessa steps sequence in *Potemkin.* After differentiation, there occurs the process of "integration" when the various elements are assembled into an organic unity. The director is not a mere recorder of reality, therefore. In fact, he works not with reality as such, but with pieces of film. Unlike the stage director, whose material consists of a scenario and actors, the film director imposes his will on celluloid fragments. As such, he reorganizes space and time to effect what Pudovkin calls "temporal concentration"; that is, the integration of basic units containing the central differentiated units: "The film assembles the elements of reality to build from them a new reality proper only to itself; and the laws of space and time, that, in work with living men, with sets and the footage of the stage, are fixed and fast, are, in the film, entirely altered" (p. 90).

Because of this release from space and time, the film director
is freer than other artists to move to the essence of the object or
scene. Pudovkin speaks about this ability of film not only to capture detail but to use the particular detail as a vehicle for a more
complete revelation of meaning; that is, he argues that the particular can lead us to the universal: "The power of filmic representation lies in the fact that, by means of the camera, it continually strives to penetrate as deeply as possible, to the mid-point of
every image. The camera, as it were, forces itself, ever striving,
into the profoundest deeps of life; it strives thither to penetrate,
whither the average spectator never reaches as he glances casually around him. The camera goes deeper; anything it can see it
approaches, and thereafter eternalises upon the celluloid" (p. 91).

Types of Editing

Pudovkin describes three kinds of editing processes. First,
he speaks of *constructive editing*, the means by which the director works like the writer of narrative fiction to let us see details in
the setting. For example, Pudovkin describes a scene in which a
passerby meets two men in a wagon and asks directions. The
scenario would include details about the condition of the wagon
and description of the three men. Accordingly, the director will
want to present these details in the film, but, Pudovkin argues,
these details cannot be rendered solely with recourse to close-
ups, for such an abundance of close-up shots would interrupt the
narrative action. It is better to let the viewer notice and observe
such details *within* the filmic context. Thus constructive editing
would involve presenting details necessary to understand the
physical aspects of the scene without overpowering the essential
dramatic thrust: "The details organically belonging to scenes of
this kind . . . must not be interpolated into the scene, but the
latter must be built out of them" (p. 51).

Structural editing is a second way of arranging the filmic
elements. In this category occur decisions about when to use
close-ups and long shots; the director makes choices in this regard
on the basis of the action of an entire scene. Thus one kind of
camera set-up would be used to film three men engaged in trying

to lift a heavy object. But if one of the three were to withdraw in order to pull out a revolver, the director would want to isolate him and his particular action with a different kind of shot. Variation from one kind of shot to another, as from a long shot to a close-up, is not to be considered an interruption in the narrative action when the shift is functionally related to the action.

The third and most important category is *relational editing*, since it is so intimately bound up with the director's ability to guide and produce emotions and associations in the viewers. Pudovkin describes five types. An example of the first, *contrast*, would occur in a film about a poor, starving man whose actions were intercut with the gluttony of a rich man. The editing process would relate the scenes to each other without any particular reference to time, space or causation. Second is *parallelism*, similar in some ways to the first. Here his example describes two events more closely related: the preparatory activities for and ultimate execution of a factory worker intercut with the activities of his employer during the same time period—both series presented with reference to time and relationship. An example of the third division of relational editing, *symbolism*, occurs in Eisenstein's *Strike* when the director alternates between shots of slaughtered workers and cattle in a stockyard. As we will see, Eisenstein calls this "intellectual montage." Pudovkin cites the last part of *Intolerance* as a good example of the fourth type, *simultaneity*. As I mentioned earlier, this occurs in the modern story as Griffith cuts from the condemned man to his wife's efforts to reach the governor with information which will save her husband. Pudovkin acknowledges that this form of relational editing has been overused, but still remarks on its effectiveness. The final type, *leit-motif* (reiteration of theme), is designed to reinforce the central theme of the film. Thus in a work directed against clerical and tsarist abuses, there recurs a shot of church bells with a pious subtitle under it, thus emphasizing the hollowness of the church (pp. 75–78).

Like Kuleshov, Pudovkin uses literary analogies to explain elements of the montage process. He points out that a word can, in itself, be more evocative than a visual image, for "in a single word often a whole complex of images is contained" (p. 37). The director translates the scenario into images of suggestive power;

and when the images are established, composition occurs: "Editing is the language of the film director. Just as in living speech, so, one may say, in editing: there is a word—the piece of exposed film, the image; a phrase—the combination of these pieces" (p. 100). Rather like Lindsay, Pudovkin identifies the personal stamp of the director in the editing process: "Only by his editing methods can one judge a director's individuality. Just as each writer has his own individual style, so each film director has his own individual method of representation" (p. 100).

The construction of images into larger units parallels the activities of the creative writer. Words are his raw materials, like the images of the director: "Hesitating, selecting, rejecting, and taking up again, he stands before the separate takes, and only by conscious artistic composition at this stage are gradually pieced together the 'phrases of editing,' the incidents and sequences, from which emerges, step by step, the finished creation, the film." Pudovkin argues that the film is "built up from the separate strips of celluloid that are its raw material" (p. 24). Thus an image as such flashed onto the screen is only a *"dead object,"* unless it can be shown to have a relationship to the other images: "Only if the object... be presented as part of a synthesis of different separate visual images, is it endowed with filmic life" (p. 25).

Acting

Turning now to the theory of film acting, we find that among our group of three Russian pioneers only Pudovkin welcomes enthusiastically the more formalized training that was then available in the acting school of Konstantin Stanislavsky. Although Pudovkin never rejects absolutely the use of non-actors, typage, in general his conception of film acting presupposes a rather sophisticated training process and an even more complex relationship between actor and director than that emerging from typage.

He believes that the film should not be merely a play put on the screen. Similar to Münsterberg, he argues that film's "path to a real art will be found only when it has been freed from the dictates of an art-form foreign to it—that is, the Theatre" (p. 27). The actor, whether in a silent or sound film, faces tremendous difficulties in the transition from stage to screen performance. Pudovkin describes the problems encountered by the actor, who must necessarily perform without benefit of an audience before him, and whose actions are broken up either in the filming or in the actual presentations before the camera at different times of filming. To counter the debilitating effects of this discontinuity, Pudovkin urges a rehearsal method derived from the school of Stanislavsky, whereby the actor learns absorption with the role and particular image, and attempts to maintain his persona for as long as possible in rehearsals before the actual filming begins. Ideally, the actor should have a sense of himself as an actor in the face of the mechanical circumstances: "The actor in his creative process first learns reality; then, together with the spectator and by means of the specific peculiarities of his art, he expresses externally the results of his knowledge in the form of a newly organised artificial behaviour composed by himself. In this work, he invariably strives to preserve in live undestroyed shape his personal existence, he strives to continue to feel himself in front of the camera a whole, living person and not a mechanised likeness of one" (p. 328).

The director can help the actor in this regard by standing in, as it were, for his absent audience. This will combat the effect of filming which makes the actor always conscious of the fact that his performance is subject to mechanical revision or alteration during the editing process. As we might expect, Pudovkin rejects out of hand any such trickery as Kuleshov describes in his experiment during which the nonexistent woman was created by assembling shots of different women in montage. Creating an artificial landscape is one thing, but, for Pudovkin, who is concerned with the integrity of the actor, simply creating actors is quite another matter. He even advises directors to include the actor in the editing process. Finally, as much as possible the director should try to reproduce in the filming process the kind of conditions which an actor is accustomed to on the stage.

Sound

Precisely because he realized that there are differences in theatrical and filmic presentations, Pudovkin joins Eisenstein and

G. V. Alexandrov in 1929 and issues a by-now famous manifesto calling for the unique utilization of sound, and rejecting its unimaginative use as it occurs in filmed theatre. He supports the use of *asynchronous* dialogue matched with shots and condemns the use of music simply as a background accompaniment to the action. Sound and image "must not be tied to one another by naturalistic imitation but connected as the result of the interplay of action. . . . Unity of sound and image is realised by an interplay of meanings which results . . . in a more exact rendering of nature than its superficial copying" (p. 184). Pudovkin describes a scene which begins with calm and culminates in a battle. Ordinarily, the musical accompaniment would follow the same pattern, and be light during the moments of calm, becoming loud and violent when the battle begins. This is what Pudovkin wants to avoid. Instead he would have the martial music dominate the entire scene: "From beginning to end the music must develop in a gradual growth of power. This direct, unbroken theme I connected with the complex curves of the image" (p. 192). We will see a much more elaborate application of that concept, "the complex curves of the image," when we discuss Eisenstein's theory of sound and his *Alexander Nevsky.*

It should be noted that Pudovkin has consistently high praise for Eisenstein's films, and cites *Potemkin* again and again for its various merits, praising variously the skill in selecting details during the massacre (p. 95), the montage of the waking lions (p. 116), and the shot full into the muzzles of the guns on the battleship (p. 154).

SERGEI M. EISENSTEIN*

Sergei M. Eisenstein (1898–1948) is one of our greatest film theorists as well as one of the world's most important directors. Those interested in learning why he leaves us so few films should consult Jay Leyda's *Kino*, Yon Barna's *Eisenstein*, and Ronald Gottesman's and Harry Geduld's *Que Viva Mexico!* There they will find descriptions of the forces that consistently frustrated the genius of Eisenstein, from within his own country (Stalin and the repressive political climate) and from without (Upton Sinclair and the devastating lack of support lent to the director during the Mexican venture). Eisenstein left only a few completed films: *Strike, Potemkin, October, Old and New, Alexander Nevsky,* and the first two parts of *Ivan the Terrible.* But he bequeathed to future generations a considerable amount of film theory. Since many of his critical comments are directed at his own films, we have the opportunity to study carefully the way in which Eisen-

---

*Key to Abbreviations:

FE = *Film Essays*, ed. and trans. Jay Leyda (New York: Praeger, 1970). © 1970 Praeger Publishers, Inc. Reprinted by permission of Praeger Publishers, a division of Holt, Rinehart & Winston. Also of Dobson Books, Ltd.

FF = *Film Form*, ed. and trans. Jay Leyda (New York: Harcourt, Brace & World, 1949). Copyright 1949 by Harcourt Brace Jovanovich, Inc.; renewed, 1977, by Jan Leyda. Reprinted by permission of the publishers. Also of Dobson Books, Ltd.

FS = *Film Sense*, ed. and trans. Jay Leyda (New York: Harcourt, Brace & World, 1947). Reprinted by permission of Harcourt Brace Jovanovich. Also of Faber and Faber, Ltd.

N = *Notes of a Film Director*, trans. X. Danko (New York: Dover, 1970). Quoted by permission of Dover Publications, Inc.

stein applies his theories to his own work, particularly to *Potem-kin*, a film which invariably turns up on lists of the ten best movies ever made. I want here to explain Eisenstein's concept of montage thoroughly: the philosophical and political underpinning, the nature of conflict and dialectics, and the various types he identifies; also, to present his views on technical matters as well as on other film artists.

Montage: The Philosophical and Political Rationale

Although he shares with Kuleshov and Pudovkin the view that montage is central to the craft of film making, only Eisenstein provides an overt philosophical framework for his conception of the montage process. It is this which explains in large part his disagreement with the other two and his criticism of their analogies of bricks and blocks to describe the assemblage of individual shots into a whole. In Eisenstein's view, their analogies are at odds with their call for an organic blending of form and content.

It is possible to identify various formative influences on the aesthetic thinking of Eisenstein, such as the Kabuki theatre, Italian futurist painting, the work of the Russian Formalists, and the films of D. W. Griffith. Perhaps the most important intellectual force informing his theoretical discussions is the concept of dialectics as formulated by G. W. F. Hegel. Essentially Hegel argues that all experience—mental, spiritual, historical, political—constitutes a unity. The various areas of human existence embody disparate elements which, upon analysis, appear in relationships of tension. We can consider the broadest and most divergent polarities in any given construct as a *thesis* and an *antithesis*. The whole itself exists by virtue of a *synthesis* of the disparate elements. In other words, unity is to be seen as the product or sum of the opposing elements and relationships in a given subject.

We are all familiar with the use to which Karl Marx has put Hegelian dialectics in his political analysis. Hegel himself has left us a brilliant theory of tragedy based on this process, in particular his study of *Antigone* by Sophocles. He explains the play's structure by isolating the claims of Creon and of Antigone. As he sees it, the tragedy here as well as the basic principle of all tragedy arises from the *collision* of these typically exclusive demands by the forces in a play.

At its best, as it often appears in Eisenstein, dialectical thinking can inform one's appreciation of the formal processes at work in art and can highlight the organic relationships that give life to individual creations. Later we will see dialectical thinking at work in the criticism of André Bazin, and, even more pronouncedly, in the structuralism of Noël Burch.

Eisenstein argues that a director must have a particular political view supportive of the collective impulse and that the politics of the artist should emerge in the very manner in which he engages in his creative activity. Thus, in a 1930 lecture at the Sorbonne, he discusses the importance of the collective movement: "The necessity of making films expressing collective values helped us smash the sacred triangle of classical theatre: husband, wife, lover."* In contrast to American and continental films, which put the love interest in the foreground while relegating politics to the background, Eisenstein boasts that the Soviet film has destroyed the "triangle tradition" by stressing the collective life of the people: "We want to enter life. If we make a movie about the life of the fleet, we go to Odessa. . . . If we do a peasant film like *Old and New*, we go to the villages and spend time with the peasants." The most important goal of art for the director trying to promulgate collective values is "to put abstract ideas on film, to make ideas somehow concrete . . . by finding directly in the image or in a combination of images the means of awakening the emotional reaction we foresaw and anticipated" (Moussinac, p. 85). This sounds like Pudovkin's comments about emotion and movement, but notice that Eisenstein stresses the intellectual element as well as the emotive; the director controls a process which leads to the presentation of ideas integrally bound up with images: "We had to create a series of images composed in such a way that they provoke an affective movement which in its turn awakens a series

---

*Quoted from *Sergei Eisenstein* by Léon Moussinac, trans. D. Sandy Petrey (New York: Crown, 1970), p. 84. This and subsequent quotations by permission of Crown Publishers, Inc. © 1970 by Crown Publishers, Inc.

of ideas. From image to feeling, from feeling to thesis"
(Moussinac, p. 86).

The cinema seems to Eisenstein the chief means of producing a synthesis of basic human drives because it embodies a
dynamic dialectical process in its inner workings: "cinema is the
only concrete art which is dynamic . . . which can unleash the op-
erations of thought." He views human history as having had, at
first, a union of what he calls magic and religion: "knowledge was
both an emotional element and an element of collective wisdom.
Then, with dualism, things got separated, and we have on the
one hand speculative philosophy, pure abstraction, and on the
other hand pure emotion. We must now go back . . . toward an
analogous synthesis of emotional and intellectual. I think film
alone is capable of making this great synthesis, of returning the
intellect to its vital, concrete, emotional sources. That is our task
and the path we have chosen" (Moussinac, p. 86).

The only man whom James Joyce could imagine making a
film of *Ulysses* also contemplates a movie on *Das Kapital*. Calling
for a cinema of the intellect, he thinks "the cinema is capable of,
and consequently must achieve, a concrete sensual translation to
the screen of the essential dialectics in our ideological debates.
Without recourse to story, plot, or the living man. The intellectual cinema can and must resolve the thematics of such matters as 'right deviation,' 'left deviation,' 'dialectic method,' 'tactics
of Bolshevism'" (FE, p. 46). This process depends on the creator
having a definite attitude toward the material, and a desire to use
the external to present the internal. To that end, the process of
creation will involve "destruction of the indefinite and neutral,
existing 'in itself' . . . and its reassembly in accordance with the
idea dictated by attitude to this event or phenomenon, an attitude which . . . is determined by my ideology, my outlook, that
is to say, *our* ideology, *our* outlook" (N, p. 124). The director
engages in a dialectical process as he examines disparate elements
of experience and attempts to bring them together. It is his attitude which sparks the creative process. In effect, creation is, for
Eisenstein, the act of manifesting an intellectual position: creation
"begins at the moment when the unrelated coexistence of
phenomena is disjoined and replaced by the casual [*sic*] intercon-

nection of its elements dictated by the filmmaker's attitude to the phenomenon, which, in its turn, is determined by his outlook" (N, p. 125). Thus the attitude which is, for Eisenstein, bound up with a political position is embodied in art through a process which involves analysis and synthesis; or, to put this in relation to Pudovkin's theory, differentiation and integration of images occur for Eisenstein inevitably in a political context which he describes in dialectical terms.

Montage Thinking

Turning now to more specifically aesthetic issues, we find Eisenstein's dialectical theory apparent in his discussion of "montage thinking." Like Kuleshov, Eisenstein is influenced by oriental ideograms as well as Japanese art in general. Notice how he describes montage thinking in relation to Far Eastern imagism in a way which illustrates the dialectical impulse we have seen. He discusses the way in which a Japanese school child learning to draw differs from that of a Russian child. The latter will try to fill a rectangular sheet of paper with a given form in its visible shape, copying its entire outline. In contrast, the Japanese drawing a cherry tree branch would not copy the branch in the form in which it appears to the eyes, but, rather, reproduce various aspects of the branch in individual drawings on the sheet of paper, thus creating various elements of the branch and its relation to the tree in *separate* drawings instead of one. In other words, Eisenstein explains, "he frames a shot." The child in the process of selecting details to draw works like a director; both use the means of copying as the organizing tool. As the child picks out details, so too does the director with his camera: we see "a 'picking-out' by the camera: organization by means of the camera. Hewing out a piece of actuality with the ax of the lens" (FF, p. 41). For Eisenstein this is "montage thinking—the height of differentiatedly sensing and resolving the 'organic' world" (FF, p. 27). Individual sections of a film deserving to be called true montage pieces will display this quality of resolution: if a shot is "really a 'montage' piece, that is, not disconnected but meant to produce an image together with other pieces, it will, at the very moment it is shot, be infused with elements which characterize its inner content and at the same time contain the embryo of the structure most suited for the fullest possible revelation of this content in the finished compositional form" (FE, p. 182).

Given the highly organic concept of the montage piece, we can understand why Eisenstein rejects as "a completely false concept" the assertions we have seen that montage proceeds "by placing single shots one after the other like building-blocks" and that rhythm consists of "the movement within these building-block shots" (FF, p. 48). Nor is montage a means of "*unrolling* an idea with the help of single shots" (FF, p. 49). For Eisenstein, montage consists of organic relationships both *within* and *between* shots. The individual shot is comparable to a cell in which various kinds of tension occur. These form the basis of the next shots, and, ultimately, synthesizing resolution shots. That is, Shot *A* juxtaposed with Shot *B* yields not merely *A* plus *B*, but filmic essence *C*.

Types of Montage Conflict

Montage *within* the shot takes various forms. Citing examples from his own films, Eisenstein speaks of *graphic* conflict, where the eye is confronted with contrasting lines of force and direction; conflict of *planes*, as in *Potemkin* when the foreground is filled with soldiers firing at the solitary figure of the mother to the right and beyond the middle ground; conflict of *volumes*, as in a shot showing different forms of roundness in breasts, a blouse and a net; *spatial* conflict in which screen space is rendered through numerous shapes that interlock compositionally to lead the eye to the point of perspective at the rear of the shot; as well as conflicts of *light* and *tempo*. He also suggests conflict can arise within the shot by the use of spatial distortion through camera angle or through actual optical distortion effected by the lens. In addition, the use of slow motion can generate conflict between the means of capturing the image and the image; that is, the disruption of the normal movement against our expectations. An example of this might be the scene in *Potemkin* where the kitchen worker breaks the bread plate. Finally, there can be conflict between the activity within a frame and the boundaries of the frame itself. I think a good example of this occurs in *October* as a bridge swings open; while the metal sections move apart, the

unmoving boundaries of the frame come into conflict with the
force of the bridge which seems about to tear into the external
frame.

Montage, then, is conflict. The kinds of internal conflict
within the frame-cell prefigure further conflict between cells; the
internal conflict creates tensions spilling over into other cells. At
various points Eisenstein uses the same description to explain the
process. He tells his students, "When the tension within a shot
reaches its limits and can increase no longer within the shot, then
the shot bursts, splitting into two editing-pieces."* Again, "Conflict within the shot is potential montage, in the development of
its intensity shattering the equilateral cage of the shot and explod-
ing its conflict into montage impulses *between* the montage
pieces." He compares a group of montage pieces to a "series of
explosions of an internal combustion engine, driving forward its
automobile or tractor; for, similarly, the dynamics of montage
serve as impulses driving forward the total film" (FF, p. 38). Certain conflicts within a frame wait only for an "impulse of intensifi-
cation before flying into antagonistic pairs of pieces: *Close shots
and long shots. . . . Pieces of darkness and pieces of lightness. . . .
Conflicts between an object and its dimension—and conflicts between an event and its duration*" (FF, p. 39).

Thus the conflict within a cell, when intensified, leads to a
splitting of the cell into its dialectical opposites, creating separate
cells which contain the opposing elements. The resolution of conflict, in line with the Hegelian dialectic, should theoretically provide a synthesis for the opposing forces. We find Eisenstein offering an explanation of this process of synthesis in his description of
the fourth part of *Potemkin*, in which the townspeople take yawls
to visit the mutinous sailors on board the ship. In a passage reminiscent of Lindsay's comments about "painting-in-motion,"
Eisenstein identifies various elements in the sequence in dialectical relationship to each other: depth and foreground; motion and

---

*Quoted in Vladimir Nizhny, *Lessons with Eisenstein*, ed. and
trans. by Ivor Montagu and Jay Leyda (New York: Hill & Wang,
1969), p. 124. By permission of Farrar, Straus & Giroux, Inc. and
George Allen & Unwin (Publishers), Ltd. Copyright © 1962 by
George Allen & Unwin, Ltd.

rest; vertical and horizontal lines interspersed with lines forming
an arch which is itself common to both the moving and stationary
forces; variation of figures, and so on. The spatial and compositional features, at times distinct and at other times parallel, constitute one means of integrating and resolving the disparate
subjects—those on land and those at sea: "At the end the two
themes are merged. The composition is basically in two planes:
depth and foreground. Alternately, the themes take a dominant
position, advancing to the foreground, and thrusting each other
by turns into the background. The composition is built (1) on a
plastic interaction of both these planes (within the frame) and (2)
on a shifting of line and form in each of these planes from frame
to frame (by montage). In the second case the compositional play
is formed from the interaction of plastic impressions of the preceding shot in collision or interaction with the following shot"
(FF, p. 116). The synthesis as such in the sequence arises from
the fact that we have passed visually from a theme of the yawls
and the shore, to the theme of *"fraternization of yawls and battleship"* (FF, p. 119).

Those familiar with the film remember that the scene ends
abruptly with the word "SUDDENLY." Dialectically, this title
functions as an introduction to the antithesis of the entire fourth
section; that is, we have just watched the union of sailors and
townspeople and will now see attempts to destroy that unity. If
we look at the entire section as Eisenstein recommends, two
units broken by a caesura or pause, it is possible to view the two
main components—unity of sailors and citizens, *thesis*; massacre,
antithesis—as themselves leading to a synthesis in the most famous montage sequence of the film, in which Eisenstein joins
three shots of stone lions to suggest the rising of the human spirit
(thesis) in the face of oppression (antithesis).

His analysis of the entire structure of *Potemkin* is illuminat-
ing. The last four sections, including the one just discussed, display a two-part structure, punctuated by a caesura which sets off
distinctly different kinds of actions: Part Two, oppressed men
under the tarpaulin, followed by the cry of "Brother," and then
the mutiny; Part Three, mourning for Vakulinchuck in the mist,
and then the anger of the crowd; Part Four, unity of sailors and
citizens, "SUDDENLY," and the massacre; Part Five, the tension

as the fleet approaches, the call of "Brother," and then triumph. The overall synthesizing element is the concept of brotherhood: "From a tiny cellular organism of the battleship to the organism of the entire battleship; from a tiny cellular organism of the fleet to the organism of the whole fleet—thus flies through the theme the revolutionary feeling of brotherhood. And this is repeated in the structure of the work"; "the organic-ness of the film, born in the cell within the film . . . moves and expands throughout the film as a whole" (FF, pp. 163–164). Put in the most basic dialectical terms, then, I think we can understand tsarist oppression and authority as the thesis, revolution as the antithesis, and brotherhood as the synthesis, particularly insofar as it is the cry of brotherhood which initiates the mutiny against the military authorities as well as uniting the sailors with those forces about to attack them at the end.

Montage and Emotion

In both *Film Form* and *Film Sense* Eisenstein talks about montage and the emotions of the spectator. Rather like Pudovkin, he says the director must "transform" the image which embodies his idea "into a few basic *partial representations* which, in their combination and juxtaposition, shall evoke in the consciousness and feelings of the spectator . . . that same initial general image which originally hovered before the creative artist" (FS, pp. 30–31). The montage process will inevitably draw in the emotions of the viewer as guided by the director: "The spectator is compelled to proceed along that selfsame road that the author traveled in creating the image"; the viewer "experiences the dynamic process of the emergence and assembly of the image just as it was experienced by the author" (FS, p. 32). Notice that Eisenstein puts more stress than Pudovkin on the creative perception of the viewer in this regard; for Eisenstein, "the spectator is drawn into a creative act in which his individuality is not subordinated to the author's individuality, but is opened up throughout the process of fusion with the author's intention" (FS, p. 33).

Eisenstein also examines the viewers' emotions in relation to montage as he explains the structure of the massacre in *Potemkin*. He wishes there to generate pathos in its more formal sense of feeling. One way is to focus on an individual in the scene and the ways in which his feelings emerge. In the sequence, Eisenstein isolates various individuals—the student, the lady with the baby, the old woman with the pince-nez—and returns to each of them at various points during the sequence. Their frenzy appears in a context of constantly shifting volumes, lines, spatial depths and conflicting movements; that is, to emphasize their frenzy, Eisenstein structures the formal aspects of the sequence to duplicate this feeling. Just as humans in the grip of this terror have no firm grip on themselves but are totally lacking in direction, so too is the manner of presentation of their frenzy purposely broken up and fragmented: "in a compositional structure identical with human behavior in the grip of pathos... the sequence of the Odessa steps is carried along with such transfers to opposites" (FF, p. 171).

Categories of Montage

The kind of effect he wants here can be understood in relation to one of the five forms of montage he identifies, *rhythmic* as opposed to another form, *metric*. Metric montage is based strictly on the metrical lengths of film; various effects derive from lengthening or shortening pieces according to some formula, whether musical or mathematical. The rhythmic montage in the massacre is distinguished from metric montage on the basis of its content; that is, the editing principle does not arise from an external proportion or formula, but from the nature of cellular and intercellular conflict: "the rhythmic drum of the soldiers' feet as they descend the steps violates all *metrical* demands. Unsynchronized with the beat of the cutting, this drumming comes in *off-beat* each time, and the shot itself is entirely different in its solution with each of these appearances. The final pull of tension is supplied by the transfer from the rhythm of the descending feet to another rhythm—a new kind of downward movement—the next intensity level of the same activity—the baby-carriage rolling down the steps" (FF, p. 74). Thus, to backtrack for a moment, the tension of the rhythmical montage in the conflict of the soldiers' movements with the cutting would be one factor contributing to the frenzy in the massacre; that is, form would be enhancing and supporting content.

A third type of montage, *intellectual*, is comparable to
Pudovkin's third category, symbolic images juxtaposed to images
in direct narrative. There are numerous examples in Eisenstein's
earlier films where he attempts with intellectual montage to
comment symbolically on the action. In *October*, shots of the
ambitious Kerensky are intercut with those of a peacock, and
shots of strumming harps are matched with those of the whining
Mensheviks. In *Potemkin*, the stone lion montage, as we have
noted, functions symbolically to embody the rising of the people
in their new unity. In our time, the director John Schlesinger has
used intellectual montage in *Midnight Cowboy*, as in the scene in
which Jon Voigt's sexual encounter with the brassy Sylvia Miles is
intercut with segments of television shows functioning as ironic
comments on the hollowness of the artificial life Joe Buck wishes
to enter.

Eisenstein also develops a distinction between two more
types of montage, *tonal* and *over-tonal*. Employing references to
both music and optics, he implies that in these categories we are
beyond mere physical movement as such, but have passed in our
theoretical concerns to a realm in which much more abstract and
nebulous essences are at issue. At the risk of simplifying what has
got to be the most elusive concept in all of Eisenstein's writings,
I suggest that we can try to understand the types by having recourse to less technical terms like "mood" and "atmosphere." He
cites the mourning section in Part Three of *Potemkin* as illustrative of tonal montage. We are not concerned with physical movement exclusively, but the manner in which every element in a
montage piece interacts to form a coherent aura or quality which
emanates from the piece: "In tonal montage, movement is perceived in a wider sense. The concept of movement embraces *all
affects* of the montage piece. Here montage is based on the
characteristic *emotional sound* of the piece—of its dominant. The
general *tone* of the piece" (FF, p. 75). Thus in the mourning, the
gentle movements of the objects within the frame—birds, ships,
vapor, etc.—are in keeping with the levels of light vibrations.
Those familiar with the scene will remember the shimmering
luminosity that pervades, whether in shots of the ships or of the
candle held by the dead man: an overall emotional tone of sadness conveyed by adjusting the elements so as to reinforce a
quiet, measured aura of finality—the mood of mourning, if you

will. Eisenstein describes it in this way: "Here the montage was based exclusively on the emotional 'sound' of the pieces—on rhythmic vibrations that do not affect spatial alterations. In this example . . . alongside the basic tonal dominant, a secondary, accessory *rhythmic* dominant is also operating. . . . This secondary dominant is expressed in barely perceptible changing movements: the agitation of the water; the slight rocking of the anchored vessels and buoys. . . . Here spatially immeasurable changes are combined according to their emotional sound. But the chief indicator for the assembly of the pieces was according to their basic element—optical light-vibrations (varying degrees of 'haze' and 'luminosity'). And the organization of these vibrations reveals a complete identity with a minor harmony in music" (FF, p. 76).

Over-tonal montage is distinguished from tonal montage on the basis of its complexity. Tonal montage arises from the dominant; over-tonal montage is characterized "by the collective calculation of all the piece's appeals" (FF, p. 78). It is as if the dominant tone set in motion vibrations which themselves produce vibrations radiating out from the central dominant: "along with the vibration of a basic dominant tone, comes a whole series of similar vibrations, which are called *overtones* and *undertones.* Their impacts against each other, their impacts with the basic tone . . . envelop the basic tone in a host of secondary vibrations" (FF, p. 66). Thus tonal refers to the primary vibrations, over-tonal to the secondary vibrations, the ultimate feel of the shot: "behind the general indication of the shot [i.e., the dominant], the physiological summary of its vibrations as a *whole,* as a complex unity of the manifestations of all its stimuli, is present. This is the peculiar '*feeling' of the shot,* produced by the shot as a whole" (FF, p. 67). This is comparable to a filmic "fourth dimension" which transcends the ordinary space-time continuum.

Perhaps an example will help clarify the distinction. One of the memorable scenes in Ingmar Bergman's *The Seventh Seal* occurs when the knight, Antonius Block, enters a cell to confess to one whom he thinks a priest; we know, however, that his confessor is Death, the knight's opponent at chess. The knight explains his strategy and describes to Death how he will win the game; Death then reveals himself, promising to remember what the knight has said.

I believe that the dominant of tonal montage could be described as "tension," since everything we see and hear exists in a series of contrasting relationships: the blond hair of the knight against the dark hood of Death; the hood itself in contrast with the chalky white of Death's face; the stark lighting against the darkness of the setting, which seems almost ready to swallow up the light; the rigid bars of the grating opposed to the supple curves on the faces presented in close-up. Even the rhythm of the camera work emphasizes the contrast, since several times we cut back and forth between the two speakers, although the knight's point of view shots are framed to exclude Death's face.

The "feeling of the shot" is the sum of the many vibrations emanating from the physiological material. Here the dominant of "tension" generates a series of oppositions which themselves bounce off the basic dramatic situation. The traditional symbolic associations of light and dark—knowledge and ignorance—are undercut. The face of Death is white but enclosed in darkness; yet, until the end of the scene, only the force of darkness has knowledge. The knight who lacks this physical darkness wants information but is in intellectual darkness. The irony in the narrative exists no matter how the scene is shot. But since Bergman has, with his photographer Gunnar Fischer, filmed the scene in this manner, we can talk about the ironic overtones proceeding not just from the scenario but, equally important, from the collected visual impressions of the scene itself. Thus its dominant tension produces over-tonal vibrations of irony which support the narrative.

Vertical Montage

Elsewhere Eisenstein proposes another example of montage thinking which includes the various elements within the frame: image, sound and color. In *Notes of a Film Director* and *Film Sense,* one can discover fascinating descriptions of his experiences working with Sergei Prokofiev on the production of *Alexander Nevsky* as they structured the images and the music. In the famous scene when the knights wait for the battle on the ice to begin, Eisenstein and Prokofiev coordinate the shapes and curves of the images and sounds so that the eye and the ear experience somewhat the same sensations. Thus in a shot depicting a horizon line, the melodic line remains fairly static, and neither rises nor falls pronouncedly. Similarly, in a shot presenting an image in which the eye is led upward, the music also ascends in a rising pattern. This is what Eisenstein means by "vertical montage"; he provides several useful diagrams which include pictures as well as the musical score. Someone looking at the pages must view the figures both horizontally and vertically, exactly as if reading a musical score for a symphony—hence the notion of "vertical montage," since both sound and image are in a vertical relationship with each other, generating their own montage effects, while the image itself exists in montage relationships with the images to which it is juxtaposed horizontally (FS, pp. 157–216).

Acting

Eisenstein finds the principle of conflict present in acting as well. Although he does not argue the point in his early comments on acting, where the main interest is in typage (FF, pp. 8–9), he later conceives of acting in terms of montage. Eisenstein argues essentially that montage in acting arises from the contrasting impulses to exaggerate and restrain, as well as from the fact that the actor has to come to terms with the frame of the film in which he is contained: "there is no inconsistency between the method whereby the poet writes, the method whereby the actor forms his creation *within himself*, the method whereby the same actor acts his rôle *within the frame of a single shot*, and that method whereby his actions and whole performance, as well as the actions surrounding him, forming his environment... are made to flash in the hands of the director through the agency of the montage exposition and construction of the entire film" (FS, p. 64).

Color and Film Techniques

Eisenstein speaks of color in much the same way as sound. In his last writing—a letter to Kuleshov on color—he talks about the need to exploit all potentials of the film; color, sound, image—all must be part of the director's orchestration. Earlier, he speaks of his experiences working with black and white film, and the kind of effects he was able to get with grays and various tones. Now, with the development of color, he speaks of a "colour line" which "weaves its way through the plot as one more independent part in the dramaturgic counterpoint of the film's expressive means" (N, pp. 123–124). Elsewhere, Eisenstein leads his readers through an intriguing discussion of color symbolism. After citing various authorities who argue that certain colors have fixed associations, he concludes that the film director must not work with this assumption. Instead, he should treat his materials more flexibly: "In art, it is not the *absolute* relationships that are decisive, but those *arbitrary* relationships within a system of images dictated by the particular work of art. The problem is not, nor ever will be, solved by a fixed catalog of color-symbols, but the *emotional intelligibility and function of color will rise from the natural order of establishing the color imagery of the work, coincidental with the process of shaping the living movement of the whole work*" (FS, pp. 150–151).

Like Bazin, Eisenstein welcomes the advances in stereoscopic film insofar as they allow for the total development of film's potential to capture reality. Such an accomplishment is an answer to "some inner urge" and "satisfies some inborn requirement of human nature." In effect, he too conceives of a "Myth of Total Cinema," since he thinks that "in striving to realize this urge, humanity has been heading for the stereoscopic film as a complete and direct expression of this striving" (N, p. 130).

Also like Bazin, Eisenstein supports the use of depth of field. This is a technique made possible by the development of panchromatic film; used with special wide-angle lens, depth of field allows all the areas on the screen to appear in sharp focus. Eisenstein is interested in the spatial conflict that can arise between the foreground and background. Not only is it possible to convey an extensive illusion of space, but also: "such composition is highly effective both in cases where the two planes are thematically opposed and where they are unified. In the first instance, this composition allows the greatest conflict of volume and space obtainable within a single shot. In the second, it expresses with utmost plastic clarity the sense of unity between the general and the particular." Its most effective use comes when both of the instances are realizable simultaneously—when "the thematic unity of the two planes is solved and their plastic (scale, colour) incommensurability is emphasized simultaneously" (N, pp. 132–133).

One advance in film technique anticipated by Eisenstein has not come to pass, though. Our generation has grown accustomed to the wide screen, to CinemaScope and to 70 mm film. But there has been no attempt to develop what Eisenstein describes as the "dynamic square"—i.e., a perfectly square screen: "the one and only form equally fit to alternate suppression of right and left, or of up and down, to embrace all the multitude of expressive rectangles of the world" (FE, p. 52). Eisenstein thinks the standard screen size of his time has resulted in the loss of certain "compositional possibilities." Rejecting any more horizontal elongation in favor (I think partially humorously) of "the male, the strong, the virile, the active, *vertical* composition," he argues with characteristic Hegelian logic that the square affords a means of synthesizing opposing vertical and horizontal tendencies. Also, he says the square screen will tend to make cinema less prone to analogies with the stage and with painting (FE, p. 49).

Practical Criticism

Some of Eisenstein's practical criticism is also worth mentioning. His essays on D. W. Griffith and Chaplin, written late in his career, are particularly rewarding. In his study of Griffith, he suggests that the director learned much from Charles Dickens, the nineteenth-century British novelist, who employed fictional techniques which function very much like cinematic devices (the dissolve and the close-up). He also presents a critique of Griffith from a socioeconomic standpoint. Griffith tends to dwell on two widely separated aspects of culture, the small town and the "Super-Dynamic America" (FF, p. 198). His use of parallel montage (the last-minute rescue and such) is a result of a dualistic view of the world comparable to Dickens', a world of haves and have-nots. Consequently, the kind of montage synthesis which Eisenstein aims at is not possible in Griffith's works: "the montage concept of Griffith, as a primarily parallel montage, appears to be a copy of his dualistic picture of the world, running in two parallel lines of poor and rich towards some hypothetical 'reconciliation'

where... [editor's ellipsis] the parallel lines would cross, that is,
in that infinity, just as inaccessible as that 'reconciliation.'"
Eisenstein contrasts this to the Russian practice: "For us the mi-
crocosm of montage had to be understood as a unity, which in
the inner stress of contradictions is halved, in order to be reassembled in a new unity on a new plane, qualitatively higher, its
imagery newly perceived" (FF, pp. 235–236).

One of Eisenstein's central critical achievements comes in a
sketch of Charlie Chaplin. In "Charlie the Kid," the dean of
montage critics presents a probing estimate of Chaplin that could
as well have come from any *auteur* critic. He characterizes the
Chaplin persona as one who looks at all experience through the
eyes of a child. In a rather infantile manner, Charlie is always
trying to escape his surroundings, which threaten his childlike
spontaneity and freedom. His "secret" is "*To see things most terrible, most pitiful, most tragic through the eyes of a laughing
child*" (FE, p. 124).

The Great Dictator, in which Chaplin plays both a poor
baker and Hitler, stands as a landmark in his development because here Chaplin effects a synthesis into *one* person of two
characteristic types that have been separated previously in his
films. On the one hand, Charlie again plays the lowly man, the
baker. On the other, as the dictator he plays a part which belongs
to a list of powerful characters who, in earlier films, have always
been threats to the more familiar Charlie figure: "The Hynkels
[i.e., dictators] of his other films were first of all policemen; then
the giant partner who wants to eat him under the guise of a
chicken in *The Gold Rush,* then many, many policemen; the con-
veyor in *Modern Times,* and the image of the terrible environment of terrible actuality in that film. In *The Great Dictator* he
plays both. He plays the two diametrically opposed poles of infantilism; the triumphant and the defeated" (FE, p. 138). This is a
subtle and useful kind of dialectical analysis; we should compare
it to Bazin's study of Chaplin's *Monsieur Verdoux* later, for both
critics attempt to explain the meaning of a particular role in the
total context of an artist's work.

Eisenstein also has an appreciative essay on John Ford,
whose work has been highly praised by *auteur* critics. He says he

wishes he had made *Young Mr. Lincoln*, marvels at the film's imagery, "daguerreotypes come to life" (FE, p. 141), and praises the organic unity. It possesses "a quality that every work of art must have—an astonishing harmony of all its component parts, a really amazing harmony as a whole." Also singled out for praise is the montage: "This film is distinguished by something more than its marvellous craftsmanship, where the rhythm of the montage corresponds to the timbre of the photography, and where the cries of the waxwings echo over the turbid flow of muddy water and through the steady gait of the little mule that lanky Abe rides along the Sangamon River" (FE, p. 140).

Although many of Eisenstein's writings still await translation, and although this summary and explication of his ideas covers only the most major points in his theory, I hope readers have a sense of where Eisenstein stands. To review briefly, he conceives of montage as conflict, specifically in Hegelian terms of thesis, antithesis, and synthesis. Tensions within a cell lead to conflicts between cells; the montage process occurs by virtue of the fact that there exists a continuous series of such explosions through the life of the film. The principle of montage includes every single aspect of the filmmaking operation—sound, color, and acting.

BÉLA BALÁZS*

Béla Balázs (1884–1949), our next pioneer, can boast of numerous significant contributions to the arts: as a librettist for Béla Bartók; as scenario writer for Leni Riefenstahl; as a film director in his own right; and as an influential film theorist. Pudovkin refers approvingly to material in *Der Sichtbare Mensch*, Balázs' first book of theory; and in his later years Balázs teaches with Eisenstein in the Soviet film school in Moscow. His early works, *Der Sichtbare Mensch* (1924) and *Der Geist des Films* (1930), have not been translated into English; but in his last study, *Theory of the Film* (1945), he includes material from the other works. The most relevant ideas in his always suggestive book concern the form-language of film, the significations of various technical devices, the place of sound in film, and the distinction between documentary and abstract films.

The Form-Language of Film

Early in *Theory of the Film*, Balázs relates two stories about individuals watching films for the first time. In one, an Englishman is unable to understand or to respond to what he sees because he does not know the basic grammar of film. In the second story, a young Russian girl becomes upset by the filmic experience. As she relates it: "Oh, it was horrible, horrible! I can't understand why they allow such dreadful things to be shown here in Moscow. . . . Human beings were torn to pieces and the heads were thrown one way and the bodies the other and the hands somewhere else again" (p. 35). She too is unable to recognize the

---

*All quotations are from *Theory of the Film*, trans. Edith Bone (New York: Dover, 1970). By permission of Dover Publications, Inc.

visual conventions that we take for granted, such as the close-up and the medium shot.

It is the fact that film possesses its own distinctive form-language of such shots, and Balázs contrasts film with theatre on this score. A spectator at a stage performance always has an un-changing position within the auditorium from which he sees the action in a fixed space on the stage at an unvarying distance. In contrast, film removes all these fixities, making the experience quite different: film changes the space in the playing area; the viewer sees the action in different sections; his angle of vision varies constantly; and, because of montage, he apprehends a "mosaic of frames" assembled into a whole which incorporates various sections of reality (p. 31). Another way of highlighting the difference between the two experiences is to imagine being pre-sent as a spectator during the actual filming of a work; even then, as party to the production, a viewer cannot experience what he will when watching the scenes projected: "Even if I am present at every shot, if I look on as every scene is enacted in the studio, I can never see or feel the pictorial effects which are the results of camera distances and angles, nor can I become aware of the rhythm which is their outcome. For in the studio I see each scene and each figure as a whole and am unable to single out details with my eye" (p. 46). As a result of film's rendering of reality, we are capable of experiencing what Balázs calls "identifi-cation." Essentially, the camera brings a viewer into the action in such a way that he sees "from the inside" and is "surrounded by the characters of the film. . . . Our eye, and with it our conscious-ness, is identified with the characters in the film; we look at the world out of their eyes and have no angle of vision of our own. We walk amid crowds, ride, fly, or fall with the hero and if one character looks into the other's eyes, he looks into our eyes from the screen, for our eyes are in the camera and become identical with the gaze of the characters" (p. 48).

Such a process of identification is made possible by virtue of the form-language unique to film. Its main elements are the close-up, the changing of camera angle and set-up, and montage. The close-up has immense aesthetic importance. Aside from the fact that it permits the camera to break away from a fixed position, as was the case with earlier films, Balázs suggests that it is a means of making man visible (the translation of *Der Sichtbare Mensch*). In that earlier work, he argues that the invention of printing made man into a word-oriented being. The advent of film and its presentation of moving images of humans using their bodies and faces to express inner feelings mark a return to the use of gesture rather than words. The camera can register every gesture and movement, and experiences and emotions which "lie in the deepest levels of the soul and cannot be approached by words that are mere reflections of concepts" (p. 40). Because of the camera, "man has again become visible" (p. 41). In his last book, Balázs acknowledges that the sound film has greatly removed the attention paid earlier to gesture and facial expression, or, as he calls it, "microphysiognomy." But the principle still holds that certain emotional states defy the use of words to present them. Such emotions, though, can be captured in close-ups which take us into a new realm of space. Balázs praises Griffith for having made use of the close-up important: "he not only brought the human face closer to us in space, he also transposed it from space into another dimension" (p. 61).

His enthusiasm for the close-up relates to his general thesis that the primary function of film must be to offer the world to us in all its aspects: "The film camera has revealed new worlds until then concealed from us: such as the soul of objects, the rhythm of crowds, the secret laughter of dumb things. But all this provided only new knowledge. . . . A more important, more decisive, more historical novelty was that the film showed not other things, but the same things shown in a different way" (pp. 47–48). Again, "when the film close-up strips the veil of our imperceptiveness and insensitivity from the hidden little things and shows us the face of objects, it still shows us man" (p. 60). His defense of film as a means of seeing into the essential nature of things should be compared to the writings of major literary critics who, like Aristotle, would reject Plato's assertion that art takes us away from reality. In particular, Balázs reminds us of both Samuel Johnson and Percy Bysshe Shelley on this issue. Johnson, defining one species of wit in the eighteenth century, speaks of it as making that which is new to us seem familiar, and, correspondingly, presenting that which is familiar as new. An even more striking parallel can be found in Shelley's *Defence of Poetry* as he explains the

power of poetry: "It awakens and enlarges the mind itself by rendering it the receptacle of a thousand unapprehended combina-
tions of thought. Poetry lifts the veil from the hidden beauty of
the world, and makes familiar objects be as if they were not familiar."

A second type of form-language is that arising from the
change of camera angle and set-up. Balázs calls this "the strongest
means of characterization the film possesses" (p. 47). In fact, he
believes that without it, film could never have developed as an
art (p. 89). Somewhat prefiguring the *auteur* critics, he argues
that the changing of camera angle and set-up permits a synthesis
or union of the artist and his subject; such a unity is necessary if
there is to be art: "Every work of art must present not only objective reality but the subjective personality of the artist, and this
personality includes his way of looking at things, his ideology and
the limitations of the period. All this is projected into the picture,
even unintentionally. Every picture shows not only a piece of reality, but a point of view as well. The set-up of the camera betrays the inner attitude of the man behind the camera" (pp. 89–
90). Specifically, camera angles and their control by the director
permit us to see the shapes and outlines of objects in the most
comprehensive manner. As a result, viewers can sense the experiences of a drunken man, as he watches houses reel before
him, become aware of the mood of a landscape through an appropriate shot, and be drawn into the rhythm of the editing process.
Balázs praises Eisenstein for the way in which he varies camera
angles in the mutiny sequence in *Potemkin,* blending form and
content by shooting the fighting through ropes and bars, and by
looking at the action from different directions, even in distorted
ways: "The gestures of the combatants cannot be made any
fiercer, but the ropes, the gratings, the rungs chop up the shots.
Men are merely at each other's throats, but the shots do more;
they dismember them, by means of set-ups and angles" (p. 101).

The Cabinet of Dr. Caligari presents a different situation.
Although Balázs finds the movie intriguing, he notes that here
the apparent distortion in the sets is, in fact, real; that is, the
physical scenery rather than the camera creates the distortion. In
other words, the camera renders the bizarre reality only secon-
darily, rather than primarily. In terms which remind us of Plato's

objections to works of art as merely copies, Balázs observes that
Caligari's images are at one remove from cinematic reality: the
"interesting physiognomic effects were *not* brought about by
camera angles and set-ups which lend the real objects of a real
world characteristic, passion-twisted outlines.... The houses
were built crookedly in the studio, the lamp-standards were set
up at crazy angles and the trees were the work of the scenery
painters.... *The Cabinet of Dr. Caligari* was a film-painting, the
picture of a picture, not primary but second-hand" (p. 106). Such
stylization, whether here or in other works using the same techniques, robs film of one of its parts of speech.

Montage, the third type of form-language, also reveals the
director's personality: "Two films in which story and acting are
exactly the same, but which are differently cut, may be the expression of two totally different personalities and present two totally different images of the world" (p. 32). In other words, the
final form taken by a work is individualized. Thus, like Lindsay
and others, Balázs acknowledges implicitly that one line of endeavor for the film critic is to examine, compare and contrast individual directorial styles by reference to their techniques.

Montage completes the process begun by the set-up, which
can only do so much in capturing the significance of the objects
photographed. Speaking in terms similar to Eisenstein's, he conceives of the shot gaining meaning through the montage process:
"The single shots are saturated with the tension of a latent meaning which is released like an electric spark when the next shot is
joined to it" (p. 118). Only montage can make the images captured by the camera into a statement: "Single pictures are mere
reality. Only the montage turns them into either truths or false-
hoods" (p. 166).

Although he lists various categories of montage, it would
seem that they all could be subsumed under the common notion
of symbolism or intellectual montage as developed by Pudovkin
and Eisenstein. As Balázs defines it, *metaphoric* montage involves
direct visual parallels, as in *Potemkin*, where we make a visual
and symbolic connection between the various parts of the ship
shot in close-up and the sailors shot in the same way: "The angry,
resolute faces of the sailors transfer their own expression to the
wheels and cranks.... An almost human consciousness seems ex-

pressed in the physiognomy of the throbbing, quivering machines" (p. 126). He cites Pudovkin's *Mother* as an example of *poetic* montage: the intercutting of the rising force in revolutionaries with the growing power of a body of water into a flood. *Allegoric* montage, unlike the previous examples, occurs when shots of storms are intercut with scenes of dramatic intensity, although the storms are not related causationally or dramatically to the immediate material, but are only visual equivalents. He also mentions *literary metaphors* and *associations of ideas* as types of montage before discussing what he specifically calls *intellectual montage*, which, for him, is not particularly desirable; such montage attempts to visualize concepts as such; an example would be the toppling of the tsar's statue at the beginning of *October*, indicating that his power has been taken away. It is difficult to see on what basis Balázs makes his distinctions, and one can, I think fairly, question this categorization process.

In contrast, his comments on the rhythm and pace of montage as it affects our sense of time and space are most worthwhile. For example, shots of unmoving characters in a tense situation may be enhanced by rapid cutting to suggest the turmoil. Those familiar with Alain Resnais' *Last Year at Marienbad* will probably remember that practice in a number of scenes in which the actors remain fairly motionless, but the rapid switching from one to another with the camera generates an immense amount of tension. Balázs describes the process in this way: "the camera shifts rapidly and excitedly . . . and the movement of motionless pictures collated by the cutting may have a swift, wild rhythm, making us feel the inner movement of the scene in spite of its outer immobility" (p. 85). Again, the rapid montage found in Russian films "often effectively conveyed the feverish pace of revolutionary happenings" (p. 129). Shifting rapidly between two competitors in a race may seem to prolong the actual time of the running, thus adding to our tension. In addition, intercutting a stationary shot between two shots of tense activity may also prolong our sense of time and anxiety.

How Techniques Signify

Balázs' discussion of the expressive possibilities of film goes beyond montage to include certain camera techniques and technical practices. Thus a pan shot, in which the camera moves in such a way as to capture the actual panorama before it, can increase the reality of the filmed object "because in moving along with the tracking camera, it enables the spectators to remain in the real space in which the action takes place" (p. 139). We will find Bazin attributing the same importance to capturing the reality of space.

Fades and dissolves are much more for Balázs than mere transition devices created in the laboratory. Though not a shot as such, a fade can contribute to mood and atmosphere: "The slow darkening of the picture is like the melancholy, slowly softening voice of a narrator and after it a pensive silence. This purely technical effect can produce in us the sadness of farewells and of the impermanence of things" (p. 143). Also, a fade contributes to our sense of time; a long, slow fade used when viewing a ship disappearing from view on the horizon contributes an added time-dimension, thus giving us two lapses of time; such a tech-nique "shows two movements: movement of the ship and move-ment of the camera diaphragm. Two times: real time of ship's disappearance and filmic time produced by the fade-out" (p. 145). As viewers of film, we ought today to take Balázs' comments into account. For example, what if a director makes excessive use of fades? We should be able to explain whether any particular effect is gained or whether the fades are simply mechanical devices. In contrast, what about the director who self-consciously refuses to use fades? We should be able to offer some reasons for this practice—as in Roman Polanski's *Chinatown*, where the only fade occurs after the hero is knocked unconscious; in the rest of the film, Polanski switches crisply from scene to scene, perhaps in this way emphasizing the compressed rather than elongated time during which the action occurs.

A dissolve for Balázs is like a word known to speakers of a common language. It indicates a close connection between the shots thus merged: "It is an accepted convention, expression, turn of speech in the language of the film, that if two pictures slowly dissolve into each other, the two are bound together by a deep, dramaturgically important, connection which may not be of a nature capable of being expressed by a series of shots depicting actual objects" (p. 146). Like change of angle and set-up, as well as montage, fades and dissolves seem to Balázs to represent the director's voice directly addressing us. He even refers to the director here as an author: "when we see . . . fades and dissolves, in other words photo-technical effects, we are no longer facing only objective reproductions of things—here the narrator, the author, the film-maker himself is speaking to us" (p. 144).

Sound

Balázs asks that the sound techniques of the film perform the same functions as the visual techniques by putting us in contact with reality. In his earlier *Der Geist des Films* he points out that an unimaginative use of sound poses a threat to the development of the film, a position which he voices again in *Theory of the Film*. He is concerned that too many films are simply photographed plays. But such use, or misuse, of sound denies its potential, for just as the visual close-up makes man visible, so too should sound function to make us hear those sounds we have missed or to which we have failed to pay attention: "It is the business of the sound film to reveal for us our acoustic environment, the acoustic landscape in which we live, the speech of things and the intimate whisperings of nature; all that has speech beyond human speech, and speaks to us with the vast conversational powers of life and incessantly influences and directs our thoughts and emotions" (p. 197). He describes sound used correctly as an "acoustic close-up," analogous to the visual close-up which gives us microphysiognomy. Acoustic close-ups will help us sort out the various impressions to which we are subject, by making us discern each of these more carefully: "The sound film will teach us to analyze even chaotic noise with our ear and read the score of life's symphony" (p. 198). To this end, sound should become an actual part of the work, a "dramaturgical element," by being given prominence as an actual causational element rather than as simply an accompaniment. He suggests the use of asynchronous sound; dissolves effected through sound and sound montage; the carrying over of sounds from one scene into the next; and the use of sounds to foreshadow sounds we will hear in later scenes. Obviously, we can tell that the practice of Orson Welles in *Citizen Kane* succeeds along the lines Balázs recommends, for Welles uses sounds imaginatively as transition devices and even creates sound montage (the links between the scenes devoted to Kane's rise in politics). More recently, Robert Altman's work in *California Split* and *Nashville* gives us fine examples of a director who experiments with sound overlaps as well as attempts to surround his audience with the impressions heard by his characters—even, in the former, to the point of using eleven microphones and numerous recording tapes during filming, so that when projected, a given scene in a small interior such as a bar seems to be registering the sounds of an entire city.

Documentary and Absolute Films

Film traditionally uses its form-language and techniques to present narrative works of art. But there are also non-narrative films such as documentary and abstract films. The first type essentially employs the objective technique of reporting with the camera and appears in newsreels, travelogues, instructional films, nature studies, and so on. These are characterized by their concern with rendering reality in an objective form.

In dialectical opposition to these are what Balázs calls "absolute films." A product of the avant-garde, works in this category display more interest in form and move inevitably toward pure abstraction. The more such films depart from objective reality, the less Balázs can find much of favor to say about them. To be fair, he twice notes that his characterization of such subjective formalism as typical of decadent, bourgeois art is meant only as a description rather than as an evaluation of the merits of the absolute film. Nonetheless, he objects strongly to works which only show us images rather than attempting to present the actual reproduction of reality. Thus, more often than not, he is cautious in accepting shots of objects taken from angles which no human could ever duplicate in normal perception, as well as the use of optical effects which become ends in themselves for the film maker; he seems less enthusiastic about films which give us images of objects that have no independent existence outside of the film. The more abstract a film, a trend he attributes to surrealism, the less life; consequently, film then ceases to perform its function in revealing nature and man to us. One can imagine Balázs rejecting the recent work of such artists as the Whitney brothers and Stan VanDerBeek, who work with pure abstraction in their films, even, in the case of the latter, using the computer to produce designs and forms. For Balázs, such endeavors would plainly be of limited value, since, as he remarks of one abstract film showing moving shapes and circles: "They existed in themselves and for themselves and if they signified anything at all, they signified only themselves. . . . There was nothing here of the redemption of the chaotic material of life by forcing it into shape at the cost of a struggle, as a result of which even the most perfect form still retains a little of the raw tang of life" (pp. 181–182). Only if the abstractions produced are used to imitate the internal action of the consciousness can there be said to be much potential for absolute film (p. 180). His call for the "redemption of the chaotic material of life" should be compared to Kracauer's theory that film affords us the redemption of physical reality, since both prize film for its ability to give us the world in all its truth.

RUDOLF ARNHEIM*

Rudolf Arnheim (1904–   ) has made extensive and long-lasting contributions to our understanding of film art. An internationally respected aesthetician and psychologist, he has written many works dealing with the nature of art and with the dynamics of perception: *Art and Visual Perception, Toward a Psychology of Art* (a collection of essays), and *Entropy and Art*, in particular, should be consulted by those who would like to acquaint themselves with his brilliant and comprehensive command of art, physiology, psychology, and science. His ability to integrate concepts from the realms of science and art provides an interesting model of intellectual activity. His criticism and theory teach us the value of considering the work of art comprehensively, as related to all facets of the human mind. We are interested specifically here in his early study, *Film as Art;* written in the 1930s, the essays contained in this work advance views which Arnheim has continued to hold in the ensuing years and which inform his later comments on film. I will discuss the following: his assessment of the difference between film and reality; the manner in which film techniques grow out of its limitations; the value of the visual element in comparison to color, sound and depth; the topics of montage, technique, acting and abstraction in images; and some practical criticism.

---

*Key to Abbreviations:
F = *Film as Art* (Berkeley: University of California Press, 1971). Reprinted by permission of the University of California Press.
M = "Melancholy Unshaped," in *Toward a Psychology of Art* Berkeley: University of California Press, 1971), pp. 291–297. Reprinted by permission of the University of California Press.
P = *Art and Visual Perception* (Berkeley: University of California Press, 1974). Reprinted by permission of the University of California Press.

Distinctions Between Filmic and Actual Perception

Arnheim begins *Film as Art* by insisting that film as such does not merely give us a mechanical reproduction of physical reality; only by seeing why this is so can we understand how film can lay claim to being art. Relying on his knowledge of physiology and psychology, Arnheim explains how our acts of perception differ considerably from the activities of the camera in coping with reality. First, when we look at two men who happen to be at different distances from us, our eyes automatically make a correction so that the men appear to be of normal size. In a photographed image, a man three feet from the camera would seem to be larger than one six feet away. Since this phenomenon, known as the "constancy of size," characterizes *real* perception and not the process occurring during photography, we have immediate evidence suggesting that photographic images are unlike the mental images caused by the direct apprehension of objects in reality.

Second, our field of vision is, as Arnheim says, "unlimited and infinite" (F, p. 17). In contrast, a picture taken by a stationary camera necessarily circumscribes this unlimited field, narrowing it to a particular angle. Even if we remain stationary, our eyes can travel more extensively than the lens of the fixed camera. It is true that a moving camera in a pan shot can survey and present a larger field of content. But here too, the eye differs from the camera. In the act of perception as we cast our eyes or turn physically to scan the four walls of a room, or survey a landscape from a 360-degree angle, we will distinguish our movement from the stationary objects before us. In a filmic pan, though, the stationary objects photographed will themselves, during the projection process, seem to move *across* the screen—another difference between actual and filmic perception.

A third significant difference between film and reality springs from the fact that our senses cooperate in the act of perception. Thus when climbing a mountain, our whole body—muscles, respiration, senses—orients us in the space and surfaces. But someone looking at a picture of one stage in the climb only has the benefit of vision to become oriented.

Fourth, the space-time continuum of human vision is fluid; we are always in real duration and actual spatial contexts, and thus are limited to the clock and to existing distances. In a film, space and time are broken up in a way unlike that of normal perception; that is, the perceived filmic reality generally will contain scenes in which space is covered in an instant (long shot to close-up), and in which a given time may be interrupted by a different space and time as the narrative cuts to different settings and events. In addition, Arnheim points out that movement and space themselves are always relative in film. Unlike the eyes, which will automatically establish our physical location in a given context, the camera must photograph phenomena in such ways that the viewers can know clearly what is fixed and what mobile, what is up and what down.

That we are not confused by the filmic reproduction of reality is due to our acknowledgment of the "partial illusion" generated by the process. On the one hand, film is like a postcard, flat and two-dimensional; on the other, by its ability to give us a sense of space and time which seem similar to the theatre, film appears to have depth and reality. It is, he suggests, somewhere between a postcard and theatre, although not exactly either one.

Film's Limitations as Source of Art

Having argued that what the film shows us is not to be described as a mechanical reproduction of reality, since in fact it does not and cannot present reality to us in the same way as we physically apprehend it, Arnheim explores in more detail how film uses its own properties artistically; specifically he considers what the film artist does with the nature of the filmic image, its reduced depth, the types of lighting and color values, the size of the objects photographed, and the absence of the space-time continuum. His thesis throughout is that "the artistic effect is bound up with the limitations of the medium" (F, p. 75). In other words, film exists as an art by coming to terms with and then utilizing its own features. What we see in a two-dimensional film is a group of solids projected on a plane surface, which inevitably results in a reduction of a sense of depth. Arnheim is interested in the way an artist overcomes a restriction like this and how such an activity forms the basis of filmic art. Here he presents examples of how our inability to see as if we were really present is used creatively. For example, he discusses a Chaplin film in which many travelers in a ship are seasick. We see Charlie leaning over the side of the rail, presumably being ill like the others. But when he turns toward the camera, it becomes apparent that he has been fishing, not vomiting. Thus the limitation, the stationary camera's inability to see around, has contributed to the comic effect: "If the scene had been taken from the waterside, the audience would have realized at once that Charlie was not being sick, but was fishing"; here, "the invention is no longer concerned merely with the subject matter but is cinematographic inasmuch as a definite feature of film technique is being used as a means to secure an effect" (F, p. 37). Again, Arnheim comments on a shot of a convict played by Emil Jannings in *Vaudeville,* in which the camera angle is purposely limited so as to give the viewers only the actor's back and prison number. Thus photographed, the number becomes a symbol. Although the scene could have been taken from a number of angles, the director necessarily has to make a decision: "this very 'limitation' yields the artistic opportunity of making the particular pictured event convey an idea" (F, p. 38).

Arnheim presents numerous examples from other films to illustrate the fact that the camera's limitations in regard to depth can lead to set-ups capable of producing significant effects. Thus, as many have observed, a low-angle shot of a dominant character can stress power; a particular angle can emphasize formal values and the intrinsic design potential of a scene; and, as Balázs notes, it can so control our attention that we see the ordinary in a new way: "The spectator is thus brought to see something familiar as something new. At this moment he becomes capable of true observation" (F, p. 44).

In addition, the projection of solids upon a plane surface results in situations where some objects obstruct others from our view. He provides examples where this inevitable opacity of objects can be used to great effect, as in the following case. Greta Garbo has just killed a man and the camera eye's point of view is that of a group of soldiers who have come to talk to their leader, the dead man. His body is positioned such in a chair that they—i.e., the camera eye—cannot see him. Garbo pretends to converse with the dead man to get his answers to the questions

posed by the group. Thus the limited view occasioned by the
filmic material is functional to the artist's aim.

More specifically, this blocking on the screen emphasizes the
reduced depth of the visual field. Arnheim generally inveighs
against the possibility of three-dimensional film because he sees it
as making montage useless and, equally important, as destroying
the ability of the film artist to compose on a two-dimensional surface. One such manner of composition involves the formal arrangement of objects; viewers must decide why objects are where
they are: if "the effect of depth is almost negligible, the perspective is conspicuous and compelling. What is visible and what is
hidden strike one as being definitely intentional; one is forced to
seek for a reason, to be clear in one's own mind as to why the
objects are arranged in this particular way and not in some other"
(F, pp. 59–60). Thus in Carl Dreyer's *The Passion of Joan of Arc*,
a monk suddenly jumps into the foreground of the screen, ultimately dominating the surface and altering the perspective while
it produces "the sudden rapid extension of the flat projection" (F,
p. 61). A more recent example we could cite occurs in *The Godfather, Part I*. Al Pacino stands before the bedside of the
wounded Marlon Brando in the hospital; suddenly a nurse enters
from the bottom foreground of the screen, first her hat and then
the rest of her becoming visible. In this tense situation, the effect
of this addition of material to an existing screen space is to make
the audience jump; a foreign and possibly dangerous essence has
intruded on the visual field.

The Case Against Color, Sound and Depth

In *Film as Art*, Arnheim is cool toward the naturalistic contributions of color, sound and three-dimensional photography.
The fact that the film artist can overcome the limitations of black
and white photography and produce particular effects impresses
him. In fact, the manipulation of black and white tones through
lighting seems a more exciting means of effecting certain results.
He argues for the symbolic richness to be gained in pitting darkness against light, the stylized look to faces that can be presented
more expressively, and, in particular, the ways in which the

human face and backgrounds can be treated with lighting: "irregular features can be made to look harmonious, a face can be
made to look haggard or full, old or young. It is exactly the same
with interiors and landscapes. Depending on the lighting, a room
may look warm and comfortable, or cold and bare, large or small,
clean or dirty" (F, p. 70). The hues one finds so clearly defined in
color film appear even *more* effective in a black and white film
because the artist has overcome the limitations of his medium:
"the special delight in getting the sense of the texture of ordinary
materials—such as dull iron, shining tin, smooth fur, the woolly
hide of an animal, soft skin—in film or photograph is also
heightened by the lack of hues"; this is so because "the effect is
more uncannily exciting when it is obtained without the aid of
color" (F, p. 71).

Arnheim is usually cited as one of the purists (in the worst
sense) who fail to go along with the inevitable development of
sound in the film. He sees the addition of sound as the first step
toward increased naturalism, and, as such, an impediment to the
progress that had been occurring in the silent film: "The introduction of sound film must be considered as the imposition of a
technical novelty that did not lie on the path the best film artists
were pursuing. They were engaged in working out an explicit and
pure style of silent film, using its restrictions to transform the
peep show into an art. The introduction of sound film smashed
many of the forms that the film artists were using in favor of the
inartistic demand for the greatest possible 'naturalness'" (F, p.
154). Again, we hear the theme stated before: film artists work
through the limitations of the medium to create art.

Still, it should be noted that Arnheim recognizes the sound
film's potential as a means of bringing culture to audiences
through filmed plays and operas. Also, he expresses the hope that
silent and sound films can coexist. Even more significant, his
essay "A New Laocoön" invites comparison with the earlier *Laocoön* by G. E. Lessing in the eighteenth century. In that famous
work, Lessing argues that we should acknowledge the individual
nature and uniqueness of the various forms of art. In his essay
Arnheim speculates on the possibilities for sound film, which for
him is an art combining two forms, theatre and film. He proposes

opera as a reasonably satisfactory model for integrating sound and image. In opera, music dominates and the libretto is secondary. If one applies this model to film, he suggests that the visual element can dominate, while sound is secondary.

The wide screen also represents, for Arnheim, a deterrent to the thorough development of film art because it interferes with the organization of filmic materials along the lines we have been discussing. Limiting the image's position in its own context and in relation to the edges of the screen can be a powerful tool for expression, particularly in the close-up. He quotes, without comment, Eisenstein's suggestion for the square screen, and then explores various effects gained by fragmenting images in the confines of standard screen space. Some may question his assumption that the wide screen would make close-ups less effective. One example of a particularly striking close-up in 70 mm occurs in *2001: A Space Odyssey* as Stanley Kubrick focuses on the menacing eye of Hal.

Arnheim also fears that three-dimensional film would destroy the value of montage, which he defines here as "joining together shots of situations that occur in different time and in different places" (F, p. 87). That is, the violation of the space-time continuum accomplished by montage would not work as successfully if we were observing a visual field that had in it the depth of reality rather than the two-dimensional surface producing a "partial illusion." In fact, "If film photographs gave a very strong spatial impression, montage probably would be impossible. It is the partial unreality of the film picture that makes it possible" (F, p. 28). The theoretical interest of this observation will probably not satisfy those readers who remember the montage (last-minute rescue variety) at the ending of the three-dimensional *House of Wax*.

Montage

Arnheim's other observations on montage and the space-time continuum deserve comment. He suggests that the montage principle pervades even the physical nature of the film, for in a mi-

croscopic sense a strip of film, no matter what the content, has
frames containing pictures which follow one another. By extension, montage as we usually conceive of it in a macroscopic sense
involves joining lengths of film, one after another. In his view,
the real revolution in the development of montage did not come
with shifting from one scene to another scene in a different space
and time (cross-cutting), but in shifting *within* a given scene: "It
was a much bolder stroke to intervene in one unitary scene, to
split up an event, to change the position of the camera in
midstream, to bring it nearer, move it farther away, to alter the
selection of the subject matter shown" (F, p. 89).

Arnheim finds Pudovkin's classifications of the montage processes inadequate; this earlier formulation fails, he thinks, to distinguish clearly enough between the subject and the manner of
editing. In its place, he proposes a more detailed scheme, too
detailed to reproduce here, but which those interested in montage theory should consult (F, pp. 127–132).

He praises Eisenstein's lion montage in *Potemkin* as an excellent example of how joining pieces of film can result in "a
stroboscobic fusion" which gives a sense of movement: "the way
the stones come to life by the help of editing is most remarkable"
(F, p. 100). In contrast to this linking of separate pieces to
suggest unity is a technique Arnheim hesitates to call montage as
such, in which the space-time continuum is broken by the disruption of a single continuous action, either by trick photography (a
man disappears from one frame to the next), or by omission of
frames to make an action seem hurried or jerky (a man walks, but
seems to move unnaturally because some of the frames are ex-
cised). We are familiar with the latter practice in the work of
various New Wave directors, Jean-Luc Godard in particular. In a
more recent essay, Arnheim praises this fragmenting of the montage process; although it overthrows normal space-time relationships, it provides a means of imitating the workings of the mind:
"The human mind . . . stores the experiences of the past as memory traces, and in a storage vault there are no time sequences or
spatial connections, only affinities and associations based on similarity or contrast. . . . By eliminating the difference between what
is presently perceived and what is only remembered from the

past, [novelists and New Wave directors] have created a new
homogeneity and unity of all experience, independent of the
order of physical things"* ("Art Today and the Film," in *Cross-
roads to the Cinema*, ed. Douglas Brode [Boston: Holbrook
Press, 1975], p. 254).

Techniques

Arnheim completes his argument about film's uniqueness in
comparison to reality by examining various devices of filmic technique: slow or accelerated or backward motion, the use of the
mobile camera, superimpositions and simultaneous montage,
change of focus, use of still photographs, and fades and dissolves.
Like Balázs, he thinks the latter are more than mere transition
devices; they can indicate subjective views and emphasize time
relationships. Later, in *Art and Visual Perception*, Arnheim draws
a brilliant conclusion connecting cubist techniques to fades in
film. Cubists wished to render the independent space attendant
on each object, and, at the same time, suggest its essential conflict with other space. They desired a "fundamental disorder,
namely, the incompatibility inherent in total space itself. . . . In
order to show that . . . superimpositions do not occur in coherent
space, the cubists used the device of making the units render one
another transparent or fade out into the neutral ground of the
painting. The psychological effect becomes evident if we remember that the same means are used in motion pictures to represent discontinuity of space. If the scene shifts from the living
room to the hotel lobby, the room fades out into spacelessness—
that is, for a moment pictorial space gives way to the physical
surface of the screen." Obviously, ordinary fades and wipes,
which can also suggest the spatial independence of the scenes, do
not necessarily carry such profound implications. But Arnheim
wisely observes that modern and experimental films have employed this principle, as did the cubists, "to obtain an integration
of discordant orders" (P, p. 302).

---

*This, and the further quotation on page 70, by permission of the
College Art Association, which orginally published Arnheim's "Art
Today and the Film."

Acting

Elsewhere in *Film as Art*, Arnheim treats other issues of
concern, such as acting. He supports the effective use of Russian
typage, particularly as it counters the effects of overacting by actors
from the theatre who are performing in film. Some of the rare
kind words he has for sound in film occur in the context of acting,
as he notes how the addition of sound has reduced the poor use
of the body to convey "the mind through the body," the title of
one of his essays. Although he would agree with Balázs on the
importance of gesture in revealing states of mind, Arnheim thinks
too much body language is self-defeating. It is better to be re-
strained and use indirect means to show states of mind; for example, a director could present a shot of an ashtray full of cigarettes
to suggest "tension" in a character without having to dwell on the
actor's face with close-ups.

Film and Abstract Ideas

In another essay in *Film as Art*, Arnheim analyzes Chaplin's
actions in *The Gold Rush* as these demonstrate film's ability to
convey abstract ideas. In particular, he suggests that the scene in
which the starving Charlie eats the boot, while displaying the
manners and behavior of a rich man relishing a fine meal, master-
fully presents a symbolic contrast between rich and poor. The
boot, nails and laces are treated like a fish, chicken bones and
spaghetti: "the great artistry of the invention lies in that such an
elemental, profoundly human theme as 'hunger versus good living' is presented pictorially by objective means that are so truly
filmic" (F, p. 145). Also singled out as examples of how the
abstract can be made concrete through purely visual means are
two scenes: one in which the other hungry miner begins perceiving Charlie as a chicken—the unfortunate (for Charlie) resemblance between human and animal flesh; and one in which Charlie, while dancing with Georgia, has his pants tied up with a rope
attached to a dog—"the ballast of bad luck is tied to him" (F, p.
146). I think we should put this kind of thinking into the context
of Arnheim's larger thesis about film working by means of operating within its limitations. It can convey information only through

its images and techniques: "Literature uses words for description; film, pictures. In both media the guiding ideas are not given in abstract form but clothed in concrete episodes" (F, p. 144). What Arnheim is discovering in the Chaplin film are examples of concrete images becoming the vehicle for abstract ideas. Comparing this to the theoretical comments of Pudovkin, Eisenstein and Balázs, we see that perhaps they have stopped short too soon, insofar as they conceive of the symbolic potential of film more exclusively through the *juxtaposing* of images than, as Arnheim notes here, the use of images in the narrative which embody abstract ideas. In other words, Arnheim points out that the symbolic aspect of an image need not be separate from its function in the action; his point here is very similar to Lindsay's comments on hieroglyphics, as well as to the thinking of later semiologists such as Christian Metz.

Practical Criticism

One is struck by Arnheim's recurring call for reality in some of his practical criticism. As noted earlier, he thinks it is important for film to show us the familiar as something new. Reviewing Siegfried Kracauer's *Theory of Film*, he argues that film is "equipped to redeem . . . the view of a boundless, indeterminate, unfathomable world" (M, p. 183). Thus one understands his praise of the avant-garde film maker Maya Deren: "she was one of the artists and thinkers who speak of the great paradox of our time; who say that, although our civilization has come closest to penetrating the secrets of inorganic and organic matter, we are less familiar with the world of tangible things than any human tribe has ever been. And, thus, in Maya Deren's film, the familiar engages us by its pervasive strangeness" ("To Maya Deren," in *Film Culture Reader*, ed. P. Adams Sitney [New York: Praeger, 1970], p. 85). Again, he praises the underwater film work of Jacques-Yves Cousteau: "These most authentically realistic pictures reveal a world of profound mystery, a darkness momentarily lifted by flashes of unnatural light, a complete suspension of the familiar vertical and horizontal coordinates of space" ("Art Today and the Film," p. 252).

ANDRÉ BAZIN*

André Bazin (1918–1958) is for the post-World War II film generation what Eisenstein was for that before the war: the most significant voice, *the* critic others must acknowledge and with whom they must come to terms. As editor of the extremely influential *Cahiers du Cinéma*, Bazin encouraged and published works by men who became the leaders of the New Wave in the late fifties: François Truffaut, Jean-Luc Godard, Claude Chabrol and Eric Rohmer. In fact, those familiar with the biography of the much-loved Bazin know that he rescued Truffaut twice—first from a reform school, and, three years later, from prison, where he had been sent for deserting the French army. Although Bazin's death at age forty, after years of illness, was a tremendous loss for the film world, he left a substantial body of criticism. Hugh Gray has translated two of the four volumes constituting *What Is Cinema?* and given readers masterful and invaluable commentary on the intellectual forces influencing Bazin, and explanations of his theories, particularly his rejection of montage, his analysis of the aesthetics of neorealism and his conception of the director as an author who "writes in film." The fullest account of his life and ideas will be found in Dudley Andrew's superb biography, *André Bazin* (New York: Oxford University Press, 1978). I will examine here Bazin's theory of reality and film, and reasons for rejecting montage and expressionism; his discussions of realism in Welles and the Italian neorealists; theory of the director as author; comments on film's relationship to other arts; and, finally, his observations on documentaries and westerns.

---

*Key to Abbreviations:
C = *What Is Cinema?* ed. and trans. Hugh Gray, 2 vols. (Berkeley: University of California Press, 1971–1972). Reprinted by permission of the University of California Press.
R = *Jean Renoir*, ed. François Truffaut, trans. W. W. Halsey II and William H. Simon (New York: Delta, 1974).

The Case Against Montage and Expressionism

Commenting on the famous montage of the stone lions in Eisenstein's *Potemkin,* Bazin notes: "By skillful juxtaposition a group of sculptured lions are made to look like a single lion getting to its feet, a symbol of the aroused masses. This clever device would be unthinkable in any film after 1932" (C, I, 32). It is not a rejection of Eisenstein the man or developer of cinema that is implicit in this dismissal, for Bazin acknowledges his predecessor's importance throughout *What Is Cinema?* What Bazin finds passé and undesirable in the montage of the lions is similar to that element which he rejects in German expressionist films like *The Cabinet of Dr. Caligari*—the use of artificial devices and techniques to create meaning. He does not want "plastic symbolism and the artifices of montage," or anything "which manifests an explicit imposition of technique on the meaning of the film," or any system of aesthetics that "places more confidence in the artifices of cinematography . . . than in the reality to which they are applied" (R, p. 105). In his famous study of "The Evolution of Film Language," he identifies two major trends in the development of film: one in which directors put faith in the image, using either montage or, as with the expressionists, the plastics of the decor (sets, lighting); the other in which directors "put their faith in reality" (C, I, 24). Having faith in reality means allowing the camera to capture and then project the reality given to us as perceivers, unaltered by any overly intrusive distortions or alterations. This need for reality, untouched or retouched by man, seems to Bazin a basic human need. As he explains in "The Myth of Total Cinema," the birth of film simply waited on technical advances, since man had for ages desired "integral realism." The desire to copy nature accurately explains the need for sound, color and depth; only such a total cinema can provide "a recreation of the world in its own image" (C, I, 21). We gain such a "recreation of the world" most effectively when the camera presents reality without interruptions and moves unobtrusively in a fluid manner through the scene of action, or else remains static and photographs what occurs in a given space.

For Bazin, montage and expressionism are, by definition, antirealistic. Since, in one sense, realism resides in "the homogeneity of space" (C, I, 50), montage, by constantly switching the angles through which reality is rendered, inevitably alters

the spatial relationships existing both within the scene and between the scene and the spectator, thus introducing what Bazin
calls "spatial discontinuity, a phenomenon foreign to the nature of
the human eye" (R, p. 89). A similar disruption of space occurs in
expressionist works like *Caligari*, where typically "the systematic
use of close-ups and unusual angles is well calculated to destroy
any sense of space" (C, I, 109).

The radical alteration of space by montage and expressionistic
techniques is only part of a larger violation of film identified by
Bazin: preserving the integrity of the shot itself from the imposition of meaning outside the shot. Thus he does not support the
principle inherent in Kuleshov's experiment with the actor and
the soup. An individual shot means nothing in that circumstance
and has to be juxtaposed before it gains meaning. In contrast,
Bazin calls for an appreciation of the shot on its own terms, "in
which the image is evaluated not according to what it adds to
reality but what it reveals of it" (C, I, 28). He notes that even at
the time when film was dominated by Russian montage, there
were directors who used the camera to reveal existing reality.
Thus F. W. Murnau, who directed *Sunrise* and *The Last Laugh*,
rates Bazin's praise: "the composition of his image is in no sense
pictorial. It adds nothing to the reality" but "forces it to reveal its
structural depth, to bring out the preexisting relations which become constitutive of the drama." Erich von Stroheim, the director of *Greed*, also aimed at capturing reality: in his films, "reality
lays itself bare like a suspect confessing under the relentless examination of the commissioner of police" (C, I, 27). Neither director gives us a fragmented and radically reassembled reality,
but, rather, images which we must confront and examine on their
own terms. Under such circumstances, when the images are not
juxtaposed or distorted through emphasis on plastics, the spectator's role in perception becomes much more active. We must
make connections and draw inferences which would otherwise be
forced on us in montage or expressionist films.

Depth of Field and Orson Welles

Instead of the abstract connections of montage, Bazin calls
for concrete associations made possible by techniques running
counter to montage. He finds examples of these in the works of

Orson Welles and neorealist directors: the former "restored to
reality its visible continuity" (C, II, 28); the latter transfer "the
continuum of reality" to the screen (C, I, 37). Both effect this
through their use of depth of field, a technique Bazin considers "a
capital gain in the field of direction—a dialectical step forward
in the history of film language" (C, I, 35). Thus, like Eisenstein,
he sees the device as having importance. As I noted earlier, with
the development of panchromatic film it was possible to use special lenses in such a way that the various fields in a given shot
would all register with equal clarity rather than appear in varying
degrees of focus (i.e., foreground in clear focus, background in
unclear focus).

Although used in the 1930s by directors such as Jean Renoir
and William Wyler, depth of field was given its most sophisticated
use to date by Orson Welles in *Citizen Kane* (1941). Examination
of Bazin's praise of that film's technique will illustrate why he
considers depth of field so important. First, because the camera is
often motionless during long takes with depth of field, Welles
generates movement from the actors rather than from montage.
In his book on Welles, Bazin describes the famous scene in which
Kane discovers Susan after her suicide attempt; the scene pictures a glass enlarged by its prominent position in the foreground, Susan on the bed in the middle ground, and Kane burst-
ing in the door in the background: "Without having seen anything
but a glass and having heard two noises of different sound levels,
we have suddenly understood the situation. . . . The dramatic
structure of the scene is essentially based on the distinction between the two sounds: the gasps, nearby, of Susan and the bang-
ings of her husband behind the door. A tension is established
between these two poles, held at a distance by the depth of
focus." Kane's entrance in the background and progress toward
the foreground act like a "spark . . . struck between the two dramatic poles of the image" ("The Originality of Orson Welles as a
Director," trans. Mark Bernheim and Ronald Gottesman, in
Focus on Citizen Kane, ed. Ronald Gottesman [Englewood Cliffs:
Prentice-Hall, 1971], pp. 128–129). Bazin speculates on how the
scene might have been filmed with traditional methods of montage, and observes that, in *one* shot, Welles resolves all these potentials into a single image: "Welles's extreme use of deep focus

tends to destroy the notion of the shot as a unity of cutting. . . .
Paradoxically, the camera's immobility becomes a very complicated movement when the scene itself is in movement" (*Focus*,
p. 129). It is true that elsewhere in *Citizen Kane* Welles uses
montage, but only to give an added meaning to the deep focus
shots, for example its function in condensing time (C, I, 36). In
general, Welles is to be praised because of his "reluctance to
fragment things arbitrarily and a desire instead to show an image
that is uniformly understandable and that compels the spectator
to make his own choice" (C, I, 92).

The second value of depth of field for Bazin lies in the fact
that the essentially static nature of such shots introduces ambiguity, that quality in life which we encounter so often and
which is so central to the interpretation of Welles's film: "*Citizen
Kane* is unthinkable shot in any way but in depth. The uncer-
tainty in which we find ourselves as to the spiritual key or the
interpretation we should put on the film is built into the very
design of the image" (C, I, 36).

In general, ambiguity as presented in deep focus forces us to
enter into a closer relationship with the material than we have
with everyday reality (C, I, 35–36). Montage rules out such ambiguity for Bazin. Kuleshov's experiment proves this, since the
facial expression on the actor means nothing until juxtaposed with
another image. With depth of field part of our active participation
involves choice, as we make connections within the image which
we view. Too often with montage images, though, the aesthetic
response demanded by Bazin is impossible. If montage only generates images, unconnected in the real world, then we as viewers
are denied the active intellectual potential given by images presented in deep focus. We are not presented with images of concrete meaning and associations, but only shots with abstract
meanings; in such a case, "the apparent action and the meaning
we attribute to it do not exist. . . prior to the assembling of the
film, not even in the form of fragmented scenes out of which the
set-ups are generally composed" (C, I, 44). In contrast, as Bazin
notes in his study of Renoir, depth of field "confirms the unity of
actor and decor, the total interdependence of everything real,
from the human to the mineral. In the representation of space, it
is a necessary modality of this realism which postulates a constant

sensitivity to the world but which opens to a universe of
analogies, of metaphors, or . . . of correspondences" (R, p. 90).

Neorealism

I have stressed the importance Bazin places on our activities
when viewing scenes photographed with depth of field because
he argues that the same kind of process occurs during our experience of neorealist films. Briefly, the term neorealist is used to
describe films and directors appearing after World War II, such
as *The Bicycle Thief* by Vittorio De Sica, *Paisà* by Robert Rossellini, *La Terra Trema* by Luchino Visconti, and *La Strada* by
Federico Fellini (the later works of Fellini are not in this category). Neorealist films are characterized by a pronounced social
consciousness on the part of their makers, a concern for the lower
classes and their despair and squalor, and a stark realism of technique relying heavily on long takes and depth of field.

Just as viewers encountering an individual shot in deep focus
must make connections in the given framework of the image, so
too in the neorealist film must we draw together the implicit
meaning and relationships existing in the work as a whole. Twice
Bazin uses the same analogy to explain the kind of mental process
he believes is at work as we watch neorealist works. Speaking of
Rossellini's *Paisà,* he points out that "the mind has to leap from
one event to the other as one leaps from stone to stone in cros-
sing a river" (C, II, 35). Defending Rossellini some years later, he
contrasts the forms of classical art and traditional realism with
those of neorealism by conceptualizing the former as bricks and
the latter as stones. Bricks are assembled into structures which
we encounter as finished products, like a house or a bridge. In
contrast, the stones in a river, even if we use them as a bridge,
are, first of all, stones: "the big rocks that lie scattered in a ford
are now and ever will be no more than mere rocks. Their reality
as rocks is not affected when, leaping from one to another, I use
them to cross the river. If the service which they have rendered
is the same as that of the bridge, it is because I have brought my
share of ingenuity to bear on their chance arrangement; I have
added the motion which . . . gives them a provisional meaning and
utility." In classical and traditional art, meaning is given a priori,

since "the house is already there in the brick." In neorealist art, meaning is a posteriori, since "it permits our awareness to move from one fact to another, from one fragment of reality to the next" (C, II, 99). In other words, both a shot with depth of field and a neorealist film share the quality that they force viewers to make sense of the reality which is there.

Also, to understand more what Bazin sees in the neorealist accomplishment, particularly its use of the long take and rejection of montage, we must grasp what he means by "ellipsis." He refers to the appearance in such films of apparent gaps and exclusions during the progress of the works. But these are to be considered quite differently from the gaps that might be encountered in a work built on montage from the Russian period of realism. In the neorealist films, the gaps function to suggest ambiguity, just as depth of field within a shot can suggest this quality: "The assemblage of the film must never add anything to the existing reality. If it is part of the meaning of the film, as with Rossellini, it is because the empty gaps, the white spaces, the parts of the event that we see are not given, are themselves of a concrete nature.... It is the same in life: we do not know everything that happens to others. Ellipsis in classic montage is an effect of style. In Rossellini's film it is a lacuna in reality, or rather in the knowledge we have of it, which is by its nature limited" (C, II, 66).

Bazin presents an avowedly phenomenological view in his discussion of neorealism; he is interested in the process of perception whereby subject and viewer are united in the aesthetic experience and in which all extraneous material between subject and viewer is eliminated. The realism we are given by Italian neorealists manifests itself in scenes having "ontological equality" (C, II, 81). That is, each scene has its own meaning in the framework of the larger narrative, and the director presents each of these in such a way that we are made party to incidents in reality, just as we would be in real life. Bazin observes that in De Sica's *The Bicycle Thief* each scene has its own "phenomenological integrity." Those familiar with the film will remember that at one point during the search for the stolen bicycle by the father and son, the boy has to urinate. Both his father and the viewer must wait; that is, we are made party to the reality of the event which interrupts the search and, equally, our following of that search. In other words, form supports content here, as well as drawing us into the reality of a human activity. The director by his choice of what to include in the film announces that there are no value judgments to be made about the experiences in life; reality is reality: "the events are not necessarily signs of something, of a truth of which we are to be convinced; they all carry their own weight, their complete uniqueness, that ambiguity that characterizes any fact" (C, II, 52).

Not surprisingly, Bazin's support for neorealism includes strong enthusiasm for the use of non-actors. We have already encountered other critics from Russia favoring the practice, typage, for its greater realistic contribution to a film. Bazin identifies several kinds of practice in this regard. The one used by Rossellini is an example of what Bazin calls the "law of the amalgam," whereby a director refuses to use a superstar, choosing instead to proceed with a combination of professional and non-professional actors. In the best circumstances, a bond will be generated among the entire cast as the authenticity emanating from the non-professionals acting out their normal activities contributes to a healthy atmosphere: "the result is precisely that extraordinary feeling of truth that one gets from the current Italian films. Their faithfulness to a script which stirs them deeply and which calls for the minimum of theatrical pretense sets up a kind of osmosis among the cast" (C, II, 24). He also acknowledges that the complete use of non-professionals can be successful, as in Visconti's *La Terra Trema.*

The "Auteur" Theory

Neorealist films tend to have a documentary quality, but are not limited simply to "documentarism" (C, II, 97). This is proved for Bazin by the fact that instead of cold and impersonal treatments of the subjects and characters, neorealist directors take stands on their materials. It is paradoxical and initially confusing for those reading Bazin for the first time to encounter his arguments for the primacy of realism, and his emphasis on the absolute objectivity of the images registered by the photographic machine. One might wonder how the most important spokesman for the *auteur* theory, which stresses the importance of the director's sensibility and contribution to the work, can champion the concept that the image captured by the camera is "unburdened by the freedom of interpretation of the artist" (C, I, 21). Again, it seems unlikely that Bazin would be saying, as he does, that there is no interference in the process of creation: "for the first time, between the originating object and its reproduction there intervenes only the instrumentality of a nonliving agent. For the first time an image of the world is formed automatically, without the creative intervention of man" (C, I, 13). To resolve this paradox, two things should be noted. First, Bazin tends to modify this rather extreme position in later essays. Second, even in this early statement in "The Ontology of the Photographic Image," he admits that inevitably the personality of the artist will play some part in the creation of the film.

The concept of the director dominates most of Bazin's criticism, whether he is writing about the neorealists, Renoir or Chaplin. Put most succinctly, "the director writes in film" (C, I, 39). Bazin thus echoes his compatriot Alexandre Astruc's famous demand "to call this new age of cinema the age of *caméra-stylo* (camera-pen)."* As such, it is possible to discuss the *auteur* as we would a literary artist and consider his central themes, patterns of imagery, and techniques while we attempt to determine his uniqueness, views, and "signature" as these can be deduced from the works.

Bazin never retreats from his position that film meets a basic human need by giving us the image of the world. But as his theories are solidified, he emphasizes more the idea that the director becomes a vitally important force in rendering this reality for us. There must be some medium which functions to effect our apprehension of that reality. This happens through the agency of a human spirit, that of the director. Thus, in his discussion of Renoir, Bazin remarks that we can define a director's style by considering the way in which he treats the "dialectic between reality and abstraction, between the concrete and the ideal. In

---

*"The Birth of a New Avant-Garde: *La Caméra-Stylo*," in *The New Wave*, ed. by Peter Graham (Garden City, N. Y.: Doubleday, 1968), p. 18. Quoted by permission of Martin Secker & Warburg Limited.

the final analysis, the principle of a director's style lies in his way of giving reality meaning" (R, p. 84).

Specifically in regard to neorealist directors, Bazin says we try to determine their outlooks by examining the images they choose to give us; in this way we can talk about reality as it is filtered through the consciousness of the authors. Neorealism "always presupposes an attitude of mind: it is always reality as it is visible through an artist, as refracted by his consciousness—but by his consciousness as a whole and not by his reason alone or his emotions or his beliefs"; that is, "the consciousness of the neorealist director *filters* reality." The selection of images presented to us is "ontological, in the sense that the image of reality it restores to us is still a whole"; "there is ontological identity between the object and its photographic image" (C, II, 98). Thus, the director's consciousness is the means by which reality is rendered through the agency of the image. For Bazin, "the photographic image is the object itself, the object freed from the conditions of time and space that govern it"; "the image . . . shares, by virtue of the very process of its becoming, the being of the model of which it is the reproduction; it *is* the model" (C, I, 14).

It is useful to remember Eisenstein's dialectical critical method as we observe Bazin's comments on various artists. For example, in his brilliant analysis of De Sica, who would seem to be his favorite neorealist director, he finds a contrast between chance occurrences and an overriding tragic structure: "it is precisely from the dialectical synthesis of contrary values, namely artistic order and the amorphous disorder of reality, that [*The Bicycle Thief*] derives its originality" (C, II, 68). Again, the film's power "resides in the paradox of its having reconciled radically opposite values: factual freedom and narrative discipline" (C, II, 76). De Sica's most important accomplishment lies precisely in the power of his dialectic, for he has "succeeded in discovering the cinematographic dialect capable of transcending the contradiction between the action of a 'spectacle' and of an event" (C, II, 60).

Fellini's style is different. It is in discussions such as these that we see how useful the *auteur* theory can be. How exactly *do* we go about explaining how the style of one director differs from

that of another? Bazin gives us a fine example. He suggests that
Fellini's themes can be conceived of "vertically" in relation to the
"horizontal" nature of the narrative. Thus the action does not unfold in accordance with typical laws of causation: "Events do not
'happen' in Fellini's world; they 'befall' its inhabitants; that is to
say, they occur as an effect of 'vertical' gravity, not in conformity
to the laws of 'horizontal' causality" (C, II, 84–85). The characters
are also differentiated from those of the other neorealists, for Fellini tends to define them solely through their appearance rather
than their behavior. We recognize them by "signs, not only their
faces, of course, but by the way they move, by everything that
makes the body the outer shell of the inner man" and by "things
such as a haircut, moustache, clothing, eye glasses" (C, II, 88).
Thus, in contrast to the other neorealists, Fellini "introduces a
new kind of script, the scenario lacking any dramatic linking,
based . . . on the phenomenological description of the characters"
(C, II, 90).

Significantly, Bazin considers De Sica as the successor of
Chaplin. Both make effective use of a child (C, II, 53–54): both
achieve extraordinary dramatic effects from essentially "neutral"
shooting scripts (C, II, 57); and both convey an incredible sense
of love, although in De Sica this is objectified in the actors:
"Chaplin concentrates on himself and within himself the radiation
of his tenderness, which means that cruelty is not always
excluded from his world; on the contrary, it has a necessary and
dialectic relationship to love. . . . He is ready to love everything,
but the world does not always respond. On the other hand, De
Sica the director infuses into his actors the power to love that he
possesses as an actor. . . . We find in De Sica the humanity of
Chaplin, but shared with the world at large" (C, II, 72–73).

The various essays Bazin writes on Chaplin bear instructive
comparison with Eisenstein's "Charlie the Kid." As I noted,
Eisenstein finds the center of Chaplin's genius in his ability to
look at the world through the eyes of a child; one force attempting to destroy that attitude comes from mechanical authority.
Bazin also identifies one of the major elements in Chaplin's work
as his relationship to the mechanical. Charlie's inability to interact
with things and tools (as in *Modern Times*) is symptomatic of his
failure to be accepted by the mechanical world. His attempts to

adapt himself to this world are failures: "mechanization of movement is in a sense Charlie's original sin" (C, I, 151).

In a more extended study of Chaplin's later work, Bazin defends the much-attacked *Monsieur Verdoux* as a logical extension
of the basic career of Charlie, in much the same way that Eisenstein explains the place of *The Great Dictator* in relation to the
characters in Chaplin's world. Having traced the evolution of
Charlie's character through the silent period up to the time of
The Circus, Bazin makes the incisive observation that the murderer Chaplin of *Verdoux* is the double and antithesis of Charlie:
"By reversing the character, the whole Chaplin universe is turned
upside down at one stroke" (C, II, 106). Society has been trying
to cast out Charlie in all the films, especially through its policemen. Here again Charlie is subject to the law, but with a difference, for this time he *is* guilty. Still, as before, Charlie continues to make us see society as guilty, for the mercantile and
social behavior he imitates as Verdoux is at the heart of the corrupt society which condemns him.

There is a decided biographical cast to Bazin's discussion of
Limelight, Chaplin's film about the aging performer; he finds it
"impossible to separate the story of Calvero from the Chaplin
myth" (C, II, 125). He wonders if in the hero's "decision to give
up the music hall in exchange for the anonymity of a street
singer, [there is] a touching self-questioning on Charlie's part" (C,
II, 126). *Limelight* reveals "beyond doubt Chaplin's most secret
heart, borne inside him over a long period, perhaps even un-
aware," a fear of failure which never in fact happened (C, II,
131). Chaplin presents this fear in his double and opposite, an
aging failure: "Calvero is at once Chaplin and his opposite. First,
and irrefutably, by the identity of the faces. . . . But, secondly,
the truth about Chaplin is the opposite of Calvero's failure: in his
art as in his life, Chaplin is a Calvero whose fabulous name has
never known eclipse" (C, II, 134). In a telling passage, Bazin
speculates that the film may have had an almost cathartic effect
upon Chaplin; the chance that he *might* have turned into a
Calvero "makes Chaplin shudder and haunts his nights—else
why would he have made *Limelight*?" (C, II, 135).

Those interested in Bazin's *auteur* criticism should also consult his study of Jean Renoir, left unfinished at his death but is-

sued through the efforts of François Truffaut and Bazin's wife.
There one will find identification of various periods in Renoir's
development, the isolation of specific themes and image patterns
(such as water), a study of the director's use of technical devices
(for example, little use of depth of field in the early films, much
more later on), and fine discussions of Renoir's masterpieces, in
particular *Grand Illusion* and *Rules of the Game.*

In an essay, "La Politique des Auteurs," written a year before his death, Bazin reassesses the *auteur* theory as it has been
used by writers for his journal, *Cahiers du Cinéma,* and presents
some cautionary and sane warnings about its use. He argues that
the theory should not be made a kind of critical free pass, as
some *auteur* critics have done with it. Critics misusing the theory
tend to view all works in a director's canon as becoming increasingly better, whether they are or not. But Bazin cannot accept
the claim that because Welles's *Mr. Arkadian* is his sixth picture
it is necessarily better than *Citizen Kane*; for him it is clearly
inferior and should be declared so. He believes that "to a certain
extent, at least, the *auteur* is a subject to himself; whatever the
scenario, he always tells the same story" and "has the same attitude and passes the same moral judgements on the action and
the characters." He accepts Jacques Rivette's suggestion that "an
auteur is someone who speaks in the first person" (*New Wave,*
pp. 150–151). But there are dangers in the policy, particularly
when it degenerates into "an aesthetic personality cult" (*New
Wave,* p. 152).

Although the equation "work equals author plus subject" may
be useful, it ceases to be viable when critics consider the author
as the sole interest, to the exclusion of the work itself. Bazin
chastises such critics: "all they want to retain in the equation *auteur plus subject = work* is the *auteur,* while the subject is reduced to zero" (*New Wave,* p. 150). Other problems with the
theory follow when *auteur* critics champion only their pet directors (like Howard Hawks or Alfred Hitchcock) while ignoring or
rejecting those directors not considered *auteurs.* Bazin suggests:
"the *politique des auteurs* seems to me to hold and defend an
essential critical truth that the cinema needs more than the other
arts, precisely because an act of true artistic creation is more un-
certain and vulnerable in the cinema than elsewhere. But its ex-

clusive practice leads to another danger: the negation of the film to the benefit and praise of its *auteur*" (*New Wave*, p. 155). His own criticism stands as a healthy example of the best that *auteur* criticism has to give us. We will see the same intelligent application of the theory later when we discuss the criticism of America's leading *auteur* critic, Andrew Sarris.

Film and the Other Arts

It is worth noting some of Bazin's comments on the relationships between film and the other arts. He is fond of using the distinction between centrifugal and centripetal forces to distinguish the spatial nature of film on the one hand, and that of theatre and painting on the other. In film, by virtue of the freedom of the camera, space is fluid and flexible; the opposite is true in the theatre. Thus the playing area cannot be conceived of as having a specific *locus dramaticus*: "There are no wings to the screen. . . . In contrast to the stage, the space of the screen is centrifugal" (C, I, 105). That is, in film we are in a situation where the space extends outward beyond the edges of the screen, in contrast to the centripetal force which is directed inward toward the middle of the stage.

Failure to recognize the contrast between these outer- and inner-directed forces in relation to the action has resulted in poorly conceived filmed plays. Those directors who adapt works unsuccessfully from the stage to the screen either simply photograph the theatrical space, a violation of film's outer-directed space, or else they add useless and heavy-handed naturalistic devices to give the appearance of a film to what is still essentially a play. The truly successful translations of a play to the screen occur when a director like Sir Laurence Olivier in his production of *Henry V* uses film to stage a play. Olivier and Jean Cocteau both acknowledge the relationship between the audience and the stage, and "adopt the viewpoint of the spectator, the one denominator common to stage and screen." Like Olivier, Cocteau, "instead of trying like so many others to dissolve [the play] in cinema, on the contrary . . . uses the resources of the camera to point up, to underline, to confirm the structure of the scenes and their psychological corollaries" (C, I, 93). That is, film is used to

enhance the action within the basic terms of the dramatic situation: "to reveal, to bring to light certain details that the stage
would have left untreated" (C, I, 91).

Bazin also examines the dynamics of actor-audience relations
as these are changed by film, and suggests that, in contrast to
previous concerns with this issue, the more important problem to
be solved when filming a play involves the decor rather than the
actor. Thus, "the basic aesthetic problem of filmed theatre is indeed that of the decor. The trump card that the director must
hold is the reconversion into a window onto the world of a
space oriented toward an interior dimension only, namely the
closed and conventional area of the theatrical play" (C, I, 111). In
other words, when filming a play, the director should not simply
photograph the stage; nor should he pretend that the stage has
the same kind of space as that of a film. Rather, he should attempt to reveal all the aspects of theatrical space with filmic
techniques, thus allowing the spectator to see more in the *given*
space.

The centrifugal-centripetal distinction holds true for film and
painting as well. Bazin notes that the use of film to reproduce
paintings in studies of painters and famous works is bound to be a
disservice to the artist, even though such studies are well inten-
tioned and usually designed for educational purposes. The space
of a painting is inner-directed, centripetal like that of the stage.
Thus a film of that space disrupts it. The camera is "aesthetically
at odds" with painting because the film maker "fragments what is
by essence a synthesis while himself working toward a new synthesis never envisioned by the painter" (C, I, 164). Thus the two
are different: "The outer edges of the screen are not, as the technical jargon would seem to imply, the frame of the film image.
They are the edges of a piece of masking that shows only a por-
tion of reality. The picture frame polarizes space inwards. On the
contrary, what the screen shows us seems to be part of something
prolonged indefinitely into the universe. A frame is centripetal,
the screen centrifugal" (C, I, 166).

Elsewhere he observes that the advent of film and photography has freed painting and the plastic arts "from their obsession
with likeness," insofar as the latter no longer need to accommo-

date the human desire for reality in art. Calling perspective "the
original sin of Western painting," Bazin suggests that since photography can so faithfully duplicate the world, the other repre-
sentational arts are now free to develop their own unique properties (C, I, 12). Painting, in particular, will be able to gain back
its own "aesthetic autonomy" (C, I, 16).

Documentaries and Westerns

Given Bazin's enthusiasm for film's ability to capture reality,
it is not surprising that he praises certain documentary films
which allow us to experience reality almost firsthand. In particular, he commends *Kon-Tiki*, in which the material we see is *real*.
He notes that there is always a paradox with the documentary
film. Either one has the real thing, as in *Kon-Tiki*, and pays for
this authenticity by having to bear with imperfect technical work
and with the limitations imposed by the circumstances—for
example, at the height of a crisis on ship nothing can be filmed
because there is no one to work the camera. Or else one must
watch a "reconstructed" action in an educational documentary,
such as *With Scott to the South Pole*, where the reality is inevitably "made up" since we are viewing a modern reenactment of
events that happened over a decade ago. For Bazin the movie
about Scott fails mainly because it engages in a fruitless task: "to
imitate the inimitable, to reconstruct that which of its very nature
can only occur once, namely risk, adventure, death" (C, I, 158).
On the other hand, since the camera is actually part of the Kon-
Tiki expedition, the events registered on film, even if limited, are
much more desirable. For example, he delights in the moment
when the camera photographs a killer whale: "the making of
[*Kon-Tiki*] is so totally identified with the action that it so imper-
fectly unfolds." We are interested in the killer whale because at
any moment during the process of photographing it, crew and
boat might be annihilated: "It is not so much the photograph of
the whale that interests us as the photograph of the *danger*" (C,
I, 161). Elsewhere, Bazin expresses his admiration for Robert
Flaherty, whose *Man of Aran* and *Nanook of the North* rely on
long takes rather than on montage to capture and convey reality
(C, I, 27, 162).

Like that of Robert Warshow, Bazin's analysis of the western
is based on the identification of a basic myth imbedded in the
structure of such films. Calling the western *"the American film
par excellence,"* he observes, in a manner anticipating that of later
structural analysis, that "those formal attributes by which one
normally recognizes the western are simply signs or symbols of its
profound reality, namely the myth" (C, II, 142). Stated briefly,
the myth pictures women as thoroughly good, whether the particular woman be the pure virgin or the warm-hearted floozie in
the dancehall. If the former, she usually faces a conflict between
loyalties to her family and to her suitor, a cowboy who is not as
good as she and who must undergo various trials to win her love;
he does so, usually by rescuing her from a dangerous situation.
Note here how Bazin identifies the basic structure while putting
the western into the larger narrative framework of medieval
courtly romance: "this outline into which one can weave a
thousand variants—for example, by substituting the Civil War for
the Indian threat, cattle rustlers—comes close to reminding us of
the medieval courtly romances by virtue of the preeminence
given to the woman and the trials that the finest of heroes must
undergo in order to qualify for her love" (C, II, 144).

The fact that even the floozie is presented as essentially good
suggests to Bazin that the western mirrors sociological conditions
of the time; that is, during the development of the frontier,
women had to be protected because they were scarce: "The myth
of the western illustrates, and both initiates and confirms woman
in her role as vestal of the social virtues. . . . Within her is concealed the physical future, and, by way of the institution of the
family to which she aspires as the root is drawn to the earth, its
moral foundation" (C, II, 145). Also in his analysis of the knights
in westerns is the insight that such films embody both tragic and
epic ethics. In addition, he points out the relevance of photographic techniques, reminding us in a way of Lindsay. For example, the set-ups emphasize "vast horizons" which underline man's
conflict with nature (C, II, 147).

In "The Evolution of the Western," Bazin describes various
kinds of westerns on the basis of the director's attitude toward the
material. There are basic westerns and "super westerns"; the lat-

ter, like *High Noon* and *Shane*, display a self-conscious use of the western forms, grafting important social and moral ideas upon them.

As in my discussion of Eisenstein, I have tried to present the most significant elements of Bazin's theories. Briefly, his demand for reality in film occasions his call for film makers to use those techniques which will give us the greatest sense of presence: depth of field and the long take. Montage and expressionism interfere with the presentation of the image, destroy real space, and prevent viewers from drawing connections between elements in the shot, thus robbing film of its ability to convey ambiguity. Reality comes to us filtered through the consciousness of the director or author. One of our jobs as critics is to determine the basic forms, themes and techniques which characterize his style.

SIEGFRIED KRACAUER*

The last major theorist to be discussed in this section of the *Guide* is Siegfried Kracauer (1889–1966), teacher and man of letters. In *Theory of Film* he argues for the primacy of external reality as the most important subject of film. Kracauer constantly displays affinities to and support of positions we have seen advocated by Béla Balázs and Rudolf Arnheim; even though he seems not to have read André Bazin, we can find striking parallels and points of agreement with the latter, especially in their shared enthusiasm for neorealism. This chapter explains two major themes in *Theory of Film:* Kracauer's distinction between what he calls the realist and formative impulses in photography and cinema; and his definition of cinematic content. In a note at the end of the chapter, I comment briefly on his other major study of film, *From Caligari to Hitler.*

The Need for Reality

Perhaps the most efficient way to approach *Theory of Film* is to consider Kracauer's epilogue, "Film in Our Time." There the reader finds the basic thesis and underlying rationale of the work stated explicitly. The key to both lies in the work's subtitle: "The Redemption of Physical Reality." Briefly, Kracauer sees twentieth-century man in a universe which has lost its ideological coherence, largely through the encroachments of science. Modern society consists only of individuals, fragments, who in their desire

---

*Key to Abbreviations:

T = *Theory of Film* (New York: Oxford University Press, 1971). Reprinted by permission of Oxford University Press.

C = *From Caligari to Hitler* (Princeton: Princeton University Press, 1974). Reprinted by permission of Princeton University Press.

for certainty and meaning find no hope in myth, which has been stripped of its validity by science, or, for that matter, in science itself, which constantly frustrates our attempts to come in contact with reality by reducing phenomena to formulae and principles. Cut off from both the mental and physical worlds, we need something which will make sense of our existence. Kracauer believes that film will effect this by bringing the material world to us, thus combatting the power of science. True, belief may be gone, but we can still establish contact with the surface of things rather than relying solely on science's abstract statements: "Film renders visible what we did not, or perhaps even could not, see before its advent. It effectively assists us in discovering the material world with its psychophysical correspondences. We literally redeem this world from its dormant state, its state of virtual nonexistence, by endeavoring to experience it through the camera. And we are free to experience it because we are fragmentized. The camera can be defined as a medium particularly equipped to promote the redemption of physical reality. Its imagery permits us, for the first time, to take away with us the objects and occurrences that comprise the flow of material life" (T, p. 300).

Kracauer thinks the traditional arts use reality in quite a different manner than film. For example, painting overwhelms and transforms nature by altering it. In contrast, film aims primarily at recording and revealing nature without changing it. Film thrives on presenting faces, streets, chance occurrences, casual glances. Its images corroborate our vision of reality.

The Realist and Formative Impulses

Since film lets us see our world, Kracauer argues throughout *Theory of Film*, the best way for the artist to proceed is by capturing "nature in the raw" in a realistic manner. He identifies two trends which developed at the birth of photography and then continued to figure in film. Artists in the *realistic* tradition acknowledge the properties of the medium and attempt to record and reveal reality. In contrast, those in what he calls the *formative* tradition attempt to alter the given reality, either because they wish to add to the purely mechanical reproduction of the image presented by the camera, or else—and more likely—because they

wish to compose and create like painters and sculptors. But
Kracauer thinks that those who try to imitate traditional plastic
arts defy the basic properties of photography and film. Of course,
he recognizes that inevitably there will be formative aspects to
any essentially realistic endeavor, and does not imagine that film
exists as just a series of random shots. Still, the only justification
for giving rein to formative impulses must be the photographer's
desire to capture nature more effectively (T, pp. 15–16).

The Affinities of Photography and Film

Kracauer explains how photography and film have basic affinities to aspects of reality, identifying four areas shared by both.
First, each has an affinity for "unstaged reality" and "nature in
the raw" (T, p. 18). This arises from the basic recording properties of the camera, and is evidenced in the history of both; photography and film begin by giving unaltered images of real
life—whether a picture of a Paris street by Eugène Atget or the
Lumière brothers' film of a train's entrance into a station. Second,
both display a tendency to present the fortuitous or "haphazard
contingencies" as evidenced by the dominance of the street as a
basic subject; this is where "the accidental prevails over the pro-
vidential" (T, p. 62). Third, we find both suggesting a kind of
endlessness. Like Bazin, Kracauer sees the frame on a photograph implying a reality beyond the borders. In film the quality
of endlessness appears in the form of a continuum—such things as
vast landscapes or complicated cause-and-effect relationships.
Fourth, he discusses the "indeterminate," a quality of incom-
pleteness which characterizes man and nature, "more or less
free-hovering images of material reality" (T, p. 71). He urges the
film maker to include objects which will suggest this, and thus
"exhibit and penetrate physical reality for its own sake" (T, p. 69).

One affinity possessed only by film is for the "flow of life."
Unlike photographs, film can show us reality in a time dimension
and use cinematic techniques to convey movement. In its capacity
as a *recorder* of surface movement, film is ideally suited to present actions like the chase, dancing, and "nascent movement"—
stopped motion which highlights the movements preceding and
following the frozen frame. In its capacity as a *revealer* of reality,

film presents objects and motions ordinarily missed by us—a feature discussed by both Balázs and Arnheim. Thus film lets us see the small and the big through close-ups and panorama shots. The former "metamorphose their objects by magnifying them" (T, p. 48). As with the case of Griffith's close-up of the desperate wife's hands in *Intolerance*, these "deepen our insight into the bodily components of the whole of her existence" (T, p. 49). Panorama shots are well suited to convey images of the masses; like Lindsay, Kracauer points to the uniqueness of film in this regard. As a revealing force, film also captures the transient movements of reality, using devices such as slow motion to present the development of plants. Third, film allows us to view things we might have missed through its use of camera angles.

Kinds of Cinematic Content: The Flow of Life

Content that is purely cinematic shows us materials that only a camera can capture; its motifs "are identical with, or grow out of, one or another property of film" (T, p. 272). Kracauer divides such cinematic films into three categories: those presenting the flow of life, those with the motif of sleuthing, and those with the motif of David and Goliath.

Included in the first category, the flow of life, are documentary and narrative films. Both of these utilize what he calls the embryonic found story, anything "found in the material of actual reality" and "discovered rather than contrived" (T, pp. 245–246). The films of Robert Flaherty, such as *Nanook of the North* and *Man of Aran*, illustrate the embryonic type inasmuch as they display the characteristics of choosing a story that admits of documentary treatment, allowing the story to emerge from the life of the subjects, concentrating on the public rather than private experiences, and, last, "eliciting the story from the raw material of life rather than subjecting the raw material to its preestablished demands" (T, p. 248).

The other type of found story, the *episode*, occurs primarily in narrative works; its "common property . . . is to emerge from, and again disappear in, the flow of life, as suggested by the camera" (T, p. 251). There are three divisions in this category. First,

he cites works like *The Red Balloon*, which have only one
episodic unit. Second, some films have more than one story unit
as such, and several are "strung together like beads so that they
attain to a degree of cohesion" (T, p. 253). I think *The Yellow
Rolls Royce* is a good example of this. The third and most complex kind of episodic film occurs when various units are integrated into one single story, as in Renoir's *Rules of the Game*, in
which "the units tend to fuse so that it is as if each film they
make up were a single episode" (T, p. 254). Many readers will
think of Robert Altman's *Nashville* here, for the dozen stories at
work simultaneously in that film tend to interweave, culminate
and converge into a single organic whole by the time of the
climax. *Nashville* also illustrates by its very indeterminateness
another aspect of the found episode film: "loose composition."
Sounding very much like Bazin, Kracauer acknowledges the artist
who is not afraid to have loose ends in the film, or what Bazin
calls ellipsis: "The episode film, then, is full of gaps into which
environmental life may stream" (T, pp. 255–256).

Other Motifs

Another category of film displaying truly cinematic content
includes works based on the motif of sleuthing. Such films display
affinities to the properties of the medium in their attention to
detail (close-ups), involvement with the accidental (the fortuitous),
the element of detection, and the chase. Citing Alfred Hitchcock's films in particular, Kracauer praises him for his "perfect
command of the ways in which physical data may be induced to
yield their possible meanings" (T, p. 276), and his use of people
and objects who do not bear directly on the plot but still contribute life: "his films culminate in material things and occurrences
which, besides being traces of a crime and offering clues to the
identity of the criminal, are pregnant with both external and
internal life" (T, p. 277). We might mention *Rear Window* as a
particularly good example of this quality, since it is James
Stewart's casual observation of life (remember, he is a photographer) which leads to his discovery of the murder.

The fifth division under sleuthing is the "search for truth,"
and affords Kracauer an opportunity to present rewarding insights

into the structure and meaning of *Rashomon* and *Citizen Kane*.
He praises the former as a Hitchcock-type thriller, and remarks
on its attention to the details of reality, singling out what many
find interminably boring and organically unjustified, the woodcut-
ter's walk through the forest, as a fine example of Kurosawa's use
of camera reality. *Citizen Kane* can be viewed in this motif as
well: it is "cinematically attractive because it conveys the esoteric
truth at its core by means of detection." The truth we look for has
to be "inferred from scattered pieces of evidence which yet fail to
reveal it. Only at the film's very end does a final material clue
casually answer the question that has motivated the search" (T, p.
280). Such a critical method as Kracauer displays here is useful,
for it asks us as viewers to examine films of one type to see the
ways in which they present or use motifs from films of another
type.

The last category he suggests, films based on the David and
Goliath motif, includes works in which film's properties can be
used effectively to show the small and the big. Thus Chaplin's
tramp represents the weaker "little fellow" or David figure. Similarly, the typical western hero can be seen to belong in the David
category, since he must overcome apparently overwhelming odds
to win, as do Alan Ladd in *Shane* and Gary Cooper in *High
Noon*.

Acting, Sound and Music

Following from Kracauer's view of the realistic aspects of film
are his comments on the place of the actor, and the nature and
function of sound and music. In all cases, he supports those elements when they are successfully integrated with the properties
of the cinematic medium.

Essentially the actor should try to suit himself to those aspects identified earlier as cinema's affinities. Thus he should emphasize the quality of "being" of the character and try to convey a
sense of unstaged nature. In addition, we should receive an impression of the casual and fortuitous, as in real life (T, p. 95). As
we have seen, Kracauer thinks it important for a film to explore
material reality in all its forms; thus it is not surprising that he

should consider the actor as only one element in the film's content, rather than the most important feature. Also, he distinguishes between the non-actor (typage), the Hollywood star and the professional. Although acknowledging the success of the Russians and neorealists in using the former, he concludes that it is probably more efficient to work with professionals when the aim is characterization in depth.

In a chapter on dialogue and sound, Kracauer considers the various kinds of relationships which can develop between the visual image and sound. Dialogue can be considered cinematic when speech is deemphasized and made an organic outgrowth of the visuals; when it is undercut by such devices as we see in Chaplin's *City Lights* and *Modern Times*—that is, keeping but ridiculing sound; and when speech itself becomes an element in the material continuum of reality explored by the film, as in *Pygmalion*, where the *fact* of speech enters into the plot.

After exploring possible systems of synchronous sound-image relations, he suggests that a fruitful way to combine these lies in the "asynchronous actual sound issuing from an identifiable source and relating contrapuntally to the synchronized images" (T, p. 130). He offers two examples of this. In the first, from Lang's *M*, we *hear* the mother's cries for her missing daughter while we *see* shots of empty stairs, a plate and the child's balloon. In the other example, he points to the scene in Elia Kazan's *On the Waterfront* when Marlon Brando explains to Eva Marie Saint his role in the murder of her brother; we *see* them talking and infer the content of his speech, but do not *hear* what he says because of the noise of the boats in the harbor.

In a discussion of music, Kracauer distinguishes between music used as background material, commentary, counterpoint, or as an actual element of the narrative. Basically an unrealistic form, the musical film can be cinematic insofar as the music occurs naturally. Thus, sometimes in Fred Astaire movies the songs and dances seem to grow out of the "contingencies" of life. When well integrated with the plot, music can become part of the action itself, as in the cymbal clash which is the climax of Hitchcock's *The Man Who Knew Too Much*, or, to offer a later example, Beethoven's Fifth Symphony in *A Clockwork Orange*. Again, music can be a component of the narrative, emerging naturally in stories about entertainers. Recent examples of this are Bob Fosse's *Cabaret* and Martin Scorsese's *New York, New York,* in which the songs occur as they are actually performed. We could add here that Kracauer would have praised the contrapuntal use of music in Miloš Forman's *One Flew Over the Cuckoo's Nest.* There the 45-RPM records played in the nurses' station offer the patients calm and melodious tunes; but the music is ironically and dialectically opposed to the tension and the actual unsettled state of affairs in the ward of the mental hospital.

The Uncinematic

Kracauer contrasts the truly cinematic with various types of works he finds essentially or partially uncinematic by definition: those with historical or fantastic subjects, theatrical films, most adaptations of novels, and many experimental films. They prove uncinematic insofar as they tend to run counter to the basic affinities we discussed earlier: the unstaged, the fortuitous, endlessness, the indeterminate and the flow of life.

By their nature, historical films depict a time outside our physical existence and temporal realm. The staginess and limited qualities of costume dramas are not in keeping with cinema's affinity for the natural or for endlessness in particular. He finds Carl Dreyer's *The Passion of Joan of Arc* and *Day of Wrath* only partly successful in attempting to shift the attention from the uncinematic content to camera reality (the attention paid to faces). Fantasy films also remain apart from our physical existence. He distinguishes between fantasies established by means of staging, by the use of cinematic techniques (trick photography), and by trying to work within the confines of physical reality. *The Cabinet of Doctor Caligari* belongs in the first category, and, as a work relying heavily on the painted sets and expressionist appearances, is a "retrogression" inasmuch as it negates camera realism (T, p. 85).

Theatrical films are basically uncinematic for various reasons. First, their central interest in human relationships precludes any concern for the objects of physical reality, those things which film dwells on for their own sake even if they are not directly involved with the action. Second, Kracauer says that the smallest units in a drama are always complex and resist analysis and decomposition in the manner effected by the camera; that is, the theatre gives us human relationships, literally and metaphorically, in the form of long shots exclusively. The essence of such works is the complex pattern of relationships which exists independently of any interest in material reality. In other words, the kind of activity which the camera engages in is not really that relevant. In contrast to a neorealist film like De Sica's *Umberto D*, in which "the story consists in what the camera makes us see," the theatrical film's "intrigue is detachable from the medium; accordingly the imagery conveying it illustrates rather than releases its meanings" (T, p. 221). Tragedy in particular seems ill-suited for the screen because of its intense interest in the inner mental world of the protagonist rather than in the material realm. In contrast to the open-ended flow of life, its world must be considered a closed cosmos. Also, its content seems impossible to communicate filmically, since the form of tragedy effects a shift from visual units as conveyors of meaning to "language-bound meanings" (T, p. 268). The finality of the tragic ending runs counter to the sense of endlessness found in cinematic subjects, especially neorealist works like *Umberto D* and Fellini's *La Strada*, which have tragic themes but are not tragedies as such.

Although Kracauer acknowledges that film and the novel have certain affinities in their ability to compress time and to render the inner point of view, he believes that adaptations will tend to be uncinematic because of the emphasis, as with tragedy, on the inner mental world characterizing the novel. He offers Renoir's film of *Madame Bovary* and William Wyler's *The Heiress* as examples of how difficult it is to capture this interior landscape. On the other hand, he thinks some novels which are somewhat cinematic to begin with can be adapted successfully to the screen; he cites John Steinbeck's *The Grapes of Wrath* as directed by John Ford as an example.

Experimental films can be seen to display two main trends, abstract and surrealist. Like Balázs, Kracauer is not enthusiastic about either. In the first, we move increasingly to pure cinema and away from physical reality, using cinematic technique exclusively for its own sake to create works of art. But this amounts to the total dominance of the formative impulse, clearly a denial of the medium's recording and revealing properties. In the second, the artist becomes absorbed with the possibility of using imagery to present the internal world of dreams and vision. This too is unrealistic, as it turns away from external reality. In particular, the symbolism of surrealist films remains private, and only "imposed from without on visuals selected or manufactured for the sole purpose of illustrating them." In contrast, symbols in truly cinematic works "are a by-product—or an outgrowth if you wish—of pictures whose main function it is to penetrate the external world." Thus the sled in *Citizen Kane* and the horse in *La Strada* can be interpreted symbolically, but so can the "life which they faithfully portray, life whose every aspect points beyond itself" (T, p. 191).

From Caligari to Hitler

Readers should also consult Kracauer's *From Caligari to Hitler* in order to discover a different but equally rewarding kind of criticism. In this work, he explores the relationship of film and the German mind, as this can be inferred, between the time of country's loss of World War I and the rise of Hitler. Underlying this study is the assumption that "what films reflect are not so much explicit credos as psychological dispositions—those deep layers of collective mentality which extend more or less below the dimension of consciousness" (C, p. 6). Again, "in recording the visible world—whether current reality or an imaginary universe—films . . . provide clues to hidden mental processes" (C, p. 7). That is, he believes it is possible, by surveying the films and various trends, to reconstruct the probable state of mind shared by the German people as a whole during this period. It is commonly agreed that Kracauer succeeds brilliantly in this partly sociological and partly psychological endeavor. What emerges from the films is the image of an exhausted collective soul ideally suited for a tyrannical strong man, exactly like Hitler, who would lead them back to power and security. Particularly fascinating are Kracauer's discussions of the genesis of *Cabinet of Doctor Caligari* and the way in which it relates to other films of the period, such as Lang's *Doctor Mabuse*. Also worth consulting is a highly complex scheme for structural analysis presented in connection with Kracauer's analysis of propaganda techniques.

PART II

CRITICISM TODAY

THE AMERICAN JOURNALISTIC CONTRIBUTION

A complete history of American film criticism has not yet been written. When it is, we will be able to observe in more detail the various trends and developments that have occurred since its inception. But, for the present, we are fortunate in having the immensely useful anthology, *American Film Criticism from the Beginnings to Citizen Kane* (New York: Liveright, 1972). The editors, Stanley Kauffmann and Bruce Henstell, have assembled a representative sampling of the major critics of the period, and have provided helpful introductions. We can read here reviews by writers known to us from literature and letters, such as Louise Bogan, Hilda Doolittle, Francis Fergusson, Paul Goodman, Robert Sherwood and Joseph Wood Krutch. More important, the anthologists make it possible to become acquainted with early significant writers who are primarily film critics. such as Alexander Basky, Gilbert Seldes and Richard Watts, Jr. Included here also are reviews by Otis Ferguson, Pare Lorentz, and Harry Alan Potamkin, writers whose commentary is available in recently published collections. By and large, these early reviewers reached their public through journals and newspapers, notably the *New Republic*, the *Nation*, the old *Life, Exceptional Photoplays, Esquire*, the *New York Post* and the *New York Times*. Reading the reviews, one rarely has a sense of the "routine" kind of column in which a hack writer gives us the stars, the plot and the gossip. Instead, we are made party to a remarkably exciting phenomenon—the emergence of a critical tradition paralleling the growth of filmic art. The critics represented in *American Film Criticism* display more than casual acquaintance with technical matters (especially Basky), are quite aware of the nature of the Hollywood industry, and generally reveal a great knowledge of film history.

In particular, Otis Ferguson, the critic for the *New Republic*, can be viewed as having set critical standards which have con-

tinued to dominate in journalistic criticism since World War II.
Robert Wilson, his editor, suggests fairly that Ferguson "influenced and taught" critics like James Agee, Manny Farber,
Pauline Kael and Andrew Sarris (*The Film Criticism of Otis
Ferguson* [Philadelphia: Temple University Press, 1972], p. xiii).
And Sarris acknowledges Ferguson's importance, citing his influence on Agee, Farber and himself, while praising him as "the
writer of the best and most subtly influential film criticism ever
turned out in America" (*The Film Criticism of Otis Ferguson*, p.
x). What Ferguson left future critics (he was killed in World War
II, at the age of thirty-three) were standards including common
sense, a readable style of smooth prose graced with wit, an eye
for cinematic beauty, and a rejection of the superficial and the
hollow. Above all, though, Ferguson promulgated an essentially
realistic aesthetic. We can see Ferguson and his heirs as upholding what Kracauer would call the realist rather than the formative
impulses, and what Bazin speaks of as having "faith in reality."

Turning to the critics to be examined here—James Agee,
Robert Warshow, Pauline Kael, Stanley Kauffmann and Andrew
Sarris—we find a continuation of the best that has occurred in
American film criticism. It is obvious that I have omitted some
well-known critics in this section devoted to the major voices in
the journalistic tradition: Dwight MacDonald, for one; and, from
the avant-garde, Jonas Mekas and Gene Youngblood. But the
writers discussed here seem to me to be the most useful for
viewers; they offer standards of judgment and methods of approach that can be adapted effectively to one's thinking about the
function and evaluation of film.

JAMES AGEE*

James Agee (1909–1955) helped develop and extend the American journalistic tradition in film criticism. A novelist (*Death in the Family*), social critic (*Let Us Now Praise Famous Men*), and screen-writer (*The African Queen* and *Night of the Hunter*), he brought to film criticism perceptive insights into the nature of filmic art. The personal quality of his writing anticipates both Pauline Kael and Andrew Sarris, two critics who share many of his interests and views. Though Agee was not a theorist as such, readers of his criticism will discover consistent and well-articulated positions on matters of interest to us throughout the *Guide*. In particular, I want to discuss his call for realism, his concept of realism and poetry, and his comments on some specific directors.

The Call for Realism

Dominating Agee's criticism is a demand for realism and a rejection of any pretentious "studio" qualities in films. For example, he praises Hitchcock's *Shadow of a Doubt* for its "real attention to what places and people really look like" (p. 26), and commends Zoltan Korda's *Sahara* because it "borrows, chiefly from the English, a sort of light-alloy modification of realism which makes the traditional Hollywood idiom seem as obsolete as a minuet" (p. 53). Two of the pictures he likes best, William Wellman's *The Story of G. I. Joe* and André Malraux's *Man's Hope*, display a lifelike quality by virtue of what Kracauer would call their indeterminateness and fortuitousness; that is, like the

---

champion of the realist over the formative, Agee thinks that
chance and the unexplained detail function as important means of
creating a sense of reality. In Wellman's picture, "there is a won-
derfully discreet and powerful use . . . of purely 'meaningless'
bits—such as a shot in which Ernie Pyle . . . sits by the road while
some soldiers straggle past—which have as great meaning as anything could have, being as immediate and as unlimited by
thought or prejudice as what the eye might see on the spot, in a
casual glance" (p. 172). In *Man's Hope*, Malraux conveys a sense
of reality by "letting things and movements into his frame which
have nothing to do with the central action or which enhance it
only queerly and surprisingly—a guerrilla's sudden skipping
change in step and his sudden hand to his sweating neck; or a
dog wandering in from one corner of a street scene while a ball
maunders in from another—little things which brilliantly lock
men and their efforts and feelings into the exact real place and
time of day" (p. 240).

Like Bazin, Agee commends the work of the Italian
neorealists for their successful presentation of reality. Rossellini's
Open City displays an "immediacy" and the "urgency of human
beings"; various scenes appear "as shatteringly uninvented-
looking as if they had been shot by invisible newsreel cameras"
(p. 195). The same director's *Paisà* demonstrates an ability to give
"the illusion of the present tense" (p. 301).

Also like Bazin, Agee argues the merits of typage, particularly as it can contribute to a sense of reality in a film. He
criticizes the standard Hollywood acting of *The Human Comedy*
because it "strangles at birth every hope of a truly vivid reality"
and rejects the use of actresses playing Mexican women when
real Mexicans could perform the same parts effectively (p. 31). In
contrast, Malraux's non-actors in *Man's Hope* convey an overwhelming sense of truth; the film proves "the superiority of
amateurs over professionals for a large and crucially hopeful part
of achievement and possibility in films. The people in this film—
Spaniards and members of the International Brigade—do and *are*
things, over and over again, which are beyond acting and utterly
different from it" (p. 239). Agee praises De Sica's use of amateurs
in *Shoeshine*; working with non-actors, and forced many times to

retake scenes, the director presents characters whom we recognize as human beings (p. 280).

Consistently rejected are practices and techniques which are at odds with realism. Agee ridicules a production shot with the visual cliché "showing the withered, rosaried hands of an old woman" (p. 41). Or he notes that a film presents a supposedly *un*modern village that looks "scrubbed behind the ears and 'beautified'" (p. 57). He praises John Huston's *The Treasure of the Sierra Madre* because it lacks any "fancy-filter stuff" (p. 291), because the director "loathes camera rhetoric and the shot-for-shot's sake" (p. 328), and because the film "does not wear its art on its sleeve" (p. 398). In such comments Agee has much to say to us today, for we too are caught in an age of showy and needlessly "arty" clichés; I expect many viewers have reached the saturation point in regard to slow-motion sequences to indicate lyrical moments, zooms in and out of a scene to suggest excitement, and generally gratuitous shots into the sun.

A particular bane of Agee's critical existence is background music. Used as a kind of transition device to link images, it disrupts the visual integrity of the film: "still worse, it weakens the emotional imagination both of maker and onlooker, and makes it virtually impossible to communicate or receive ideas" (p. 164). As potentially damaging to the realism of the film is technicolor. Although it can add a useful degree of realism to documentaries (p. 82), and to musicals if used effectively, Agee does not think it should be used in all films: "color is very nice for costume pieces and musical comedies, and has a great aesthetic future in films, but it still [in 1943] gets fatally in the way of any serious imitation of reality" (p. 48).

Some of Agee's most enthusiastic comments go to documentary films, especially those revealing the dismal reality of war's effects. He argues strongly that the American public be allowed to see two films being withheld by the War Office, *The Battle of Britain* and *The Battle of Russia*, because these convey the truth about war (p. 56). A March of Time documentary presents "the fullest image of occupied Europe . . . an image of a world, a phase, which we shall never see by any other means" (p. 95). Those

wanting to experience the reality of war would do well to avoid
fictional films altogether, and rely on documentary war films, in
which they will encounter a "petrifying immediacy" (p. 99). And
the documentary need not be about war to arouse his enthusiasm;
he recommends Georges Rouquier's *Farrebique* because the director "realizes that, scupulously handled, the camera can do
what nothing else in the world can do: can record unaltered reality" (p. 296).

Realism and Poetry

Throughout his essays Agee talks about film in terms of
realism and poetry, but these should not be taken as polarities.
He conceives of the well-made realistic film as itself constituting a
poetic statement and, like poetry, using images having universal
appeal which will draw all viewers. Thus Rouquier displays an
ability to "communicate, in full unaltered power, the peculiar
kinds of poetic vitality which blaze in every real thing and which
are in great degree . . . lost to every other kind of artist except the
camera artist" (pp. 296–297). Agee finds D. W. Griffith's images
to be virtual archetypes: those of *Birth of a Nation* realize "a
collective dream of what the Civil War was like" (p. 313). Griffith
remains a "great primitive poet . . . intuitively perceiving and per-
fecting the tremendous magical images that underlie the memory
and imagination of entire peoples" (p. 314). Huston's accomplishment in *The Treasure of the Sierra Madre* lies partly in approaching "folk art," and through his story presenting characters
and an action which "yield revelations of their own, political,
metaphysical, moral, above all, poetic" (pp. 290–291). In such
comments, Agee can be said to anticipate current attempts by
structuralist critics to examine the nature of the image (such as
Pier Palo Pasolini) and to consider it in relation to archetypes
(Peter Wollen, to be discussed later).

Directors

There are many directors who draw Agee's praise, both classical and modern: Griffith, Huston, Vincente Minnelli, and, from

the B-movie category, Val Lewton. Particularly worth noting are
his comments on Chaplin, Eisenstein and Jean Vigo.

In a famous essay on "Comedy's Greatest Era," originally
published in *Life*, Agee distinguishes the unique qualities of silent films' greatest clowns, noting Buster Keaton's deadpan expression and his anti-sentimentality; Harry Langdon's very *un*-
physical brand of comedy; Harold Lloyd's dependence on story
and situation; and, above them all, Chaplin, whose genius appears in "*inflection*—the perfect, changeful shading of his physical and emotional attitudes toward the gag" (p. 9). Agee points to
the presence of "the finest pantomime, the deepest emotion, the
richest and most poignant poetry" in the early works (p. 10). And,
significantly, Agee, like Bazin, argues for the merits of the much
criticized *Monsieur Verdoux*; in fact, he even devotes three col-
umns to its defense. He is conscious of an underlying metaphori-
cal structure informing the controversial film; he assesses Verdoux's murderous actions in relation to mercantile activities, and
his personality in terms of modern life, and regards the film "as a
metaphor for the personality, and through that metaphor, as a
metaphor for the personality as the family as business as war as
civilization as murder" (pp. 261–262). He sees a connection between Verdoux and the earlier tramp figure (p. 288), but does not
elaborate as fully as Bazin on the evolution of Verdoux in relation
to the entire canon.

Eisenstein's early work rates Agee's enthusiastic support, but
he finds in the later films like *Alexander Nevsky* "a kind of
speeded-up, fluent, operatic style which was like watching a
handsome, well-organized funeral cortège carry his free genius to
its grave at a cheerful forty miles an hour" (p. 247). As far as I
know, Agee is probably one of the first critics to speak of the later
Eisensteinian manner as "operatic"; the term has stuck, certainly,
for *Alexander Nevsky* and both parts of *Ivan the Terrible*. Agee
sees the first part of the latter as displaying the same mannerism,
and also failing to communicate ideas very effectively: "considering the illusion Eisenstein manages to create of expressing many
complex ideas, densely and continuously, it is remarkable how
little actually gets expressed, and how commonplace most of it is"
(p. 249). Still, Eisenstein remains "a great hero" for Agee, who

leaves us a touching tribute to the director, sadly observing "the death and tragic life of Sergei Eisenstein, in whom so many of the greatest possibilities conceivable in the medium were for a long while imprisoned and tormented, and now lie buried" (p. 299).

Having seen *Zero for Conduct* and *L'Atalante* by Jean Vigo, who would be such an influence on New Wave directors years later, Agee remarks on the director's power to penetrate reality: "Vigo gets deeper inside his characters than most people have tried to in film, [and] is not worried about transitions between objective, subjective, fantastic, and subconscious reality, and mixes as many styles and camera tricks, as abruptly, as he sees fit" (p. 263). Observe that Agee is quite receptive to the experimental element in Vigo's films because the director's aim is to render reality as fully as he can on all levels—thus the need for techniques and devices which are not traditionally realistic. The issue raised here is significant; essentially Agee is saying that a film may not be "realistic" in a documentary sense, but extremely realistic as regards its ultimate purpose. Like Truffaut and others who would honor Vigo later, Agee sees the director's importance in the history of film when he says that *Zero for Conduct* (a major influence, we know, on Truffaut's *The 400 Blows* and Lindsay Anderson's *If...*) is a film "which worked deeply within pure motion-picture style, and... extended the possibilities of style and expression as brilliantly, and germinally, as the best work of Griffith, Chaplin, Eisenstein, Dovzhenko, and Murnau" (p. 287).

ROBERT WARSHOW*

Robert Warshow (1917–1955) contributed major discussions of film and its genres to *Commentary* and *Partisan Review*. One of his eventual aims was to have been an analysis of the "immediate experience" in one's viewing of films; he wanted to define film culture and the uniqueness particular to the witnessing of movies. Although he did not live to complete that project, he has left us important studies of gangster and western films, as well as an interesting estimate of Chaplin. Important also is his discussion of realism, which in his view is not merely cinematic fidelity to the external world, but also faithfulness to ideas. Throughout his writings we find a sociological concern for the cultural influences on film that reminds one of Kracauer's *From Caligari to Hitler*, a work which Warshow respected but found somewhat limited in approach.

Gangster Films

Warshow describes the characteristics and appeal of such films while effectively explaining the uniqueness of the genre. Essentially the gangster hero belongs to the city—not a *real* city, but the imaginary centers that have been created out of Hollywood mythology. Caught up in the success ethic, he is incapable of overcoming the obstacles particular to his type: loneliness, lack of choice, melancholy. A gangster like the hero of *Scarface* can be considered tragic in a romantic sense, in that his doom is a response to "the outrageous presumption of his demands" (p. 143).

The gangster has a special appeal for American culture because he and the genre afford us a means of coming to terms with

---

*All quotations are from *The Immediate Experience* (New York: Atheneum, 1971). Used by permission of Paul Warshow.

a spiritual dilemma. From Warshow's cultural perspective,
Americans seem to be bound to a cult of optimism to which they
pay lip service, but in which they do not really believe; that is,
there exists a painful gap between our actual feelings and our
apparent cheeriness. Gangster films allow us to deal with these
mixed feelings by letting us identify with the hero's drive for success in an indifferent world and, simultaneously, relish his failure.
Thus, "the gangster is the 'no' to that great American 'yes' which
is stamped so big over our official culture and yet has so little to
do with the way we really feel about our lives" (p. 136). In fact,
our sense of tragedy, which is always struggling to make its appearance in the midst of official cultural optimism generated by
the state, can be satisfied through the gangster film, a kind of
disguised reenactment of our frustrations. He speaks of "a current
of opposition, seeking to express . . . that sense of desperation and
inevitable failure which optimism itself helps to create"; notes
that this opposition usually appears in a sublimated form when it
enters art; and concludes: "the gangster film is remarkable in that
it fills the need for disguise . . . without requiring any serious distortion" (pp. 128–129). A similar emotional use of the gangster
film figures in our experience of the violence. We can be involved in a gangster's violence while we reject it: "we gain the
double satisfaction of participating vicariously in the gangster's
sadism and then seeing it turned against the gangster himself"
(pp. 131–132).

Warshow speaks incisively about some of the conventions in
the gangster film with a full knowledge of its typical features and
of audiences' expectations. Thus a gangster who appears alone, as
in the opening scene of *Scarface,* is automatically sensed to be in
danger: "we understand from this immediately that he is about to
be killed. No convention of the gangster film is more strongly
established than this: it is dangerous to be alone" (pp. 132–133).
We can think of two examples of this in Francis Ford Coppola's
The Godfather, Part I: Marlon Brando's visit without bodyguards
to the market section, and James Caan's solitary automobile ride
to reach his sister. In both cases, Coppola relies on our acceptance of the convention to build both tension and dramatic in-
evitability. Warshow here speaks in much the same terms as
Erwin Panofsky does about conventions which we have come to
respond to in film.

Westerns

Like Bazin, Warshow offers a rewarding analysis of western conventions and the hero. Although the cowboy shares certain characteristics with the gangster (another lonely and melancholy man with a gun), he differs from the latter in that he has more insight into his own existence and a greater sense of positive moral purpose. Both the gangster and the cowboy are driven men, in the sense that they *must* do certain things, but what the cowboy "has to do" is, finally, to maintain and defend "the purity of his own image" (p. 140). When there is tragedy in westerns, it arises from the hero's attempt "to assert his personal value," and is classical in conception rather than romantic, as is the gangster's attempt "to extend his dominion" (p. 143). The women the hero encounters either display insight into his problems (the prostitutes and dance hall girls), or remain ignorant of his situation (the good, marriageable girls from the East).

The western has its own conventions and patterns. Viewers accept the introduction of realism to the conventionalized form when it enhances the basic pattern without altering it essentially: "the spectator derives his pleasure from the appreciation of minor variations within the working out of a pre-established order. One does not want too much novelty" (p. 146). Still, there have to be enough modifications to satisfy a need for variety; we want the "same form" but not "the same movie" (p. 147).

Two major westerns of the 1950s which go too far for Warshow in introducing variations in the form are Fred Zinnemann's *High Noon* and George Stevens' *Shane.* The first film presents a "social" element in a rather clumsy manner and attempts to impose it on a basic conventionalized form: the hero forced to defend himself against overwhelming odds, the two women (one "bad" and understanding, one "good" and imperceptive), the showdown, etc. The film errs in trying to explain the hero's isolation at the climax, a standard convention, with a secondary social drama in which the townspeople are exposed for their lack of moral fibre. Thus the movie muddles the form: "to explain *why* the other townspeople are not at his side is to raise a question which does not exist in the proper frame of the Western movie, where the hero is 'naturally' alone" (p. 149). *Shane* fails in another way, through its overindulgence of the aesthetic tendency. By making the hero almost a "Spirit of the West," and by staging and sets which deny the actual conditions of the West, the film is as out of keeping with the form as John Ford's *My Darling Clementine*, in which we have "a superficial accuracy of historical reconstruction, but so loving in execution as to destroy the outlines of the Western legend, assimilating it to the more sentimental legend of rural America" (p. 149).

Warshow also connects the violence in this genre with our culture. The western allows us a "serious orientation to the problem of violence" in a special way (p. 151). Although we condemn violence, we still feel a fascination for it. The western offers violence, but, by presenting it in connection with a hero who is generally characterized as being self-restrained, *deflects* our participation in the acts from the violence to the *style* itself of the acts. Warshow did not live to see recent westerns in which the kind of sublimated experience of violence he describes is less possible; the spaghetti westerns of Sergi Leone or Sam Peckinpah's *The Wild Bunch* deflect attention away from the style of the cowboy to the style of the director in the depiction of violence. All cinematic means are used to illustrate or expose the nature of violence—gallons of blood, slow-motion sequences for deaths, severed hands, etc.

Chaplin

Warshow offers a sensitive and perceptive defense of *Monsieur Verdoux* by relating it to the former works in the Chaplin canon. In the early Tramp films, the hero and society exist in a relationship of enmity which is more casual than purposeful; that is, simply by his anti-social presence, the Tramp elicits negative but not downright hostile responses from society. From about the period of *Modern Times* onward, though, the relationship becomes more tense; society *intends* its attacks on the Tramp. In the hero of *Monsieur Verdoux*, the murderer who operates according to the business ethic of his society, the Tramp and society itself are combined in one figure: "with Verdoux, the opposition between the individual and society has lost its old simplicity. The society has flowed into the individual, and the two

have in a sense become co-extensive; the struggle is now an
internal struggle, full of ambiguities and contradictions; it is man
himself who is corrupt, both as individual and society" (p. 211).

Throughout Chaplin's career, the actor/tramp/comedian has
been asking the audience to "love me" (p. 223). In *Limelight*, the
Calvero figure embodies this call while revealing the basic dilemma of all clowns who must always be humiliated personally
while trying to maintain a separate identity distinct from their
absurd creations: "In *Limelight*, as in *Monsieur Verdoux*, Chaplin
has got caught in this paradox. He has grown reluctant to submit
directly to humiliation and is anxious to be accepted as something
'more' than a clown" (p. 229). The split in Calvero's personality
between being a person and being a professional clown suggests
"there must be such a division in Chaplin's personality; if there
weren't, he would be insane" (p. 230). Like Bazin, then, but with
a somewhat different attitude toward Calvero/Chaplin, Warshow
identifies the two: Calvero "is Charles Chaplin 'in person' presid-
ing at the telling of his own story and not for a moment relin-
quishing control" (p. 231).

We notice in Warshow a curious mixed attitude toward
Chaplin; in some ways he admires Charlie, but in other ways he
seems repelled by him—a duality that emerges most clearly when
Warshow qualifies the opinion Eisenstein had advanced earlier,
that Chaplin sees the world through the eyes of a child. Warshow
adds that there is a "coldness of heart which seems to belong
inextricably to Chaplin's genius." Even though he is like a child,
"he is also imprisoned within the limits of his own needs and
understanding, and can express no true relation with others. Precisely the lack of such a relation makes him a clown—the most
childish kind of entertainer—and gives him his clown's subject
matter" (p. 231).

Reality and Ideas

A constant theme in Warshow's criticism is the need for a
true image of the world, achieved through the camera's activities
and also through what the film maker says about man. His discussions of several films illustrate this demand clearly. Unlike

most of his contemporaries, Agee for one, who praise William
Wyler's *The Best Years of Our Lives*, Warshow condemns it for
its essential hollowness. Although he finds a multitude of examples where the film presents the surface of reality (the look of a
city, the contents of apartments, the interiors of banks and
drugstores, conversations which sound like real speech), he argues that the film never goes beyond superficiality: "what you see
is all there is" (p. 157). Missing is any serious examination of
social conditions. In fact, the film seems to manufacture a
nonexistent issue (the problem faced by returning veterans) while
it ignores "the reality of politics" (p. 158). We get only "evasions
and distortions" in regard to human relationships, since the film
pretends that questions of finance, equality and politics are
merely issues of "personal morality" (p. 159).

Rossellini's *Paisà*, which so impressed Bazin, also offends by
its exclusion of ideas. Warshow likes half of the six episodes, but
in general he finds the film inadequate. In particular, he inveighs
against the long take, because, by simply registering events, the
technique does not permit interpretation of them. We remember
that Bazin sees the long take with deep focus as a means of allowing spectators to choose and to sort out the ambiguities in the
scene. But for Warshow, "the neutrality of the camera tends to
exclude the possibility of reflection and thus to divorce the events
from all questions of opinion" (pp. 253-254). In the desolation of
the final sequence with its pervasive imagery of death, "again
there is no room for ideas" because the spareness of neorealist
techniques excludes them (p. 254). He laments what he sees as a
stripping away of intellectual depth: "the rejection of ideas is also
a rejection of principles" (p. 257).

But it is not only neorealist techniques which can, used in
this way, interfere with the communication of ideas for Warshow.
He also criticizes Eisenstein's approach to rendering reality. He
speaks of the "intolerable pedantry" in the Russian's criticism,
and considers the montage method in the bridge sequence of *October* as a sign of "essential and dangerous frivolity." Even while
granting the effectiveness of the Odessa steps sequence in *Potemkin*, and acknowledging elements of greatness in the film, Warshow's praise of Eisenstein and the other Russian masters is
grudging at best; the films are "crude, vulgar, often puerile, but

yet full of sudden moments of power" (p. 271). The montage of
the stone lions which we have heard praised throughout the
Guide is condemned by Warshow because it emphasizes the "art"
of film rather than the reality which the medium is capable of
capturing: "The use of the stone lion is, indeed, a clever and
'artistic' idea, but it is also fundamentally cheap, and in both re-
spects it is characteristic of Eisenstein, and of the Soviet cinema
generally. What we want most, that cinema rarely gives us: some
hint of the mere reality of the events it deals with. The important
point about the lions is that all the 'art' of their use depends on
the fact that they are not alive" (pp. 272–273).

Whether or not one accepts Warshow's objections to
neorealist or montage techniques, it is important to understand
the relevance of his argument. Essentially he says that the manner of presentation is linked to the communication of ideas; in
other words, the form can affect the content—in these cases robbing the actual subjects of their full potential meaning, either by
not focusing our attention or by artificially structuring our vision.
Thus, as critics, we would want to ask whether in a given film the
director employs techniques and methods that allow the full presentation of the subject and its implications, or whether the manner of communication is at odds with the subject, and actually
self-defeating. For example, in *The Passenger*, Antonioni's latest
picture, the long take near the end of the movie has provoked
much discussion. With a complex mechanical arrangement involving a gyroscope, Antonioni takes his viewers from inside a bedroom, through a window grating, and onto the street outside the
room—all in a single and remarkable take lasting seven minutes.
Although it is possible to argue that the sequence has aesthetic
implications in regard to neorealism itself, and although one cannot deny the technical virtuosity of it, there is still the nagging
question of artistic validity; viewers must decide if the long take
finally contributes to the meaning of the scene, if it draws attention to itself as sheer wizardry, or if it actually proves destructive
to Antonioni's intent here.

PAULINE KAEL*

The immensely popular and influential Pauline Kael (b. 1919), long on the staff of *The New Yorker*, is the only film critic ever to win the National Book Award (for *Deeper into Movies*). For many years, she has been directing the attention of her readers to the cultural and economic elements in film production, as well as sociological and psychological aspects of audiences' responses to films—topics to be examined here. She fears the potentially destructive control of the medium by businessmen, and also explains how television contributes to the erosion of film art. Her rejection of the *auteur* theory relates, in large part, to her view of how Hollywood distorts production values. Readers can also find first-rate and cogent criticism and analysis of hundreds of films in her various collections of reviews and essays.

Economic Forces

In a famous 1974 essay "On the Future of the Movies" (R, pp. 309–331), Kael presents a scathing denunciation of the way

---

*Key to Abbreviations
C   =   *The Citizen Kane Book* (New York: Bantam Books, 1974). "Raising Kane," copyright © 1971 by Pauline Kael, originally appeared in *The New Yorker*, reprinted as introduction to *The Citizen Kane Book*. Quoted by permission of Bantam Books, Inc.
D   =   *Deeper into Movies* (New York: Bantam Books, 1974).
G   =   *Going Steady* (New York: Bantam Books, 1971).
K   =   *Kiss Kiss Bang Bang* (New York: Bantam Books, 1969).
L   =   *I Lost It at the Movies* (Boston: Atlantic Monthly Press, 1965).
R   =   *Reeling* (Boston: Atlantic Monthly Press, 1976). Quotations from the last five titles by permission of Little, Brown, and Co. in association with the Atlantic Monthly Press.

forces in Hollywood control film production, distribution and advertising. The essay contains themes that have dominated her criticism for many years. She calls for independent directors to band together and form their own distribution agency as a means of combatting current practices which inhibit the healthy development of the medium.

She explains how advertising plays a crucial role in film distribution, and how this affects all kinds of films. On the one hand, she observes that simple word-of-mouth advertising, which used to be able to help a film, has been transformed into elaborate advertising campaigns which bludgeon the public, usually in connection with mediocre pictures. The hard-sell strategies for films like *Walking Tall* and *The Great Gatsby* are designed to make individuals feel personally inadequate unless they have seen the film that, so the advertisers tell them, "*everyone* is talking about." On the other hand, the executives have the power to make or break a film by limiting advertising. This usually happens with directors and films that, it is feared, are too arty or advanced for the public. Kael mentions Martin Scorsese and Robert Altman, who, until recently, had to be content with half-hearted support from their studios because of the experimental and non-traditional elements in their films.

It all comes down to what the financial powers think will sell. The appearance of *The Poseidon Adventure* generates a stream of "calamity" pictures because of the assumption that this is what will be bought at the box office: "the studio heads are setting up disaster epics like kids reaching hand over hand up a baseball bat—all because of the success of *The Poseidon Adventure*, which probably had about as much to do with a public interest in apocalypse as Agatha Christie's old *Ten Little Indians* had" (R, p. 318). That is, the industry cashes in on the success of one film by making others like it, and by using advertising to create an atmosphere in which these films *must* be seen.

Another aspect of Hollywood's control which distresses Kael is the sheer cynicism of the operation. Not only does the industry turn directors into hacks, and pander to a taste which it creates, but it also sells out by seeming to condemn mercantile values—for a profit. Thus a film like Arthur Penn's *The Chase* really exploits while seeming to condemn: "the attitudes of the moneymen behind movies show through the film's attack on moneymen. They try to make a big action picture that will 'expose' the attitudes of white Southerners in lavish cross-section and at the same time they want to make sure the picture makes money, so they play up all that dirty rotten white Southern sex they're condemning" (K, p. 186). Another example of this duality appears in the advertising campaign for Lindsay Anderson's *If...* , a film about youthful rebellion which ends with a massacre of authority figures. Here the moneymen "are turning 'youth' on to armed revolt" and jumping on the bandwagon of counter-culture films. She astutely notes a paradox in this regard: "one of the contradictions in capitalism that Marx did not foresee: the conglomerates that control the mass media are now selling 'youth' the violent overthrow of the Establishment for the suicidally simple reason that they can find and develop a demand for it" (G, p. 348). For another and more extensive examination of the relationship between the commercial interests and a given film, viewers should consult her study of the filming of *The Group* (K, pp. 83–124).

Cultural Observations

Very often Kael will include in her criticism commentary on the audience's reaction to a given film. This practice follows from her interest in the dynamics of response and its relation to a larger issue, the sociological, political and psychological implications of certain films and genres.

For example, she notes that the western genre has long been exhausted as any kind of viable form in and of itself. Still, the moneymen and the production companies (often owned by western stars) continue to make them: "Westerns are money in the bank" (K, p. 56). Instead of the traditional western myth, Hollywood creates a new mythology for the public out of the "stars who have aged in the business, who have survived and who go on dragging their world-famous, expensive carcasses through the same old motions. . . . The new Western is a joke and the stars play it for laughs, and the young film enthusiasts react to the heroes not because they represent the mythological heroes of the Old West but because they are mythological movie stars" (K, p. 53). It is hard not to think immediately of John Wayne at this

point; readers will be able to identify other stars whose presence
in films constitutes—literally—the whole show; Vincent Price in
horror films, for example.

Kael also explores audiences' reactions to violence. She explains the enthusiasm of the young who respond to Alexandro
Jodorowsky's "horror circus," *El Topo*, with its carnage and perversion as a result of drugs (D, p. 421). The film seems "no more
'real' than the experiences they have in their skulls on drugs.
That's why the blood doesn't bother them" (D, p. 426). Other
recent films which contain excessive violence testify to a disloca-
tion of values. In *The Cowboys*, a western in which John Wayne
initiates young boys into the world of manhood, there is a marked
deemphasis of sex, so that the film can get a "GP" rating, but the
violence is perfectly acceptable: "the boys must be virginal killers;
sex would make them dirty boys" (D, p. 492). Or a movie can, as
it were, hedge its bets, the way she detects *The French Connection* playing for all political elements in the audience. In the
film's conception and in the unglamorous hero, she sees a
"right-wing, left-wing, take-your-choice cynicism" which is really
"total commercial opportunism passing itself off as an Existential
View" (D, p. 402). *Dirty Harry* is clearly right wing, "a deeply
immoral movie" (D, p. 488). The hero stands for "vigilante justice" since his experiences seem to prove the inadequacy of the
social system (D, p. 487). He can't get the killer, "this walking
rot, because of the legal protections, such as the court rulings on
Miranda and Escobedo, that a weak, liberal society gives its crim-
inals. Those are the terms of the film" (D, p. 486).

Although she does not think much of the work of Siegfried
Kracauer (L, pp. 269–292), her comment that we consider a picture like this as representative of a period certainly reminds us of
the earlier theorist: "when you think back on the movies of the
past, or when you watch them on television, they're like
samples—swatches of cloth—of the period in which they were
made: *In the Heat of the Night* belongs to the Lyndon Johnson
era as clearly as *Dirty Harry* belongs to the heyday of the Nixon
era" (R, p. xiii). Consider also her speculation on the reasons for
the appeal of lushly romantic films in 1970. At that time the "desire for a reassuring moral universe" explains why audiences are
drawn to *Ryan's Daughter* and to *Love Story;* the latter "may

satisfy a national (perhaps international) longing. It deals in private passions at a time when we are exhausted from public defeats, and it deals with the mutual sacrifice of a hard-working, clean-cut pair of lovers, and with love beyond death" (D, p. 275).

Other evaluations of films and the audiences' reactions to them can be found in her essay, "The Glamor of Delinquency," on the alienation theme in *On the Waterfront, East of Eden* and *Blackboard Jungle* (L, pp. 44–62); her stunning discussion of *Bonnie and Clyde* (K, pp. 59–79); and her analysis of "Trash, Art and the Movies" (G, pp. 105–158), in which she points out the validity of "trash"—popular entertainment which makes no pretensions at being "art" but which can teach audiences what "art" can be.

Television

Kael considers television a real threat to films and suggests several ways in which it contributes to their diminishment, both in regard to content and technique. Traditionally, directors would learn their trade working on "B" pictures in Hollywood. But with the breakup of the large studios there are many fewer such opportunities. As a result television writers and directors go directly into films without the usual background training in the medium itself. What they bring from television are uncinematic notions of how to create films.

For example, the pacing of the average television show, with its necessary breaks for commercials, may be contributing to a "destruction of the narrative sense—that delight in following a story through its complications to its conclusion" (L, p. 9). In place of traditional narrative structure, television directors grow accustomed to scripts with "thin, one-dimensional characters and situations, almost continuous dialogue, sharp visual contrasts, quick jabs at the emotions, and lots of climaxes" (G, p. 24). There is no depth: she sees "nothing underneath the situations, nothing behind or around the foreground action, no sense of a life going on to support the events" (G, p. 25). The characters lack life: "if no character in a movie seems to have a past, one can be pretty sure it was written and/or directed by people from television. The characters are not likely to have much present, either" (G, p. 27). The technical aspects are just as inadequate. Television directors now making movies "just keep the actors shouting in close-up" (K, p. 93). Instead of using the camera to capture physical reality, these directors regard "the camera as a recording device for staged action." For the audience, "there's *nothing* on the screen for your eye to linger on, no distances, no action in the background, no sense of life or landscape mingling with the foreground action. It's all in the foreground, put there for you to grasp at once. It's all in the surface, it's jumping out of the frame at you" (K, pp. 102–103). Kael specifically singles out Sidney Lumet, director of *The Group*, as an example of a television-trained director who brings to film the unfortunate aspects of his earlier trade. But viewers might want to consider the validity or pertinence of her remarks in relation to more recent directors who have gained their training in television. Steven Spielberg, for one, may not seem at all guilty of the various offenses Kael fears; very few viewers consider Spielberg's *Jaws* to be an overblown TV show. Those scenes early in the film where he does indeed rely on tight framing and apparently excessive shots in which the action remains in the foreground are perfectly functional inasmuch as they suggest the tension and paralysis of the terrorized townspeople. It should also be noted that one of Kael's favorite directors, Robert Altman, began by working in television.

Critical Standards

Kael thinks the good critic should "help people see what is in the work, what is in it that shouldn't be, what is not in it that could be" (L, p. 308). Films should be "judged in terms of how they extend our experience and give us pleasure, and... our ways of judging how they do this are drawn not only from older films but from other works of art" (L, p. 309). She finds criticism "a balancing act, trying to suggest perspectives on the emotions viewers feel, trying to increase their enjoyment of movies without insulting their susceptibilities to simple, crude pop" (R, p. xiii). Both André Bazin and James Agee rate her praise as excellent critics.

Even though she thinks highly of Bazin, she condemns the *auteur* theory as it is formulated, not by Bazin, but by Andrew Sarris. She acknowledges that with any art, critics will be interested in "the way artists borrow from themselves (as well as from others) and how the same devices, techniques, and themes reappear in their work" (L, p. 294). But, she asks, do we need the *auteur* theory to engage in such critical activities? Rather like Stanley Kauffmann, she would explore the issues of repetition and thematic consistency in a director without recourse to a specific theory as such.

The three premises suggested by Sarris (to be discussed in more detail later) make little sense to her. She rejects the first, that a director must display "technical competence," as a criterion of value when it becomes more important than thematic concerns. Of the second premise, that our ability to *detect* a director's "signature" in his films through his habit of repeating certain techniques and themes should be a standard of judgment, she asks, "how does this distinguishable personality function as a criterion for judging the works?" (L, pp. 297–298). In fact, if the movie makes us conscious of the director's personality rather than the narrative content, it is probably not a good work of art. Even the identifiable tricks of Hitchcock may not give us *his* personality so much as his "personal theory of audience psychology" (L, p. 298). She finds Sarris' call for "an élan of soul" particularly weak and condemns it for the same reason Bazin urged against the *Cahiers* critics: "élan as the permanent attribute Sarris posits can only be explained in terms of a cult of personality" (L, p. 301).

The notion that we ought to be able to detect "interior meaning . . . extrapolated from the tension between a director's personality and his material" appears to her to be, at bottom, a defense of the studio system and typical moneyman pressures. That is, our ability to see a director stamping routine films with his personal touches and signature as he works in the confining atmosphere of the studio suggests that we are dealing with a hack: "their ideal *auteur* is the man who signs a long-term contract, directs any script that's handed to him, and expresses himself by shoving bits of style up the crevasses of the plots. If his 'style' is in conflict with the story line or subject matter, so much the better—more chance for tension" (L, p. 302). Elsewhere she calls the *auteur* theory "a defense of the studio system—and especially of such studio products as Westerns and action pictures—on the ground that those directors who were artists transformed their assignments into works with a personal vision, that they were *auteurs* who could fulfill themselves within the commercial system. It was on the basis of this theory of the superior hack as hidden artist that the movies of men like Raoul Walsh and Samuel Fuller were acclaimed" (D, p. 98). The theory, thus conceived, is "dangerous" because "it offers nothing but commercial goals to the young artists who may be trying to do something in film" (L, p. 316).

She agrees with *auteur* critics that the director should have "creative control" of his picture (D, p. 98). But "creative control" does not mean *absolute* power; realistically that would seem impossible. There is, first of all, the presence of the screenwriter, in most films someone other than the director. A director has to have a well-written script in order to make a good movie; on the other hand, a good script does not guarantee that a film will be well directed (K, p. 75). "Worship" of the director as the sole creative force behind a film fails to inform us of the true conditions that exist: "such worship generally doesn't help in sorting out what went into the making of good pictures and bad pictures" (C, p. 68).

"Raising Kane"

Her fascinating study of the creation of *Citizen Kane*, "Raising Kane," serves as an outstanding example of her concern for "sorting out what went into the making of good pictures." In this controversial essay, which has been severely criticized by Andrew Sarris and Peter Bogdanovich for its thesis and errors in research, she describes in detail all the elements that went into the creation of the film. The main thrust of her argument is to prove that the script was in fact created by Herman J. Mankiewicz, although Orson Welles probably made various suggestions along the way, and that the expressionistic visual style of the film owes much to

Gregg Toland. The essay exists in large part to refute Welles's comment that "theatre is a collective experience; cinema is the work of a single person" (C, p. 9).

For her the film is not the work of a single person, Welles, but "a superb example of collaboration" (C, p. 110). This kind of creative experience happens when the director is indeed in control—not doing everything himself but acting as a force to "liberate and utilize the talents of his co-workers, who languish (as directors do) in studio-factory productions" (C, p. 109). The truly free director who says "a movie is totally his" should be viewed as an artist who "wasn't interfered with" and who was "free to use all the best ideas offered him" (C, p. 109).

Readers of "Raising Kane" will find interesting commentary on the Hollywood scene in the 1930s; parallels between William Randolph Hearst, Kane and Welles; Mankiewicz's strategic error in releasing the script; and the events surrounding the opening of the film. Also present are some perceptive objections to various aspects of the film, which Kael finds "a *shallow* masterpiece" (C, p. 4), more properly considered in terms of the newspaper-muckraking film genre than as tragedy. Many points are worth consideration. She wonders how Raymond heard Kane's dying word, "Rosebud," when there was no one present; notes the uselessness of the bridge shot before the reporter visits Leland; finds overly precious the first meeting of Susan and Kane; and suggests the roughness in staging of the newpaper office scenes as well as problems of characterization in both wives and in Leland as an old man.

Practical Criticism

Kael displays a most impressive knowledge of film history and is receptive to the merits of traditional directors as well as to more experimental artists. Thus she praises Carol Reed as well as Jean-Luc Godard. The latter, in a phrase which reminds us of Agee, "aims for the poetry of reality and the reality of poetry" (K, p. 139). Among the avant-garde artists, she praises Bruce Baillie, Carroll Ballard, Jordan Belson and Ed Emshwiller (K, p. 16, and R. p. 323). Her pre-release tribute to Bernardo Bertolucci's *Last*

Tango in Paris created something of a sensation itself, particularly her claim that the movie signalled a new direction for film, much as Stravinsky's "Sacre du Printemps" did for music. Particularly valuable in that review is her suggestion about Bertolucci's references to other films; in a brilliant observation, she suggests that "Bertolucci uses a feedback of his own—the feedback of old movies to enrich the imagery and associations"—and identifies the presence of Renoir; the Godardian nature of Tom; the resemblance of Tom's movie to Vigo's *L'Atalante;* the lighting of Josef Von Sternberg; and the tracking camera of Max Ophuls: "Bertolucci draws upon the movie background of this movie because movies are as active in him as direct experience" (R, p. 33). Her review of *Nashville,* again prior to its release and, to the annoyance of some, prior to the final editing, is also worth consulting (R, pp. 446–452). Viewers interested in her opinion of documentaries should read her favorable discussions of Frederick Wiseman's films *High School* and *Hospital* (D, pp. 24–30, 126–128, and 261–267), particularly in the light of her suspicions about the use of *cinéma vérité* in a film like the Maysles brothers' *Gimme Shelter.*

STANLEY KAUFFMANN*

Film and drama critic for the *New Republic*, Stanley Kauffmann (b. 1916) is, with Pauline Kael and Andrew Sarris, one of the top three film reviewers today. He brings to his task experience as a teacher, novelist and playwright. His comprehensive knowledge of film history and his objectivity result in commentary and reviews which offer standards of excellence as well as useful information for lovers of film. We will examine his views of the *auteur* theory; his rejection of facile techniques he finds in recent films and in the New Wave; and his discussion of film and theatre.

The "Auteur" Theory

Like Kael, Kauffmann rejects those critics whose formulation of the *auteur* theory leads to worship of the director's personality and to an emphasis on style over content. Nonetheless, his own discussions of a particular director's themes and style stand as a model of the best kind of criticism that can emerge when one examines a work in the context of an artist's total development.

*Key to Abbreviations:
F = *Figures of Light* (New York: Harper & Row, 1971).
      Copyright © 1967, 1968, 1969, 1970, 1971 by Stanley Kauffmann.
L = *Living Images* (New York: Harper & Row, 1975).
      Copyright © 1970, 1971, 1972, 1973, 1974, 1975 by Stanley Kauffmann.
W = *A World on Film* (New York: Delta Books, 1966).
      Copyright © 1958, 1959, 1960, 1961, 1962, 1963, 1964, 1965, 1966 by Stanley Kaufmann. All quoted by permission of Harper & Row, Publishers, Inc.

First, he points out that in many cases the *auteur* works with
scripts provided by someone else; how, then, can we argue for
the director's fondness for particular themes when he is simply
filming what he was assigned. Even though he might have had
the right to decline a script, and even if his films over the years
do indeed present "a graph of his temperament and talent," still,
the director did not search out his subjects the way other artists
do: "he didn't have to find his subjects himself—certainly not *in*
himself" (L, p. 39). The fact that many directors revered by *auteur* critics work with scripts written by others is crucial for
Kauffmann. For example, he thinks Don Siegel, a favorite of such
critics, is a better director when he has been supplied with a
better script (L, p. 241). And a major hero, Hitchcock, succeeds
only insofar as he has good material to work with: "all of Hitchcock's successes are primarily writers' films—expertly directed,
but overwhelmingly dependent on their scripts" (L, p. 122).

Second, he criticizes François Truffaut and other *Cahiers* critics who elevate the critical value of being able to detect a director's "imprint" in the style of a film (L, p. 39). He cannot accept
that emphasis on "manner over matter," or the idea that "manner
is all: that Samuel Fuller's *Shock Corridor* and Nicholas Ray's
Party Girl and Preminger's *The Cardinal* and Hitchcock's *The
Birds* and Hawks's *Hatari!* are excellent art works because of the
directors' styles, that objection to the tacky stories is misplaced
because the film is not in the story but in [quoting Gavin Millar]
'the relationship between the director and his material' " (F, p.
99). The critic must consider content as well as technique and
style, and not ignore film's "cultural heritage—the cinematic *and*
the literary and theatrical and psychological and social-political"
elements (F, p. 163). Kauffmann cites approvingly Bazin's criticism of the *Cahiers* critics, noted earlier; Bazin had, we remember, inveighed against the kind of criticism which reduces
the subject to zero in the equation *auteur* plus subject equals
work.

Third, *auteur* critics ignore discussions of the financial interests which often play a dominant role in shaping a film. He cites
Max Ophuls' *Lola Montez* as an example. The economic background of the work, actually commissioned as a star vehicle for
Martine Carol, never gets mentioned by critics who maintain a

"hierarchy of film values" emphasizing style: "a chief motive behind the hierarchy is to avoid discussion of the strictured elements forced on film making by the ever-present money men."
Instead of acknowledging this, *auteur* critics look the other way,
and "concentrate on Ophuls' marvelous décor, detail, and camera
movement and, by the simple act of appropriate omission, presto,
we have a masterpiece" (F, p. 163).

Still, viewers should be aware of how Kauffmann, again and
again, offers outstanding examples of what we might call the
Bazinian cast of *auteur* criticism, in which the technique of a film
never is enough for the critic who asks that there be structural
coherence, organic unity and good acting, as well as efficient use
of the camera. Any number of directors whom Kauffmann reviews
over the years would provide good evidence of his ability to assess a film's individual merits, point out its relationship to other
works by the director, and fix it thematically and sometimes bio-
graphically in the artist's career. Three of the best examples are
Michelangelo Antonioni, Ingmar Bergman and Charlie Chaplin.

Unlike the critics Bazin condemns for assuming that a director's latest picture is his best, Kauffmann evaluates directors fairly
and objectively, noting where there seems to be a falling off, a
temporary lull, or, in the case of Antonioni, a continuing slide.
The latter's contribution to film in *L'Avventura* and in the trilogy
Eclipse, La Notte and *Il Grido* are outlined in a masterly series of
reviews which identify his particular achievements: "he is reshaping the idea of the content of film drama, discarding ancient and
less ancient concepts, redirecting traditional audience expectations toward immersion in character rather than conflict of character. He is reshaping time itself... taking it out of its customary
synoptic form, wringing intensity out of its distention, daring to
ask us to 'live through' experiences with less distillation" (W, pp.
305–306). But *Blow-Up*, although great, seems not as good as the
earlier films of the trilogy. Kauffmann speculates that the next
film, the disastrous *Zabriskie Point*, may have arisen out of Antonioni's attitude toward the political situation: "it may be an attempt to exorcise a guilt for having been politically quiescent in
his recent work, just as the whole film may be an attempt to
exorcise a guilt about being middle-aged" (F, p. 244). Kauffmann
finds the director's latest picture, *The Passenger*, "even more dis-
appointing" (*New Republic*, 19 April 1975, p. 22).

His discussions of Ingmar Bergman are even more illustrative of this objectivity. In well over a dozen reviews and a long essay on *Persona*, we can examine Kauffmann's respectful and useful analyses of the director—all tempered with a determination to evaluate fairly. He notes that Bergman creates works which are "manifests of. . . inner life" (L, p. 57). Films of the middle period, such as *Wild Strawberries* and *The Magician*, reveal his poetic potential, although they lack a firmly wrought structure. Perhaps Bergman's experience in the theatre accounts for a looser treatment of dramatic structure: "he looks on the film as a free form, an opportunity for rhapsody and for that psychic exploration dear to the Scandinavian spirit and difficult on the stage" (W, p. 272). *The Magician* can be read as an autobiographical allegory, but Kauffmann finds much of it incomprehensible and lacking artistic control. *The Virgin Spring* seems to him another interesting failure, and raises the issue of whether "his films have become essentially arenas of spiritual wrestling for the author through his characters, rather than disciplined artistic experiences whose prime purpose is emotional involvement of the audience" (W, p. 279). Kauffmann does not see progress in the trilogy— *Through a Glass Darkly*, *Winter Light* and *The Silence*—since they reveal problems in motivation, symbolism, and, in the second film, a literariness at odds with the cinematic aims of film (W, p. 286).

In contrast, *Persona* is a triumph; all its elements cohere: acting, structure, direction. Here Bergman "has found an answer in art to what lately has been troubling his art." Perhaps the director "had become disheartened; by a sense of irrelevance, *his* irrelevance." It was as if Bergman "was keeping a kind of private journal in public" (F, p. 15). But this film signals a mastery over any inner problems bothering Bergman as an artist. The next films, *Hour of the Wolf* and *Shame*, falter, although Kauffmann shows how they interlock with the director's other films in respect to setting, character, names and themes. *The Passion of Anna* gives more evidence of the coherence in his work; this and all his "new films grow organically out of his preceding ones: in continuity of locale, of associates, of almost diaristic closeness to the director's inner experience. . . . Bergman wants this continuity to be seen as part of his esthetics" (F, p. 267). The point here is that for Kauffmann, Bergman's latest film is by no means always his best. But readers of his criticism will be given a means to see

how a film fits into the director's career. In fact, there are more
qualified reviews with reservations about Bergman than outright
commendatory ones. We can compare this phenomenon with
Kauffmann's claim that Lindsay Anderson is "the most gifted director in British film history," even though his reviews of the
director's films have been increasingly negative (L, p. 204).

Like so many of the critics we have discussed, Kauffmann
posits a theory about the development of Chaplin and the Tramp
figure. *The Gold Rush* reveals the Tramp's essential qualities of
"innocence and an unwitting faith in the power of that innocence"
(L, p. 301). The Tramp affects us because of Chaplin's ability to
make us accept him as a "comic character whose standards are
better than our own, just as his body in motion is more beautiful
than our bodies" (L, p. 306). Kauffmann does not like *The Great
Dictator* or *Monsieur Verdoux*. And in *A King in New York*,
Chaplin's last film, he detects the ultimate disintegration of the
Tramp figure: "it shows most vividly how schizoid the later Chaplin had become" (L, p. 248). In *The Great Dictator*, Chaplin
splits into two roles, Hitler and the Tramp. The last speech,
which signals a division between the serious and the comic, initiates a bifurcation extending into *Monsieur Verdoux, Countess
from Hong-Kong,* and *A King in New York*, perhaps because of
Chaplin's "fear that the clown, whose very persona had won him
his claims to seriousness, was no longer serious enough." In the
last film, the division seems different; here the king "represents
not only Chaplin's politically and socially conscious self but Chaplin himself as King—the King that the Tramp has made him!"
The cause of the split probably lies in the coming of sound to
films; that is, the later Chaplin persona cannot be imagined in a
silent film: "he split his world-worshipped character in two and
made the 'serious' half a vehicle for talk" (L, pp. 248-249).

The New Wave

Although initially receptive to French New Wave directors,
many of them *auteur* critics for *Cahiers du Cinéma*, Kauffmann
has not been very enthusiastic over the years since they appeared. He likes Philippe de Broca, Truffaut's *Jules and Jim*, and
Godard's *Breathless* (W, pp. 233, 226-230, and 238-241), but
grows increasingly weary of certain devices and techniques used

by New Wave directors, in particular what he calls chic "in"
jokes, tributes to earlier directors, or self-indulgent references to
themselves—aspects which for him are merely surface gloss and
which ignore the real business of film. He provides an ironic
"formula" for how to be a New Wave director, including a rec-
ommendation to acquire a good cameraman (the most important
aspect); a good story (this does not matter much); a pretty girl for
the star (she need not be an actress); and then, "lay it on. 'It' is
the New Wave repertoire of stunts, camera techniques, and cutting." He includes as faults such things as "long walks through a
city, preferably Paris," whether or not these function organically;
casual overheard dialogue; some of the techniques of Alain
Resnais, and "some silent-film burlesque" (W, pp. 252–253). The
latter figures prominently in many Truffaut films with iris-in and
iris-out transitions and dissolves, silent style wipes, and altered
motion. Or, to take another New Wave director whose films generally displease Kauffmann, Godard in *Pierrot le Fou* provides his
"usual... barrage of devices, standard even by 1965: verbal-visual
puns... editing that goes backward, forward, and sideways in
time; saturation in film references.... In short, more grist for
movie-buff mills" (F, p. 139).

Thus he attacks elements which draw attention to issues outside the organic structure of the work. Clearly his point should be
considered carefully, not only with New Wave films but with any
work; he notes, for example, a Resnais imitation, to no purpose,
in Dennis Hopper's *Easy Rider* (F, p. 188). As viewers we must
ask what function tributes to earlier directors and films serve, and
what useful effect is gained by techniques which draw attention to
themselves. We do not want to reject such things out of hand,
though, for, as we saw with Kael's discussion of Bertolucci, references to film can play a significant part in the director's conception. And Kauffmann himself demonstrates in a brilliant analysis
of *Last Year at Marienbad* how intercutting, repetitions, zooms
and other camera tricks can matter organically (W, pp. 246–251).

The Ugly and the False

Like Agee, Kauffmann points out various set pieces which
have been used so often that they are merely cinematic clichés.

The prime, but not exclusive, offenders in this regard are usually British and American directors. He criticizes John Schlesinger for copying Tony Richardson's heavy-handedness in *Darling;* at the end of the film we move from a news report on the princess (Julie Christie) to an image of a crone singing "Santa Lucia": "it is ugly enough, but what does it signify? Weren't there toothless street singers in more decorous epochs?" (W, p. 208). *Inadmissible Evidence* makes facile use of obvious and clichéd images with "walks along ugly streets, with ugly faces, to show how debased modern life is" (F, p. 92). Haskell Wexler takes the easy way out in *Medium Cool,* giving us "the usual hallmark of the worried realist—facile ugliness: a dwarf attendant at the derby, a badly crippled orderly at the hospital" (F, p. 194). *Easy Rider* is not without its set pieces as well; examples of "arrant triteness and falseness" include the meal with the rancher ("third-rate Steinbeck"), a nude swimming scene ("a very weary objective correlative for purity of heart"), and the New Orleans sequence ("a glimpse of a whore on crutches, ready for business, that looks like Terry Southern's homage to Max Ophuls") (F, p. 187). In Jerry Schatzberg's *Scarecrow,* "there is no move missed toward fake symbolism. Hackman's Denver sister runs a junkyard (*oh,* boy)" (L, p. 196). And Robert Altman fumbles in *Thieves Like Us* as he tries to suggest the hero's relation to society "in terms of minutiae—a soundtrack décor of contemporary radio programs (by now a painfully trite device), the drinking of Cokes, etc." (L, p. 264).

   I have listed a large number of such clichés and examples of easy ugliness (there are many more in Kauffmann's reviews) because they point to one of his chief merits. Only someone with a vast and impressive sense of film history is in a position to identify such things for us as overworked. If we lack the experience and good fortune to have seen thousands of films, at least we owe it to ourselves to consult someone who has, for such a person can alert us to a dimension we ought to consider; that is, the really knowledgeable critic can prevent us from praising a cinematic image as "original" or "fresh" by noting its worn status, and can also encourage us to consider films with an eye to realizing how easily a director chooses patently obvious images to convey meaning.

Film and the Stage

Kauffmann's experience in the theatre puts him in an excellent position to compare the two forms, and in reviews and an essay devoted to the transition from stage to film, he offers extremely useful comments. In "Notes on Theater-and-Film," he makes the following points. The stage director has to work harder to capture our attention, while the film director has it by virtue of the medium. Although film's ability to alter normal time is an advantage, theatre's "real" time benefits insofar as it becomes a structural component. He rejects the usual compulsion to "open up" a play when it is filmed, because it is illogical in relation to the ultimate aim of each form: "fundamentally, the film takes the audience to the event, shifting the audience continually; the theater takes the event to the audience, shifting it never" (L, p. 355). Each has a different kind of thrust. Plays have a vertical dimension: "to assume that the film's extension of a play's action is automatically an improvement is to change the subject: from the way the theater builds upward, folding one event on another in almost perceptible vertical form, to the film's horizontal progression" (L, p. 356). As for the type of comment Bazin makes about framing—the centrifugal aspect whereby the viewer recognizes an extension of the screen material outside the borders of the frame—Kauffmann asserts that film audiences are as aware as play audiences of the equipment outside their immediate view: cameras, microphones, booms, etc. One definite difference and an advantage film has over the stage is its ability to use things which, like the sled in *Citizen Kane*, can become actors in the narrative.

He rejects the argument that stage actors work more than the film actors who have mechanical aids available to them—retakes, make-up, camera angles that intensify their speeches, etc. But it is true that, unlike the stage, films tend to fix actors into roles; that is, we can imagine a succession of actors playing the same role in a given play over the years, but cannot accept as easily the idea of a film role as a vehicle for different actors: "a film role has no separate existence; most theater roles are apprehensible as entities, even during original productions, because the theater is a place where actor and role meet and, eventually, part" (L, p. 360).

Some practical criticism will help to expand his observations. The film of Eugene O'Neill's *Long Day's Journey into Night* does not succeed for Kauffmann: "this theatrical whale has been stranded on the beach of another medium"; it is an "essentially unadaptable" play, and director Sidney Lumet's use of the camera does not make it cinematic (W, p. 75). Similarly, an attempt to film a classic like George Bernard Shaw's *The Doctor's Dilemma* seems doomed from the start. It is better to "make a filmed play, not a film" when dealing with works like this: "you cannot adapt a great dramatist's work to another form because if he was truly great, he has built his work into the form and vice versa" (W, p. 90). In particular, he thinks filmed versions of Shakespeare's plays generally fail, citing as evidence Franco Zeffirelli's *Romeo and Juliet*, which "proves again that the film medium and Shakespeare are born antagonists" (F, p. 113). Although Roman Polanski's *Macbeth* succeeds rather well in its editing, and in its treatment of the witches and of Ross, Kauffmann still voices "the old inescapable complaint about Shakespeare films. The text is slashed, to make time for the pictures. But the tragedy is in the words. Those words *cannot* (repeat: CANNOT) be transmuted into pictures, no matter how gorgeous, nor into action, no matter how exciting" (L, p. 92).

Other Criticism of Note

Readers should consult various essays and reviews in which Kauffmann discusses the current "film generation" (W, pp. 415–428) and shows its relationship to the development of the "personal film" in the United States: for example, his essays on Bob Rafelson's *Five Easy Pieces* and *The King of Marvin Gardens* (L, pp. 11–15 and 146–148); and Martin Scorsese's *Mean Streets* (L, pp. 229–231). Also worth consideration are his mixed views of documentary and *cinéma vérité* techniques: *Warrendale* (F, pp. 102–105); *A Married Couple* (F, pp. 226–229); *Derby* (L, pp. 53–54); and *Marjoe* (L, pp. 131–132).

The latest collection, *Living Images*, contains long and rewarding essays on *Potemkin*, with a brilliant analysis of its visual structures; *Rashomon; Persona*; Griffith and melodrama; and Jean Renoir's *La Grande Illusion*. In the latter, which is particularly rich and suggestive, he discusses Renoir's use of the moving camera and depth of field. He believes Bazin is too "generous" in assigning so much importance to Renoir's use of depth of field, since it can be found in film as early as Edwin S. Porter's *The Great Train Robbery* (1903): "more important, the point that Bazin and other deep-focus theorists have tended to disregard is that the deep-focus principle is about 2500 years old and is usually called 'the theater.' Renoir, who has written and directed plays, simply combined the flow of cinema with the relationships within a frame that are standard practice in the theater" (L, p. 315).

ANDREW SARRIS*

For the last twenty years Andrew Sarris (b. 1928), the most important spokesman in America for the *auteur* theory, has contributed to our knowledge of film with articles in major film journals, reviews in the *Village Voice*, courses of instruction at major university film departments, and editorship of the English edition of *Cahiers du Cinéma*. His knowledge of film is encyclopedic, his insights into the nature of the medium impressive, and his formal analysis of the structure of various films worthy of close analysis. We will examine his explanation of the *auteur* theory and the manner in which he employs it in his practical criticism; consider his views of structuralism and semiology; and note various other matters of interest throughout the *Guide*.

The "Auteur" Theory

Sarris represents the ultimate development of the journalistic tradition in American film criticism and can be considered the heir of Otis Ferguson, James Agee and Robert Warshow; he acknowledges all these predecessors throughout his writings. A

*Key to Abbreviations:
A = *The American Cinema* (New York: Dutton, 1969). Copyright © 1968 by Andrew Sarris. Reprinted by permission of the publishers, E. P. Dutton.
C = *Confessions of a Cultist: On the Cinema, 1955–1969* (New York: Simon & Schuster, 1970). Copyright © 1970 by Andrew Sarris. Reprinted by permission of Simon & Schuster, a Division of Gulf & Western Corporation.
P = *The Primal Screen: Essays on Film and Related Subjects* (New York: Simon & Schuster, 1973). Copyright © 1973 by Andrew Sarris. Reprinted by permission of Simon & Schuster, a Divison of Gulf and Western Corporation.

major influence has been André Bazin, whom Sarris once called
"the greatest film critic who ever lived" (P, p. 42). He has,
though, lately qualified this extreme praise (*The Village Voice*, 19
December 1977, p. 96). Although he accepts only with qualification Bazin's thesis that we should evaluate the filmic image on the
basis of what it reveals of reality, he praises him for two great
contributions: "the restoration of interest in the integrity of visual
space" and "his audacious assertion that the camera could be most
faithful to itself by being faithful to the theatricality of the plays it
adapted to the screen" (P, pp. 87 and 103). He presents an extended analysis of Bazin's critique of *auteur* critics, noted earlier,
and shares with him (and, as we see, with Kauffmann) a fear of
the excesses that can follow from their extreme attitudes (P, pp.
41–46).

Sarris explains what the theory means for him in various
writings, most notably in "Notes on the *Auteur* Theory in 1962,"
an essay which prompted Pauline Kael's attack on him. There he
introduces points which continue to figure significantly in his discussions of the theory. First, he assumes as a standard of evaluation "the technical competence of a director" (P, p. 50). If a director has nothing remarkable to offer in this category, he does
not qualify for Sarris' "Pantheon" of great directors. Included in
this category are the following: Charlie Chaplin, Robert Flaherty,
John Ford, D. W. Griffith, Howard Hawks, Alfred Hitchcock,
Buster Keaton, Fritz Lang, Ernst Lubitsch, F. W. Murnau, Max
Ophuls, Jean Renoir, Josef Von Sternberg and Orson Welles (A,
pp. 39–81). Second, he believes that our ability to discern the
personality and signature of the director in his films can be
another standard of value. It is easy to misinterpret him here; he
is not saying simply that mere evidence of directorial personality
guarantees anything about quality in a film, but rather that good
directors will inevitably stamp their works indelibly with signs of
their presence: "over a group of films a director must exhibit certain recurring characteristics of style which serve as his signature.
The way a film looks and moves should have some relationship to
the way a director thinks and feels" (P, p. 50). For example, we
can detect the signature of Pantheon director Howard Hawks.
Noting that Hawks never loses his "personal identity" in the Hollywood atmosphere, Sarris suggests that his technique amounts to
an extension of his personality; Hawks does not use technique as

much as other directors to evaluate the action, but when he does, he is economical: "Hawks consciously shoots most of his scenes at the eye level of a standing onlooker. Consequently, even his spectacles are endowed with a human intimacy which the director will not disturb with pretentious crane shots. Hawks will work within a frame as much as possible, cutting only when a long take or an elaborate track might distract his audience from the issues in the foreground of the action." This kind of technique "has served ultimately to express his personal credo that man is the measurer of all things" (A, p. 55).

A third assumption made by Sarris pertains to a film's "interior meaning," that which "is extrapolated from the tension between a director's personality and his material" (P, p. 51). Neither an attitude nor a vision, this quality can be likened to "an élan of the soul." That is, a Pantheon director not only demonstrates technical competence and stamps his films with his signature, but also makes us conscious of his presence by offering us films which reveal an *inner* content, a sense of his relationship to their material which we determine by close examination of the films. We are thus able to determine his uniqueness, how he speaks to us the way no other director does.

In other words, when we have studied a director's works, we will know them, but we will also be able to comprehend the creative force which has overseen the creation of them, the intelligence which pervades the universe constituted by the films. Pantheon directors "have transcended their technical problems with a personal vision of the world. To speak any of their names is to evoke a self-contained world with its own laws and landscapes" (A, p. 39). For example, consider his estimate of Orson Welles and the way in which he characterizes the distinctive aspect of all the director's works: "apart from *The Magnficent Ambersons* . . . every Welles film is designed around the massive presence of the artist as autobiographer. Call him Hearst or Falstaff, Macbeth or Othello, Quinlan or Arkadin, he is always at least partly himself, ironic, bombastic, pathetic, and above all, presumptuous. The Wellesian cinema is the cinema of magic and marvels, and everything, and especially its prime protagonist, is larger than life. The dramatic conflict in a Welles film often arises from the dialectical collision between morality and megalomania, and Welles more often than not plays the megalomaniacal villain without stilling the calls of conscience" (A, p. 79).

The "Auteur" Theory and Film History

Sarris refuses to accept the position of some *Cahiers* critics, condemned by Bazin, that the worst picture of an *auteur* is necessarily better than a good picture by a mediocre director. For Sarris, "the worst film of a great director may be more interesting though less successful than the best film of a fair to middling director" (A, p. 17)—"more interesting," but not better.

He takes this position because the theory itself does not exist chiefly as a means of fixing directors forever in some value scheme. The theory's prime merit for him is that it allows critics to bring order to their consideration of the thousands of movies made since the birth of the medium. That is, the *auteur* theory serves him primarily as a *historical* tool. Sarris rejects John Russell Taylor's categorization of films from the 1940s on the basis of trends, subjects and genres. To rely on such divisions and to sort out cinematic developments in this way is to cloud over the complexities and richness of any period of film making: "After rummaging through hundreds of films of this period quite recently, I can find no sensible alternative to directors' retrospectives in organizing the period" (P, p. 34). Such an approach will combat what he calls the fallacious "pyramid" theory of film history by which precursors are linked together at the base of a structure leading to specific pinnacles of achievement. For example, a pyramid theory of the silent film considers movies from 1895 to 1925 in relation to their preparation for and explanation of the arrival and genius of Eisenstein: "this fallacy consists of viewing the history of cinema as a process by which approved artisans have deposited their slabs of celluloid on a single pyramid rising ultimately to a single apex, be it Realism, Humanism, Marxism, Journalism, Abstractionism or even Eroticism" (P, p. 25). In place of this, he calls for an "inverted pyramid opening outward to accommodate the unpredictable range and diversity of individual directors. The time span of the cinema can then be divided into the career span of its directors, each of whom is granted the options of a personal mystique apart from any collective mystique of the cinema as a whole" (P, p. 27).

He makes no special claims for the theory as a magic key for evaluation, calling it "a theory of film history rather than film prophecy" (A, p. 26). The ranking of directors will, he thinks, "establish a system of priorities for the film student" and make up for "the absence of the most elementary academic tradition in cinema" (A, p. 27). Again, he sees his approach "not so much a theory as an attitude, a table of values that converts film history into directorial autobiography." He believes that the *auteur* critic "looks at a film as a whole, a director as a whole. The parts, however entertaining individually, must cohere meaningfully" (A, p. 30). Because of the concern for wholeness, the critic must—as Sarris clearly does—have an immense knowledge of films; only then can the critic say with certainty that "director X" uses a particular technique for the first time. Unfortunately, such an encyclopedic knowledge is hard to attain. But the critic must try to broaden his knowledge by seeing as many films as possible: "nothing should be beneath criticism or contempt. I take a transcendental view of the role of a critic. He must aspire to totality even though he knows that he will never attain it" (A, p. 34). Finally, the theory offers "a system of tentative priorities, a pattern theory in constant flux." The critic must "take the long view," as if every film would survive forever, for the approach "implies a faith in film history as a continuing cultural activity" (A, p. 34).

The Director and the Screenwriter

In response to critics like Pauline Kael and Richard Corliss who challenge the director's exclusive claims for the creation of a film, Sarris argues that we should recognize the unique role of the director without forgetting *any* of the other formative elements. He calls for common sense in evaluating the contributions of the screenwriter and director, beginning with the assumption that "the director is the hypothetically dominant figure in the filmmaking process until a pattern of contributions has been established." The director becomes a kind of focal point, "a field of magnetic force around which all agents and elements of the filmmaking process tend to cluster" ("Preface" to Richard Corliss, *Talking Pictures* [New York: Penguin Books, 1975], p. xiv).* Sarris refuses to make hard-and-fast assessments of the director-screenwriter relationship in the "no man's land of narrative and dramatic structure," and accepts the notion advanced by Joseph L. Mankiewicz, who conceives of screenplays as directed movies, and directed movies as screenplays: "that is to say that writing and directing are fundamentally the same function" ("Preface," p. xv).

Citing the story of "Little Red Riding Hood," Sarris suggests that the manner in which the basic plot might be filmed would affect our interpretation of the story. To film the girl consistently with close-ups and the wolf with long shots would be to interpret the material in one way: "the emphasis is shifted to the emotional problems of vestigial virginity in a wicked world." On the other hand, to concentrate on the wolf with close-ups would be to express concern "primarily with the emotional problems of a wolf with a compulsion to eat little girls." That is, the manner in which the director films and edits can itself be a condition and element of the story. Analogously, modern directors like Hawks and Hitchcock, who do not write their own scripts, nonetheless interpret someone else's story through their technique and methods of presenting the material: "each of these directors has created a world of his own on film, a world no less unique for having been filtered through the varying verbalizations of scores of scriptwriters" (C, p. 361).

With cutting and set-ups the director provides "a consistent point of view" for the material (C, p. 362). Only this force "is capable of preserving formal order in all the chaos of filmic creation" (C, p. 363). Conceiving of the director as a magnetic force in no way denies the contributions of others: "To look at a film as the expression of a director's vision is not to credit the director with total creativity" (A, p. 36). Again, "the search for meaningful authorship on the screen does not denigrate the roles of writer, actor, composer, cameraman and editor" (C, p. 364).

---

*Copyright © 1974 by Richard Corliss. By permission of the author and The Overlook Press, Woodstock, N.Y. 12498.

As for the charge that it is fruitless to search for a style or personality in directors like Ford or Hawks working under the stifling atmosphere of the Hollywood studio system, Sarris suggests that a director probably escaped more easily than the screenwriter whose words and narrative ideas were always subject to pressures from studio bosses or censors: "even the vaunted vulgarity of the movie moguls worked in favor of the director at the expense of the writer. A producer was more likely to tamper with a story line than with a visual style. Producers, like most people, understood plots in literary rather than cinematic terms" (A, p. 31). Finally, he observes that the *auteur* theory "was never intended to enthrone all directors above all writers, but rather to identify the source of a style in movies worthy of memory" (P, p. 123).

Sarris has continued to articulate his views of the theory, and, in some recent writings, offers viewers refinements of earlier positions. In a recent book, he surveys the career of John Ford, and notes how the early films, *Four Sons* and *The Iron Horse*, establish a dialectic of the expressionistic and naturalistic which figures in relation to the later films. He stresses that critics must consider any film not only in terms of the director's works, but also in relation to *all* films: "Hence authentic auteurism, far from narrowing the historian's focus on film to the dimension demanded by the frame-by-frame heretics and the stilted structuralists, must inevitably expand into an encyclopedic awareness of not only the universe of film itself, but also the exact position of film in the universe" (*The John Ford Movie Mystery* [Bloomington: Indiana University Press, 1975], p. 18.)*

Were he formulating the theory again, he assures us, he would have emphasized style more than he did previously, and would now pay less attention to the personal element. He seems to be attempting to objectify the theory as he makes clear that "auteurism and Sarrism are not identical" ("The Auteur Theory Revisited," *American Film*, 2:9 [1977], 51). In yet another recent comment he addresses himself to the importance of the actor in film. The actor is inevitably a collaborator in the production in-

---

*Quoted by permission of Indiana University Press and of Martin Secker & Warburg, Ltd. (reprinted from their Cinema One series).

sofar as he participates in the merger of reality and fiction in the role. Sarris is not warm to the implications of the Kuleshov experiments we described earlier. Instead of saying, as he once did, that "feelings are expressed *through* actors, not *by* actors," he argues: "Though I still believe in a cinema of directors, I have come to believe also that the actor constitutes much of the language of the cinema" ("The Actor as Auteur," *American Film*, 2:7 [1977], 17).

Semiology and Structuralism

We will discuss semiology (the study of signs) and structuralism (the exploration with linguistic, anthropological and psychological methods of the nature of man) in more detail in the last chapter. Here I want to point out why Sarris rejects these as critical tools for himself.

To generalize about these most complex processes for a moment, we could say that semiologists and structuralists who turn their attention to film want to explore the nature of cinematic language, explain how signs convey meaning, and consider narrative in terms of inner patterns as well as its relation to larger external phenomena. Such critics are often interested in images and symbols as these belong to an extended system of social and cultural relationships outside the immediate work. They do not necessarily deny an interest in the organic nature of a work, but their methodology very often leads them away from the work to forces outside it, whereas formal analysis, such as Sarris employs in connection with his *auteur* criticism, takes one inside the work and the mind of the director. We will see that Peter Wollen attempts a synthesis of *auteur* criticism and semiology. But Sarris, in a phrase that many will find unfair, laments "the dangerous botulisms of semiology" which may arise if the approach gains more force, particularly in quarters inhabited by critics who know very little about film history (*The Village Voice*, 11 August 1975, p. 66).* He resents the semiologist's "addiction to charts and dia-

---

*This and subsequent quotations from the *Voice* reprinted by permission of The Village Voice. Copyright © 1974 and 1975, The Village Voice, Inc.

grams at the expense of flowing prose." More important, he rejects any semiologist who does "not seek to understand the meaning of the artist, but instead . . . strives to extract from the work of
art the elements which properly belong to the society at large"
(*Voice*, p. 64). By so doing, he charges, the critics lose sight of
the creative process.

For example, Sarris considers the striptease sequence in
Robert Altman's *Nashville*. He speculates that a semiologist
"might interpret this sequence in terms of how audiences traditionally interpret the spectacle of the striptease" (*Voice*, p. 66).
In fact, Roland Barthes, a leading figure in semiology and structuralism has just such an essay on the subject. For semiologists,
Sarris thinks, "a striptease is a striptease" (*Voice*, p. 63). But, for
him, Gwen Welles's abasing performance provides an occasion to
think of other screen stripteases: "there is pride in her performance, but not the professional pride of Lola Albright's stripper
in 'Cold Wind in August,' nor Natalie Wood's ugly-duckling-
turned-stripped-swan pride in 'Gypsy,' nor Joanne Woodward's
existential pride in 'The Stripper,' nor Patricia Owen's sexually
liberating pride in 'Hell to Eternity'" (*Voice*, p. 64). As an *auteur*
critic "more concerned with the director's attitude toward the
spectacle" than the spectacle itself, Sarris offers a sensitive evaluation of the striptease in respect to Altman's technique: "Altman's
camera stumbles with her and temporarily obscures part of her
performance. . . . Altman does not cut away abruptly from the ultimate revelation, but neither does he linger. He does not cut in
to the girl's face to separate it spiritually from the shamed body.
She remains a whole person, her pride intact in the presence of
her tormentors. We are all trapped together, Altman seems to be
saying, and, stylistically at least, he does not take a cheap shot at
the figures in his frame" (*Voice*, p. 66).

Presumably, he believes, a semiologist would not be interested in the differences in the various stripteases: "is not
semiology inherently hostile to the extraordinary allusiveness of
film?" (*Voice*, p. 63). He starts "groaning under the enormous
weight of the methodological machinery" when semiologists "begin drawing charts with such headings as sign and signal, index
and icon, system and syntagm" (*Voice*, p. 64). Readers may find
his attacks on semiology as limited as Kael's attacks on his *auteur*

criticism for its assumptions; what we find is that both *auteur* critics and semiologists have something to offer us.

The Ugly, the Beautiful and the Chic

It is instructive to observe the way Sarris and Kauffmann, who both operate out of an aesthetic upholding realism, share a distaste for the facile and obvious devices used by directors to suggest "truth" and "meaning." For example, Sarris catalogues the typical "mannerisms of realism," which include: "no background music. Unprofessional actors. Bad sound recording. An emphasis on exteriors. A concern with the social problems of the lower classes. Black and white, small screen, and oodles of montage. Above all, realistic movies must pretend not to be movies at all, but impersonal documents of reality" ("A Movie Is a Movie Is a Movie Is a," in *The Emergence of Film Art*, ed. Lewis Jacobs [New York: Hopkinson & Blake, 1969], p. 314).* He criticizes Martin Ritt's *Hud* for "that hungover look that is almost invariably confused with honest realism. Here the visual correlative of decadence is dust, even though Texas was dusty long before the Alamo" (C, p. 90). John Schlesinger's *Midnight Cowboy* also offends in this respect: "A director can suggest all sorts of problems simply by letting his camera stare at almost any urban street scene, and Schlesinger has gone to even greater lengths ... to make modernity seem meaningfully meaningless. All the luridly neonized flora and fauna on Forty-second Street don't necessarily foreshadow the decline and fall of American Civilization" (C, pp. 442–443).

In another vein, Sarris notes the empty use of stunning shots in David Lean's *Dr. Zhivago:* "full of beautiful shots of ice and snow and moon and sun and fields and flowers and trees and spires, but the shots spill out on the screen like loose beads from a broken necklace. There is nothing holding the effects together, not an idea, or a feeling, or a mood, or even much of a plot" (C, pp. 227–228). In other words, effects which exist merely for themselves, without organic relation to the plot, are to be rejected.

---

*Quoted by permission of Andrew Sarris.

But, like Kael, and in contrast to Kauffmann, Sarris defends various tributes or *hommages* as being more than simply chic devices thrown in by the director. Here he has much to say to us. For example, he notes that in *Contempt*, Jean-Luc Godard's inside jokes and allusions to other films and directors actually represent a position—Godard's rejection of Bazin and the *Cahiers* School to which he had formerly belonged (C, p. 188). Godard in particular employs *hommages* in which "subtler meanings may be lurking beneath the surface frivolity" (C, p. 168). An outstanding example of this occurs in *Weekend,* as Godard alludes to Salvador Dali's and Luis Buñuel's *Un Chien Andalou,* and the scene in which an androgynous girl, observed from a window by a man and woman, is run over by a car. In *Weekend,* "the three bourgeois characters look down from their balcony at a street accident culminating in a violent brawl between the two drivers involved. Godard stages the brawl from such an insistently overhead viewpoint that he creates a metaphor for bourgeois detachment from social turmoil. The verticality of the viewpoint is sustained long enough to remind the educated moviegoer of a similar metaphor in Luis Buñuel's and Salvador Dali's more overtly surrealistic classic. . . . Whereas Buñuel and Dali treated apparent moral indifference as actual metaphysical liberation, Godard treats idle curiosity as immoral complicity. The difference between Buñuel-Dali and Godard is therefore the difference between irony and allegory" (C, p. 402). This kind of comparative criticism provides a useful model for viewers; first, by its perceptive and synthesizing intelligence; and second, by its built-in lesson—know as many films as possible so that it will be possible to recognize and judge the value of a cinematic allusion.

Theatre and Film

As I noted earlier, Sarris applauds Bazin's suggestion that the best way to translate a play into film is by staging the work with a camera and retaining the theatricality of the dramatic work. Sarris views as unfortunate the naturalistic bias toward deemphasizing speech and stressing the visual elements (P, p. 103). He believes that speech as such can always be cinematic, and defends the validity of speech as a dominant element in a film, as in Marcel Carné's *Les Enfants du Paradis,* in which characters "talk and they talk and they talk, poetically, flamboyantly, personally. Is this cinema? Of course it is. Cinema is everything. Image, sound, music, speech, color"; "there is no greater spectacle in the cinema than a man and a woman talking away their share of eternity together" (C, p. 227).

Sarris criticizes Mike Nichols for "opening up" *Who's Afraid of Virginia Woolf?* in a naturalistic manner: "he has underestimated the power of the spoken word in his search for visual pyrotechnics. . . . There is no need to jump up and down with the camera every time a character suggests humping the hostess or getting the guests or humiliating the host. Nor is there any need to take the action outside, where the hypnotic spell of an alcoholic mood can be dispelled by the fake emptiness of exteriors. Nichols gained nothing in the way of genuine cinema with his screeching station wagon" (C, p. 261).

Formal Analysis

One of the most rewarding experiences for readers of Sarris comes from encountering some of his brilliant analyses of the organic structure of various films. In particular, I recommend his various studies of *Citizen Kane*.

In an early essay, *"Citizen Kane:* The American Baroque," he systematically and convincingly refutes the charges that the film has an unnecessarily complicated structure, that its technique is showy, and that the ideas are superficial. He identifies two themes: "the debasement of the private personality of the public figure, and the crushing weight of materialism"* (*Film Culture Reader*, ed. by P. Adams Sitney [New York: Praeger, 1970], p. 103). The first theme is developed through the film's verbal element, the second through its photography and technique. The opening newsreel deserves praise for its economy, since it sets up the biographical framework without recourse to the typical mon-

---

*This and the following three quotations are reprinted by permission from *Film Culture Reader*, ed. by P. Adams Sitney (New York: Praeger, 1970), copyright © 1970 by the Film Culture Non-Profit Corporation.

tage devices used to compress lives. Even more, through this newsreel, "Welles frees his flashbacks from the constricting demands of exposition, enabling his main characters to provide insights on the external outlines of the Kane biography" (*Film*, p. 104). Sarris also defends the ending, and the revelation to the audience of the identity of "Rosebud": "the burning sled is apt not only as a symbolic summation but also as a symbolic revelation. The reporter, the butler, the workman, the friends, the enemies, the acquaintances of Kane never discover *Rosebud* because it is lost amid the 'junk' of Kane's materialistic existence" (*Film*, p. 105). By virtue of Gregg Toland's camera angles, Kane appears diminished by "a universe of ceilings. . . . He becomes the prisoner of his possessions, the ornament of his furnishings, the fiscal instrument of his collections" (*Film*, p. 106). Any superficiality in *Citizen Kane* springs from the nature of the character himself, rather than from a faulty artistic conception.

Later, Sarris responds to Pauline Kael's charges in "Raising Kane" that Herman J. Mankiewicz and not Welles actually wrote the film, attacks her argument and research methods, while striking out with new insights about the film. Particularly worth noting is his discussion of the symbolic nature of the sled: "'Rosebud' reverberates with psychological overtones as it passes through the snows of childhood . . . into the fire, ashes, and smoke of death. Indeed, the burning of 'Rosebud' in Xanadu's furnace represents the only instance in which the character of Kane can be seen subjectively by the audience. It is as if his mind and memory were being cremated before our eyes and we are too helpless to intervene and too incompetent to judge" (P, p. 118).

More recently, Sarris proposes an interesting view of the suicide scene which Bazin praises for effective use of deep focus. The latter notes how the technique economically resolves in one shot material that traditionally would have been presented in several shots. Sarris observes that "Bazin's stylistic dialectic involved two different stories. The choice that Welles made with his deep focus and derisive distortion throws all the guilt on Kane for his wife's attempted suicide. The multiple-shot montage treatment of this same episode would shift the moral emphasis somewhat to the husband's active concern over the fate of his wife. The action of the rescue in Bazin's imaginary 'traditional' treatment thereby absolves the husband of much of the responsibility for the wife's suicide attempt whereas the actual Wellesian approach tightens the moral noose around Kane's neck" (*The Village Voice*, 25 April 1974, p. 76). We are back again with the possibilities noted earlier, in his discussion of Red Riding Hood and the wolf; the way a director chooses to unveil the action to us is part of the meaning of the story. Here Welles's technical treatment of Kane is itself a statement about the hero: form supports content.

FEMINIST CRITICISM

A recent development in criticism has been the attention paid to women in film. The journal *Camera Obscura* is concerned primarily with this topic, and other publications have also considered the issue, among them *Jump-Cut, Ciné-Tracts* and *Quarterly Review of Film Studies*. I want to discuss the work of three leading critics who analyze the image and role of women in film. Molly Haskell and Marjorie Rosen follow historical developments and trends in film as they point out the psychological and sociological significance of the treatment of women; Joan Mellen provides equally useful insights while emphasizing individual directors and films rather than particular historical developments.

It should be noted that none of these critics writes exclusively on feminist issues. Viewers can find excellent essays and reviews by them considering film from many other aspects: historical, formal, genre, etc. Still, I have chosen to limit my discussion to those works specifically aimed at women and film. In many ways, their criticism reminds us of Plato's objections to art and his charge that the artist gives us a work which is at two removes from the ultimate truth. For these critics, most films have distorted the image of women; in Rosen's words, Hollywood has "held a warped mirror up to life."

MOLLY HASKELL*

Molly Haskell (b. 1939), a widely read critic (*The Village Voice, Ms., New York Magazine*), considers the role of women in films in *From Reverence to Rape* by employing the *auteur* theory in connection with psychological and archetypal constructs derived from Sigmund Freud and Carl Jung. In this extremely rich study of trends, she identifies various images of women and tries to account for their presence. We will proceed by examining some of the types she isolates; the reasons for their existence; patterns over the years in the portrayal of women; and comments on some noteworthy *auteurs*.

The Typing of Women

Haskell believes that the manner in which male directors present women provides an index to their inner lives, either their fantasies or values: "women, by the logistics of film production and the laws of Western society, generally emerge as the projections of male values. Whether as the product of one *auteur* or of the system ... women are the vehicle of men's fantasies, the 'anima' of the collective male unconscious, and the scapegoat of men's fears" (pp. 39–40). For example, she argues that, primarily for Oedipal reasons, males project a dominant image of women as mother or virgin. Man's attempt to purify women arises from a desire to eliminate any reminder of the father's sexual power: "mother's purity, the most sacred and crucial image of our culture, is entirely a wish fulfillment invented by man, an Oedipal attempt by the son to banish the hated image of sex with the father" (p. 119). But to foster this image is to deny female sexual-

---

*All quotations are from *From Reverence to Rape* (New York: Penguin Books, 1974). Copyright © 1973, 1974 by Molly Haskell. Reprinted by permission of Holt, Rinehart and Winston, Publishers and of New English Library, Ltd.

ity and to make of woman a lesser being, even while seeming to
elevate her.

In contrast to this process of purification is its opposite, a
debasing projection of woman as vamp. In this case, it is man's
sense of weakness which explains the phenomenon. The terms
themselves, "vamp" and "sex goddess," seem to her a kind of
strategy, "magical words, incantations invented by men to explain
the inexplicable, and . . . to locate the source of destruction within
the 'mysterious' sex" (p. 104). The same applies to the sexy and
murderous seductresses of the films of the 1940s; their "power to
destroy was a projection of man's feeling of impotence" (p. 191).

Sometimes an actress functions in a complex way as the
anima, or female principle, for a director, as Marlene Dietrich
does for Josef Von Sternberg: "she is Sternberg's creation, his
anima, and yet she absorbs so much of him into her that she is
not an 'other' as object . . . but an androgynous subject." A star
like Mae West, who essentially creates her own image, becomes
both "anima and animus"—that is, embodies both female and
male principles of strength and being. Greta Garbo is such a
strong personality that, as anima, she belongs neither to one director nor even to the collective unconscious of her audience, but
must be considered, rather, as "a natural force, a principle of
beauty that, once set into motion, becomes autonomous" (p. 107).

Haskell discusses a number of types to be found in film,
some emerging from fiction, but most, ultimately, from actual social conditions: the earth goddess, the enigmatic woman, the
mother, the whore, the flapper, the vamp, etc. She connects the
iconography of virgins and vamps to the typage theory advanced
by some of the Russian critics we discussed earlier. In American
films of the 1920s, typage involved a moral rather than a political
version of this practice. Actresses were chosen on the basis of
their physical affinities to the moral image of vamp, mother,
virgin, and woman of the world. For example, a virgin type
would not only be fair, but also smaller than the mother type.
The woman of the world would incorporate the external appearance of the vamp, while retaining certain aspects of the virgin's
spiritual suggestions.

With or without the use of typage, the camera's activity inevitably makes woman an object by virtue of the medium itself.
Haskell thinks "the first principle of the aesthetic of film as a
visual medium" is the fact that woman becomes an "idol, art object, icon, and visual entity" (p. 7). Because of film's involvement
with external behavior—that is, what it can film—it "prefers surfaces to essences and types to individuals" (p. 47). In this sense,
one can view all film allegorically, inasmuch as one must go from
the surface icons and their patterns to the underlying relations
represented by these surfaces. Film is also a sensual medium.
She notes the difficulty faced by any director who tries to film a
beautiful woman *without* turning her into a sex object; that is,
the process of filming, with its revealing tendency and use of surfaces, can actually perpetuate the concept of woman as object by
presenting her to us *as* an object, an idol or type without any
interior life of her own.

This combination of psychological factors, by which women
become merely projections of male feelings, and the nature of the
medium, which emphasizes the surface of reality, tend to account
for the fact that women lack inner life on the screen. Only rarely
does an actress like Katharine Hepburn or Joan Crawford or
Bette Davis reach the status of "superwoman" and convey a sense
of independence and of the ability "to achieve her ends in a
man's world, to insist on her intelligence, to insist on using it" (p.
230). Again, only a few, like Hepburn or Rosalind Russell, have
been able to present lives based on our sense of moral rather
than merely romantic sensibilities. She applauds such women:
"Our approval has everything to do with the degree to which a
woman, however small her part, is seen to have an interior life: a
continuum which precedes and succeeds her relationship with
men and by which she, too, defeats time temporarily and transcends her biological fate" (p. 203).

From the 1920s to the Present

In general, Haskell argues that women achieve their greatest
treatment in films of the 1930s. Prior to this, the dominant images which emerge from the films of D. W. Griffith and of Mary

Pickford are not strong. The former portrays woman as "Holy Grail" (p. 57); still, he does present her as having some "emotional complexity" (p. 55). The child worship of the Pickford heroines relates, in a negative way, to an American phenomenon—the desire to escape adult responsibilities, especially those connected with marriage, either by remaining a child or by escaping from society. The latter theme figures significantly in our cinema, particularly in westerns and comedies. She considers the films of Laurel and Hardy offensive and detects overt misogyny in their womanless world. The flappers and suffragettes of the 1920s display only apparent freedom, since their liberation is more emotional than sexual.

In the 1930s two important developments help explain the favorable presentation of women: the full arrival of sound and the instituting of the Production Code. A heroine of the previous decade lacked "the very instrument of her emancipation— speech. . . . The conversational nuances of an intelligent woman can hardly be conveyed in a one-sentence title" (p. 76). As sound made woman articulate, the Production Code contributed to her stature. In the early part of the decade, largely in response to pressures for censorship from the Hearst press and from citizens outraged at the films of Mae West, the code was created under the direction of Will Hays. It provided extremely restrictive moral guidelines as to what could or could not be shown. As a result of this, Hollywood avoided dealing with sexual matters directly or with female sexuality. Portrayals of women shifted from interest in her as a sexual object to depictions of her as an active being in the world. Romance was not eliminated, but it became only one aspect of a complex of details in a woman's life. Thus, paradoxically, by getting woman "out of the bedroom and into the office" (p. 30), the code contributed to an important development in film history, since now there was definite interest in her as a member of the working force—for example, *Take a Letter, Darling,* in which Rosalind Russell plays the employer of Fred Mac-Murray. Equally important to Haskell is that in the 1930s we see something approaching equality in the love relationships. Women appear capable of genuine sexual feeling. And in films like *The Awful Truth, It Happened One Night,* or the Fred Astaire-Ginger Rogers musicals, she finds an "equilibrium, a world in which male authority, or sexual imperialism, is reduced or in abeyance, while the feminine spirit is either dominant or equal" (p. 131).

Haskell argues that the "Woman's Film" of the 1930s and 1940s should be considered a genre in itself. So often excluded from the main action in predominantly male-oriented western and gangster films, women in this genre become "the center of the universe" (p. 155). The heroine is usually in the middle class, economically and intellectually, and locked in a repressive code. She relies for her happiness "on institutions—marriage, motherhood—that by translating the word 'woman' into 'wife' and 'mother,' end her independent identity" (pp. 159–160). She categorizes various kinds of films about women, some dealing with "ordinary" and others with "extraordinary" beings. In the first, women are generally substitutes for the bulk of their female audience and "defined negatively and collectively by their mutual limitations rather than by their talents or aspirations" (p. 160). In the second, heroines played by Katharine Hepburn, Rosalind Russell, and Bette Davis are "aristocrats of their sex," serving as models rather than as surrogates. Typical themes of the woman's film include: *sacrifice*, for children or husband—*Madame X, Back Street*; *affliction*—the physically ill or doomed heroines of *Magnificent Obsession* or *Dark Victory*; *choice*—a film like *Daisy Kenyon* in which the woman must decide between two men; and *competition*—films in which the woman fights another woman for the same man. Throughout all these Haskell believes we can detect underlying patterns of consciousness that explain the psyche of the audience: "Because the woman's film was designed for and tailored to a certain market, its recurrent themes represent the closest thing to an expression of the collective drives, conscious and unconscious, of American women, of their avowed obligations and the unconscious resistance" (p. 168).

There are some positive images of women in 1940s films: in the works of Howard Hawks, in Hepburn movies, and in some war stories' attractive characterizations of the "Fighting Women" or the "Waiting Women." But, by and large, the decade's films reveal a rejection or dark qualification of the advances seen in films of the previous decade. In contrast to the previous equality, Haskell sees "fatalism," "pessimism," and "social disaffection" (pp.

193–194). This is particularly true in the *film noir*, when female sexuality is linked to evil, as in *Double Indemnity;* or in melodramas when love relationships are dominated by mistrust, "fear and suspicion, impotence and inadequacy," as in *Gaslight* and *Suspicion* (pp. 195–196).

The 1950s represent another step downward in the portrayal of women. Female sexuality is increasingly distorted, whether in the unreal images of the ingenue as "professional virgin" (Debbie Reynolds) (p. 263), or in the grotesqueness of Jayne Mansfield, "a cartoon of overblown sex appeal" (p. 255). Even if Hepburn appears positively, and even if, in films by Douglas Sirk, there is an occasionally attractive portrayal of women, the negative images dominate. Significantly, interest in showing women in roles *playing* actresses almost becomes a metaphor at this time: woman *as* actress. Although women must assume roles in their lives, the version this takes on in films of the fifties strikes Haskell as "an insidious implication" since it supports the idea that "acting is role-playing, role-playing is lying, and lying is a woman's game" (p. 243).

The years since 1960 have seen no improvement in the depiction of women. Directors whose misogyny had been covert now present their feelings directly. She finds Sam Peckinpah and Stanley Kubrick particularly apt examples of a hostile attitude, especially in the former's *Straw Dogs*, where the sexuality of the heroine, played by Susan George, seems more a male fantasy of the director than anything corresponding to reality. Some of the negative images of women may be the result of a backlash against the advances gained through the women's movement. Certainly women seem to be increasingly excluded from films about male activities—in works like *Dirty Harry* or the two parts of *The Godfather*—or films where the basic interest is male relationships—*Easy Rider* or *Midnight Cowboy*. There appears to be little or no evidence of the advances of women's liberation, and even the best roles for actresses have been essentially debasing: "the great women's roles of the decade, what are they for the most part? Whores, quasi-whores, jilted mistresses, emotional cripples, drunks. Daffy ingenues, Lolitas, kooks, sex-starved spinsters, psychotics. Icebergs, zombies, and ballbreakers. That's what little girls of the sixties and seventies are made of" (pp. 327–328).

Feminist Criticism and "Auteurs"

As Haskell studies various *auteurs*, she demonstrates most convincingly the truth of her assertion that she is "a film critic first and a feminist second"; for her "art will always take precedence over sociology, the unique over the general" (p. 38). That is, although her prime interest here is with the issue of the treatment of women in film, she succeeds in keeping artistic judgments separate from sociological observations.

Some of her most enthusiastic praise goes to Howard Hawks; although his earlier films do not deal effectively with women, as he develops there is an increasing tendency to consider women as equals in male/female relationships. Particularly impressive is his treatment of Lauren Bacall *To Have and Have Not* and *The Big Sleep*, and of Rosalind Russell in *His Girl Friday*. He directs an actress in a way that allows her to appear in a positive light: "for the Hawks' heroine, the vocal quality, the facial and bodily gesture are the equivalent of the literary heroine's words, and with these she engages in a thrust-and-parry as highly inflected and intricate as the great love duels of literature" (p. 211). Even in male-dominated films like *Hatari!*, Hawks employs women prominently: "the men are generally seen in relation to women, and women are the point of reference and exposition" (p. 208).

Haskell believes that the true *auteur* confirms Freud's theory about artistic compensation: "to the extent that he is an artist, the director is driven to create by some maladjustment, however minor; by the wound, the stutter, the irritation, the limp that keeps him out of step with the world's drummer" (p. 34). Any such limitation will appear in his art, and his treatment of women will suggest various aspects of the forces that go to shaping him as an artist: "women will be made to reflect his puritanism, his obsessions, his hostility" (p. 35).

Ingmar Bergman provides an illustration of the *auteur* whose women reflect his inner turmoil. He has, she believes, presented "some of the most complex and sensually intelligent women of cinema" (p. 316). But the manner in which he uses them must be considered in the light of his personal relations to some of the actresses themselves, with whom he has been lover and/or husband: "since his work is also a progressive burrowing into the self, it follows that as he becomes older and more despairing (and less sexually vital) his women will suffer the consequences" (p. 316). Even though he has not taken women lightly in his films, the later works present us with "tortured, stifled women, increasingly imprisoned by the images Bergman has given them" (pp. 314–315). Like Joan Mellen, Haskell criticizes the treatment of women in *Cries and Whispers:* "Bergman the artist controls them like puppets, abusing them for being what he has made them: Thulin—neurotic, intellectual, and repressed; Ullmann— beautiful, vain, sensual; and frustrating any attempts at interrelationships by silencing their conversation and aborting sensual overtones between them" (p. 315).

MARJORIE ROSEN*

In *Popcorn Venus,* film critic Marjorie Rosen (b. 1944) considers the ways in which movies have reflected and/or distorted the image of women since the birth of the medium. We shall follow Rosen's examinations of various developments over the years, stereotypes and genres.

Distorted Images

The "Popcorn Venus" which constitutes the title of her most readable book refers to "the Cinema Woman . . . a delectable but insubstantial hybrid of cultural distortions" (p. 10). This amalgam can be analyzed in numerous ways as we observe the various forms taken by or imposed on women in film. The "cultural distortions" identified by Rosen figure prominently throughout all the media. Often she cites from newspapers and magazines to illustrate how contemporaries view women; to a great extent we find her sources depicting women as helpless entities whose proper functions should be limited to homemaking and mothering. Also presented, though, are figures and data illustrating what women have, in fact, accomplished or suffered in the last seventy years, information which has generally failed to be reflected in films. For the most part, she argues, films have not come to terms with women realistically; instead, they have suppressed facts, maintained stereotypes or created unrealistic figures. Only rarely have movies revealed genuine interest in or presented sympathetic treatments of women.

For example, in films of the 1920s we can find portrayals of working women, but those we see are predominantly blue-collar

*All quotations are from *Popcorn Venus* (New York: Avon Books, 1974). Copyright © 1973 by Marjorie Rosen. By permission of the author and of Coward, McCann & Geoghegan, Inc.

workers or chorus girls. By showing such images, Hollywood "held a warped mirror up to life" (p. 81), since, in reality, women at that time were represented in more important jobs: in science by zoologist Delia Akeley; in politics by Annette Adams; in sports by Gertrude Ederle; and in the arts by painter Georgia O'Keeffe, author Willa Cather and dancer Isadora Duncan. In the 1930s films begin to present women "working by their wits" as secretaries, detectives and reporters, but now, Rosen thinks, the object of such portrayals is escapism rather than any genuine desire to acknowledge women contributing significantly to the working force. Even at that, the presentation comes ten years late. Worse, the actual economic problems afflicting women in the 1930s never receive adequate emphasis but are lost in the charm of films about girl reporters and those which perpetrate a false image of security and comfort (p. 144). As in the previous decade, films fail to reflect significant accomplishments of such notable figures as Secretary of Labor Frances Perkins, and Nobel Prize winners Jane Addams and Pearl Buck.

With the arrival of World War II, films actually register more realistically than before the conditions faced by women— certainly, Rosen argues, because so many in the audience were women. Still, even though there are many films about women war workers (the Rosie the Riveter genre), after the war Hollywood ignores the plight of women who lose their jobs to returning soldiers and focuses on the psychological problems of adjustment faced by the men rather than the emotional and economic hardships of women who wanted to continue working.

Further examples of cinematic distortions and failures to present the actual conditions of women occur in bobby-soxer pictures of the late 1940s and after. The image of boy-crazy girls whose only interests are romantic is untrue to the facts, which indicate that, even prior to the war, more and more women were attending college. With some exceptions, films of the 1950s fail to mirror the kinds of women's accomplishments evident in the movies of the previous decade. In most of the genres, the female image which is elevated, directly or indirectly, is that of the happily married woman—itself a distortion, since the divorce rate was beginning to rise significantly in the 1950s. Rosen argues convincingly that a number of films about unmarried females, the

Woman Alone genre, treat her "as if she were a national subver-
sive. Was she the Establishment's allegory warning against deviation from the norm?" (p. 276).

Hollywood's apparent interest recently in showing women as
independent beings seems to have been guarded, although some
portrayals such as Doris Day's executive in *Pillow Talk* and Shirley MacLaine's secretary in *The Apartment* suggested potential
advances earlier. Rosen is not impressed generally with the image
of women conveyed in films like *Joanna* and *Sweet November*, or
in her exclusion in the masculine-dominated worlds of *Easy
Rider*, *Midnight Cowboy* and *Mash*.

Stereotypes

One of the most interesting aspects of *Popcorn Venus* is Rosen's identification of a specific stereotype and examination of its
subsequent manifestations. Although she makes no claims to be a
structuralist critic, it is worth noting that her analysis of the original vamp and child characters and their various later appearances
parallels the typical kind of activities seen in anthropological or
literary studies in which researchers identify an archetype,
whether a character or a motif, and then examine the transformations which the type undergoes over the years. Rosen does
not here cite the obvious, that the vamp herself is a transformation of the archetypal woman of mystery, "la belle dame sans
merci," who derives from the Circe figure of mythology. In films,
the type makes its first major appearance in Theda Bara's *A Fool
There Was* (1915). Representing "enticing notions of depravity
and wanton lust" (p. 60), the darkhaired and exotic vamp lures
men to their destruction. Curiously, the vamp's sexuality was not
viewed as genuinely threatening by patrons of the films because
the figure was so unrealistic and so great a distortion. Rosen
thinks Bara helped ease the transition from the Victorian image of
the pure woman to the image of the unfettered flapper of the
1920s. But she nonetheless "managed a permanent disservice to
women" insofar as she conveyed such a negative image of woman
in general as "the vagina with teeth" (p. 61). Also important, Bara's vamp became the cinematic ancestor of "the *femmes fatales*,
the Mysterious Women, the Impenetrable Bitches of later screen

generations" (p. 61), and, as a result, served women poorly because of the unrealistic and reductive nature of the type. Later
vamps appeared in less extreme form than Bara; since they
seemed more realistic, they necessarily received more criticism
and prompted more censorship. Transformed from the pure cari-
cature of the vamp, certain actresses became either the *femmes
fatales* like Pola Negri or, in later transformation, the Evil
Woman who turns up as the gun moll in 1930s gangster films and
as the heroine of 1940s melodramas.

   More significant modifications of the type occur in the films
of Greta Garbo and Marlene Dietrich, who convey various degrees of mystery and passion: "enigmatic incarnations of all that is
mysterious to man—all that he wants to conquer, subjugate, and
destroy" (p. 169). In a particularly effective observation, Rosen
suggests that we consider the Bette Davis of later 1930s films as a
kind of synthesis of the other two: "as self-aware as the Swede, as
unyielding as the German, and more calculating than either" (p.
177). It is with Davis that the myth begun with Bara reaches its
fullest embodiment, for female power is seen essentially as evil
passion. In turn, Davis is the ancestor of the heroines of 1940s
film noir in which women appear as genuine threats. Rosen lists a
host of scheming bad women and/or murderesses including those
in films like *Double Indemnity*, *The Postman Always Rings Twice*,
and Davis' own *Beyond the Forest*—the film with the now famous
complaint (thanks to Edward Albee), "What a dump!" The women
in films of this type more often than not wreak their havoc because of "avarice and controlled loathing" (p. 239).

   Turning aside from the archetypal aspect of the vamp figure,
Rosen speculates that the appearance of the type in the 1940s
may be Hollywood's response to women's rise in the business
community: "such movies may even have been in part a consequence, signifying that women were finally a threat to the status
quo. Hollywood simplistically interpreted this shift in the only
terms it could understand: power, the quest for love or money"
(p. 238). Compare this observation with the one noted earlier by
Haskell, who sees the poor treatment given current heroines as a
response to the advances of the women's movement.

   Another stereotype figuring in film over the years is that of
the child. Its most important early appearances are in the films of

D. W. Griffith and Mary Pickford. In particular, the latter, who
performed little-girl roles many years beyond her childhood, conveyed a sense of woman that, for Rosen, seems "to stultify the
growth of women's self-image" (p. 34). As the child who does not
alter existing circumstances, suggest immorality, or radiate sexuality, Pickford continued and perpetuated Victorian values and
opinions of women. It is only *because* Pickford's heroine is a child
that, in a film like *A Poor Little Rich Girl*, she can be bold and
forthright. No adult woman in a film of the time could have done
this, since the Pickford/child's demands, "coming from a real woman, would have been too aggressive and threatening." Rosen
argues that this is why women so loved Pickford; she gave them
"an outlet for all their repressed energies and fantasies" (p. 38).

In the 1930s Jane Withers (most recently Josephine, the
plumber, on television commercials), Deanna Durbin and, above
all, Shirley Temple continued to maintain the child image. Again,
because of the child/female's youth, audiences accepted her with
delight and did not take her seriously as a woman. Temple succeeded in her demands and activities precisely because she was
"a neuter": "her opinions *counted* in areas where no adult woman
would dare venture, much less be heeded" (p. 194). As such,
Rosen suggests, she represents a version (or in structural terms a
transformation) of the Pickford heroine.

In her later manifestations, the child appeared as the bobby-
soxer or the "teen-age Cinderella" (p. 300). Various actresses portrayed this type: June Allyson, Pier Angeli, Janet Leigh, Jane
Powell, Debbie Reynolds, Natalie Wood, to name a few. They
shared a collective impotence in matters of any significance besides marriage, in one sense mirroring woman's loss of status after
World War II. The waif, urchin and tomboy of the 1950s were in
marked contrast to heroines in the Rosie the Riveter mold of the
previous decade. All of the newer women's lives appeared to be
"defined solely by their men"; they had virtually no independent
existence of their own (p. 301).

A more recent transformation of the child/female occurred at
the end of the 1950s and after in films about musical stars, Elvis
Presley in particular. The way women appear in films like *Loving
You* and *Jailhouse Rock* offers a standard which is not encourag-
ing. As similar to each other as the Cinderellas of the 1950s,

these women share the same unprogressive qualities, alike useless
in advancing any positive ideas for young women: "Ann-Margret,
Jill St. John, Debra Paget . . . and other flossy, plastic, heavily
made-up, man-crazy females served as ideals, living handbooks on
how to win such a special sexy heart as Elvis'. Those lucky
heroines—confusingly alike in appearance—were pretty, peppy,
good dancers, brave motorcycle backseaters and hot-rod maidens"
(pp. 308–309). The Sandra Dee who replaces Debbie Reynolds in
the *Tammy* pictures is a continuation of the Shirley Temple figure who solves everyone's problems: "all on the up and up, with
no sex, please—but much burgeoning wistfulness and the kind of
saccharine patience bestowed only on professional virgins" (p.
310).

Genres

Another useful aspect of Rosen's study is her discussion of
genres and her analysis of how and why some of these surface and
then fade. Particularly worth noting is her description of some of
the genres of the 1940s. As noted, the war occasions the Rosie
the Riveter genre in which independent women contribute to
winning the battles here and at the front: as factory workers—
Ann Sothern as *Swing Shift Maisie,* and Claudette Colbert in
Since You Went Away; and as service women—Betty Hutton in
Here Come the Waves. One important theme emerging from
these and similar films is the strength of women and the love and
camaraderie possible between them—as opposed to images of ir-
responsibility or nastiness.

In contrast, the Woman as Victim, another genre of the
times, conveys a very bleak picture of women's power, for,
whether sufferers of illnesses or potential murder victims, women
appear helpless, especially when undergoing mental cruelty and
oppression. This list includes Bette Davis in *Dark Victory* (dis-
ease); Barbara Stanwyck in *Sorry Wrong Number* (the wife as
murder victim); and Ingrid Bergman in *Gaslight* (her husband
tries to make her lose her mind). Rosen singles out Hitchcock for
his "antifemale thrillers" (p. 237), noting such films as *Rebecca,
Suspicion* and *Notorious,* although *Shadow of a Doubt* with
Teresa Wright is an exception.

Other Notes

Other comments worth directing readers to include Rosen's
discussion of the way in which women have been portrayed as
sexual objects: from the beginnings, up through the pin-ups of
the 1940s (Betty Grable, Rita Hayworth and Lana Turner), with
the "Mammary Madness" directed at Jayne Mansfield and Marilyn Monroe, and the current decadence of soft- and hard-core
pornography. She attributes the pin-up phenomenon to Hollywood's interest in separating any human qualities from sexuality, a practice which has reached its ultimate manifestation in
Deep Throat, a work which testifies to "a masculine preference
for the alienated sex experience" (p. 351). In that film sex is totally divorced from feeling. Even worse, the film's gimmick—the
heroine, Linda Lovelace, has her clitoris in her throat—results in
the effective loss of value of a woman's normal sex organs (p.
353).

Finally, readers will observe that the star or heroine of *Popcorn Venus* is Katharine Hepburn. She appears to be the most
independent woman in the history of Hollywood. She has re-
mained this way as a woman, and her screen roles have generally
perpetuated this image, especially *Adam's Rib*. There, playing
the part of a lawyer, she successfully defends Judy Holliday on a
charge of attempted murder against the arguments of the prose-
cuting attorney—her husband, played by Spencer Tracy: "Hepburn has won, professionally and privately. Having inconsider-
ately humiliated her husband, she nevertheless manages the impossible feat rarely allotted to screen females: She has her cake
and eats it" (p. 211). Even in the Woman Alone genre, her
heroines are different. Rosen thinks that four of her films in this
category—*The African Queen, Summertime, The Rainmaker* and
Desk Set—"did not really depart from the decade's premise that
the middle-aged unmarried female was just half a person." Even
so, her presence enhances this essentially negative aspect: "Hepburn, however, brought to this genre her usual intelligence, stoi-
cism, and energy, and if we are to articulate the differences between her spinsters and others, it would be that during the
course of the film they are awakened sexually perhaps for the first
time in their lives—and it is a positive, not a destructive force"
(p. 274).

JOAN MELLEN*

Teacher and critic Joan Mellen (b. 1941) shares the view of Haskell and Rosen that current films are definite regressions from those of earlier periods when stars like Katharine Hepburn and Bette Davis appeared as human beings capable of genuine and significant achievements. In *Women and Their Sexuality in the New Film* she discusses many pictures which present women in negative and reductive ways. Only a few psychologically and politically oriented films even begin to do justice to women and their sexuality. Viewers should also be aware of her studies of the embodiments of female sexuality, Mae West and Marilyn Monroe.

The Negative Image in Today's Films

Like Kael, Mellen believes that the production forces and moguls exploit fashionable issues for their own financial interests. She sees Hollywood using the women's movement in a particularly pernicious way by giving audiences women who are either co-opted by the stories or made to serve as actual underminers of liberation. In the first category is Julie Christie in Robert Altman's *McCabe and Mrs. Miller.* The independent businesswoman on the western frontier appears as an opium-smoking prostitute. Although liberated, she is, ultimately, only a "Super Whore" (W, p. 28). Similarly, in *Diary of a Mad Housewife*, the heroine Tina seeks sexual meaning in her life, but is presented to us in such negative terms that the liberated impulse is weakened.

---

*Key to Abbreviations:
W = *Women and Their Sexuality in the New Film* (New York: Horizon Books, 1973). By permission of Joan Mellen.
M = *Marilyn Monroe* (New York: Pyramid Publications, 1973). Quoted by permission of Joan Mellen.

The film robs her sexuality of any satisfying elements and seems to deny that Tina or any woman can hope to achieve sexual balance. In these films "the industry has it both ways. While it seems to raise issues of concern to women, in reality it proceeds to undermine and demean liberated alternatives" (W, p. 27). In the second category is Barbra Streisand's Margaret in *Up the Sandbox*. Here Mellen finds the industry not merely co-opting the women's movement, but attempting "a full-scale demolition of the entire radical period" (W, p. 244) and offering "counter-revolt rather than pseudo-reform" (W, p. 247). By making the forces of radicalization ridiculous (the "Castro" figure), by playing on racist fears, and by affirming the values of home and motherhood, the film "deprives the insights of the women's movement of conviction or coherence" and is "insidious towards any female aspiration beyond that of baby-machine or caretaker" (W, p. 244).

Mike Nichols' *Carnal Knowledge* is another recent film which fails to present women fully or in part as capable of "a mature, mutually satisfying relationship with a male who recognizes her as a valuable individual" (W, p. 73). It offers desperate and narrowly conceived women like Ann-Margret's pathetic Bobbie and Rita Moreno's prostitute Lilian. Candice Bergen's Susan plays only a minor part. By and large we are given "no alternative of a sexually alive and simultaneously intellectually and emotionally vibrant woman" who would suggest by her presence that there exists an alternative to the unfair "assessment of women as castrating bitches" offered by the film (W, p. 69). Even films by women directors and writers can fail to indicate that there are healthy women alive in the world today. Mellen criticizes Elaine May severely in this regard for *The Heartbreak Kid*, in which her own daughter, Jenny Berlin, as well as the other female characters are all unappealing (W, p. 44).

With only a few exceptions, the cinematic treatment of lesbianism has been negative. Generally films dealing with the subject present lesbians either as predators or as maladjusted neurotics, and refuse to consider that "homosexuality may not be the organizing principle" in the lesbian's life (W, p. 75). In addition to the voyeuristic and exploitive *Lickerish Quartet* and the sensationalized *The Killing of Sister George*, she examines Claude Chabrol's *Les Biches*, which uses lesbianism as a "metaphor for

extreme self-centeredness" (W, p. 84), and *The Fox*, Mark
Rydell's adaptation of D. H. Lawrence's novella. In the latter,
Rydell loses much of the richness of the author's suggestions
about the unconscious, and adds explicit sex scenes not in the
original. He also builds up Sandy Dennis' Banford as a
stereotype, "fussily domestic, simultaneously self-pitying and
self-righteous" (W, p. 217), as well as an "oppressive lesbian for
whom her mothering makes up the whole of her life" (W, p. 96).

Ingmar Bergman and Women

Like Haskell, Mellen is concerned about the way in which
Bergman treats women on the screen, calling him "a retrograde
force in world cinema" (W, p. 52), and an obstacle who "stands in
the way of a liberated image of women in film through a rigidity
that ought not to escape notice because it is rooted in a pseudo-
philosophical determinism which passes as profundity" (W, p.
126). Only in *Persona*, with his examination of the relationship
between the nurse Bibi Andersson and her patient Liv Ullmann,
does he reveal anything that seems to Mellen to be positive.

Generally, she argues, Bergman presents men as the in-
tellectuals who pursue ethical issues, while the women appear in
a "biological" realm: "their lives lack meaning because they are
rooted in biology and an inability to choose a style of life independent of the female sexual role" (W, p. 107). Ester in *The
Silence* and Karin in *Cries and Whispers* seem to her as rebels
from Bergman's usual definition of women: "instinctual, passive,
submissive, and trapped within the odors and blood of her geni-
tals" (W, p. 108). The director exploits his women, using them as
symbols to convey a dismal view of existence, particularly in
Cries and Whispers. There the dying Agnes (Harriet Andersson)
symbolizes mankind. The scrutiny of her physical suffering by the
camera suggests that Bergman is "a man for whom not only sexuality or its intimations of need are vile, but most particularly, the
female functions" (W, p. 111). The positive consolation and minis-
tering of the servant Anna amount only to an "animal consolation
of physical nearness—all, Bergman says, of which woman is capable" (W, p. 113). Even though appalled at Bergman's vision of
women in the film, Mellen offers viewers an acute and perceptive

analysis of its structure: in particular, notice her comments on the function of the color red and the nature of conventionalized behavior.

Some Encouraging Signs: Rohmer, Buñuel, Bertolucci

Although Mellen offers an overwhelming amount of evidence to prove how poorly women fare in current films, she finds, nevertheless, that there are directors who attempt to grapple seriously with issues pertaining to women and sexuality. One such film maker is Eric Rohmer, whose six films comprising the "Moral Tales" deal engagingly with male and female relationships. Mellen considers his subject as "what woman is and what she can be, as seen through the inadequacies of bourgeois man" (W, p. 49). She analyzes *My Night at Maud's, La Collectionneuse, Claire's Knee* and *Chloe in the Afternoon* to document her argument that Rohmer's men encounter contrasting women and make the wrong choice, usually by taking the "safe" route out of relationships with women superior to them. The heroes of the first three films (Jean-Louis, Adrien and Jerome) are all revealed as inadequate. Mellen wonders why Rohmer is content only to raise the issue of their tendency to hide true emotions under the guise of rationality, rather than going deeper and trying to explain why the men act in this way.

Luis Buñuel's *Tristana* presents a heroine whose life is controlled by the institutionalized repression of church and state in Spain. The political dimension of the film is important for Mellen, since she generally applauds attempts by film makers to consider sexuality in as wide a context as possible. It is important to note, however, that in no way will she praise political treatments of women and radicalization simply *because* this dimension is present, as is indicated by her rejection of propagandistic Chinese films and Dusan Makavejev's *WR: Mysteries of the Organism*, a work she finds incoherent. But in *Tristana*, Buñuel provides an ordered examination of bourgeois values and their connection to church and state as he uses the relationship between the aging lecher Don Lope and his young ward Tristana to embody the corruption of the Spanish government and to analyze the results of social dependence. The heroine, played by Catherine Deneuve, attempts fruitlessly to escape her guardian/seducer. Exploited and demeaned in an oppressive relationship, she eventually contributes to his death. Certainly she would not seem to be a very liberated woman; still, "the movie itself offers a revolutionary conception of woman by locating Tristana's 'fall' in the patriarchy dominating Spain at the time she comes into womanhood. . . . Tristana's perversion becomes an expression of that of Spain in the last moments of the republic" (W, p. 49).

Mellen's brilliant discussions of two films by Bernardo Bertolucci offer further examples of her interest in the ways in which films utilize political elements to comment on sexuality. One merit of *The Conformist* is its treatment of lesbianism as only one aspect of a woman, Dominique Sandra's character Anna Quadri. Married to an old man about to be assassinated by fascist Jean-Louis Trintignant, she is captivated by the murderer's wife and, as an indirect result of her infatuation, is also murdered. Although her homosexuality controls her life to a great extent and accounts for her vulnerability, the director does not treat it as "a blight, or as a perversion." Instead, "that her lesbianism becomes so overt and dominating at this moment in her life may in part be attributed to the ineffectuality of her husband. . . . Above all, he is the weak father who fails her. Ann's [sic] lesbianism can be seen as part of her overall victimization, and her death, not as a punishment for lesbianism, but damage done to her and many others by a hostile social milieu—fascist even for those who believe they are escaping in exile" (W, p. 91).

Even though she has reservations about *Last Tango in Paris*, Mellen still finds it "a brilliant study of male-female sexuality" (W, p. 49). The film's limitations follow from the fact that Bertolucci makes Jeanne (Maria Schneider) essentially passive, thus allowing all the "tormented struggle" to Paul (Marlon Brando) and suggesting that a successful relationship can arise only with an active male and passive female structure. In addition, Mellen thinks the film offers too limited a conception of human potential to be a "great" film.

These qualifications notwithstanding, she presents an exciting and cogent interpretation of the film, explaining its themes and plot in relation to Bertolucci's attempt to combine Freud and

Marx. Essentially, she argues that Paul wants to establish a community with Maria away from the bourgeois world of family and institutions, and outside political and historical realities. In the external bourgeois world is violence, symbolized by the pistols belonging to Jeanne's father—one of which will eventually kill Paul. Both characters demonstrate the futility of trying to escape the devastating effects of family relationships (Paul's wife and parents, Maria's fiancé and family). Mellen sees a Freudian/Oedipal relationship between Jeanne and her father, but suggests that this psychological element informs rather than controls the film; characters act "as they do, not because they are determined by Freud's model for all of human nature, but because they have been socialized by the repressive bourgeois family" (W, p. 131). The relationship between Paul and Maria cannot last because human beings lack the ability to ignore external life: "the very necessity to leave their hideaway and re-enter the time, space and reality of the outer world foredooms them." The political dimension of this situation comes from Bertolucci's vision of "tragedy and capitulation to the world as inexorable in this age, what Marx called the 'prehistory of man'—a capitalist era incapable of humane relations" (W, p. 132). In addition to her interpretation of the film, only sketched out here, readers should note her perceptive comments on the technique as well (see especially W, pp. 130, 135, 138–141).

Mae West and Marilyn Monroe

Mellen also considers two of the entertainment industry's most famous sex symbols, Mae West and Marilyn Monroe. Insofar as the former plays on her role as granter of sexual delights to fortunate males, Mellen thinks she perpetuates a negative kind of image in which female liberation itself seems to be equated with openness about risqué matters (W, p. 229). But, on the positive side, West has used this very exploitation of her own sexuality to undermine traditional myths and, in fact, assert the power of women. First, her aggressiveness functions to put men "off-balance" as she turns the tables on them by treating men as objects of *her* desire and by making "sexual allure on the part of women into an item of pride, power and autonomy" (W, p. 230). Second, she stands as the antithesis of the weak or disingenuous coquette; she is the boss who decides whom she will favor: "Mae West thus deploys her own brand of sexism to create an image of liberated woman—and Hollywood is her vehicle" (W, p. 232).

Besides the effective use of sexuality to suggest the power of women, Mellen points to other significant aspects of West and her career. She has been a diligent and successful writer; she has assumed roles normally given to men, such as her lion tamer in *I'm No Angel;* and she has appeared as a woman who makes her own living, independently of men. Her strengths are pitted against equally strong masculine forces, rather than against weak strawmen in opposition to whom even a milder and weaker woman might look good. Finally, she rarely fails to convey a sense of complexity and "self-irony"; that is, there is more to her than merely sex: "West's values transcend her sexual role" (W, p. 238).

Mellen's treatment of Marilyn Monroe is a welcome relief from many of the sensationalized and tasteless studies which continue to appear. Here viewers will find a compassionate and objective consideration of Monroe and the films, the best of which for Mellen are *Bus Stop* and *The Misfits.* Particularly in the latter, where as Roslyn she asserts herself in the famous horse-trapping scene, Monroe is "truly at the center of one of her films; it is from her character that the capacity for justice expressed by Gay [Clark Gable] springs" (M, p. 138). But in most of her films Monroe appears as nothing but a body, while the story is controlled by a man and his concerns, as in *The Seven Year Itch.* Until her part as Roslyn, Monroe was denied "a role as a woman of intellectual inquiry" and did not face "either conflicts of consciousness, problems of decision-making, or dilemmas of moral choice" (M, p. 105).

Probing into the relationship between Monroe the star and the woman, Mellen suggests that, unlike Mae West, whose persona of sex symbol permits her freedom, Monroe's persona as sex goddess was actually characterized by "exaggerated subservience and incapacity"—unfortunately a persona of "an empty-headed wide-eyed dumb blond enticing men but rarely earning their respect for her talent or character" (M, p. 24). Mellen believes the persona was actually a pose which Monroe affected as a defense mechanism to avoid exploitation and victimization as a human being and to escape the sadness and meanness of her formative years. But, ironically, by adopting the persona of sex-goddess— the dumb blond with the sexy voice—she bound herself to her created role: "Marilyn herself became the prime victim of this image" (M, p. 22). The snide jokes about the pitiful attempts in her private life to rise above both her background and screen image underscore the futility of Monroe's life.

STRUCTURALIST CRITICISM

The term "structuralism" is used with varying degrees of precision to refer to a number of related critical and scientific activities that have come to dominate modern culture. Put most simply, structuralism investigates the interrelationships of parts in given constructs: whether sentences, works of art, or cultures. Structuralists try to determine the ways in which the surface manifestations of phenomena such as speech, dress, and codes of kinship relate to larger underlying patterns of linguistic, psychological and sociological behavior. Thus the thrust is both horizontal—describing the phenomena as they exist in time and space—and vertical—showing how the phenomena cohere with other elements in interrelated systems.

This is not the place to attempt even a brief history of structuralism, but it should be noted that most advocates of the method would acknowledge the primary importance of the following seminal thinkers whose theories have shaped and sustained the growth of the activity: philosopher and economist Karl Marx; linguist Ferdinand De Saussure; linguist and literary critic Roman Jakobson; anthropologist Claude Lévi-Strauss; semiologist Roland Barthes; and psychoanalyst Jacques Lacan.

The theorists to be examined here can fairly be classed as structuralists. Noël Burch's study of the operation of film and the interrelationship of filmic elements can be considered the counterpart of the kind of analysis Jakobson performs on the operation of literary language. Christian Metz's analysis of film language owes much to the work of De Saussure, as well as to other linguists like André Martinet, Louis Hjelmslev and Emile Benveniste. And Peter Wollen's anthropological *auteurism* derives largely from the work of Lévi-Strauss, while his use of semiology (the science of signs) owes much to C. S. Peirce. These men are not alone in their basic structuralist orientation. The interest in the anthropological model seen in Wollen can also be found with modifications and variations in Jim Kitses, *Horizons West,* and Will Wright, *Sixguns and Society.* Attempts to explain the language of film along the lines of a linguistic model appear in the works of Gianfranco Bettetini, *The Language and Technique of the Film,* as well as in the writings of Pier Paolo Pasolini and Umberto Eco. The three structuralists to be discussed here are the most important and influential proponents of each approach represented. The method itself, whether the emphasis be on language or on the nature of cinematic meaning as embodied in signs or on the interrelationship of parts, is of immense importance for current film studies.

NOËL BURCH*

Film maker and teacher Noël Burch (b. 1932) deserves attention here because of the usefulness of the particular kind of structuralist criticism he offers in *Theory of Film Practice*. Like Metz, he wants to map out the terrain of film, providing specific tools of analysis for discussing the relationships between parts. Since he is a film maker, one is not surprised to see him emphasizing the potentialities in the editing process. I want to explain his use of the term *découpage* by examining his comments on spatio-temporal articulations, editing and space. We will see as we proceed that Burch conceives of the film in very Eisensteinian terms as a construct composed of various dialectical oppositions. Considered in relation to the pioneer theorists, Burch belongs to the Eisensteinian rather than the Bazinian tradition, particularly with his rejection of what he calls the "zero point of cinematic style."

Dialectics

Burch argues that any given structural relationship existing between elements in a film can be viewed in dialectical terms. In fact, he equates "structure" and "dialectics": "for structures almost always seem to occur in dialectical form—that is to say, a structure necessarily evolves within a parameter defined by one or more pairs of clearly delineated *poles*" (p. 66). The concept of "structure" applies not only to traditional organic links, but to every element: "a structure exists when a parameter evolves according to some principle of progression that is apparent to the

---

*All quotations are from *Theory of Film Practice*, trans. Helen R. Lane (New York: Praeger, 1973). English translation © 1973 Praeger Publishers, Inc., a division of Holt, Rinehart and Winston. By permission of Holt, Rinehart and Winston and of Martin Secker & Warburg Ltd. (reprinted from their Cinema Two series).

viewer in the theatre, or perhaps only to the film-maker at his editing table" (pp. 66–67). There are as many parameters as there are elements in a film—everything from lighting to the handling of time.

Dialectical Parameters

Burch identifies at least a dozen basic dialectical opposites operating in films and divides these into basic categories. The first, *legibility and duration*, refers to the opposition between the appearance of an image on the screen and the length of time it is visible. Two images, one with static content and one with a scene of activity, will, when projected for the same amount of time, *appear* to be of different lengths of time, since it is harder to comprehend totally the active scene in a short period of time; that is, the latter will seem shorter, even though it is not. Similarly, a shot of a static scene will seem longer because of the inactivity. This dialectical relationship between legibility and duration can affect us emotionally and induce such feelings as frustration or boredom, given our ability or inability to grasp the image.

The second category, *photographic parameters*, includes such technical aspects as the contrasts between soft and sharp focus, black versus white, and color versus black and white. To illustrate how the latter contrast involves creation of "a structure centering around these two poles, a structure functioning independently of the narrative structure though dialectically related to it" (p. 55), Burch describes the film *Exemple Etretat*, in which the viewer alternately sees examples of every kind of color. Another example we might mention here is Lindsay Anderson's *If . . .* , in which the switching from color to black and white (sometimes within a scene) can produce an effectively jarring note quite in keeping with the psychological aim of the film.

Another category, *organic dialectics*, concerns the image in two ways. First, we can encounter a dialectical relationship set up by the image's absence and presence, as in Ken Jacob's *Blond Cobra* where the blackened screen is pitted against projected images. Or, second, we can point to kinds of movement in a frame

related to the central subject (subject stationary with other elements in motion; or subject moving while other elements in
frame are stationary). Burch cites Chris Marker's remarkable *La
Jetée* in this context. In this twenty-five-minute work, the only
movement within a frame occurs once as a young woman opens
her eyes. This movement exists in dialectical opposition to every
other scene in the film, which consists of photographed stills.

Another major category is that of *narrative time*, the relations between past and present, flashbacks and flashforwards. The
director's treatment of time can create an important structural
element in itself, and be more than just a narrative dimension, as
in Alain Resnais' *Last Year at Marienbad,* "whereby each sequence (or rather each sequence shot) refers to one or several
other sequences in what is perhaps the past, perhaps the present,
or perhaps the future 'tense.' This dialectic of ambiguity with its
several variables in itself engenders complex structures that are
independent of the film's narrative structures (thematic variations
on the statue, the woman at the balustrade, and so on) or its
plastic values (the organization of camera movements, shot size,
ellipses, and so on)" (p. 62).

Still other categories identified by Burch include sound and
image, live as opposed to animated shots, different acting styles,
and contrasts in décor. In these, as in the other categories, his
thesis is again that various polarities exist through a film, independent of but still related to the main narrative action.

Découpage

The various dialectical oppositions of individual elements discussed by Burch have their counterparts on a larger scale in the
workings of the complete film; it is in connection with this that he
explains *découpage.* The term can refer to the working script of a
film, or to a more detailed prefilmic breakdown of the work into
shots and sequences. But as he uses the term here, it refers to
"the underlying structure of the *finished* film" and "what results
when the spatial fragments, or, more accurately, the succession of
spatial fragments excerpted in the shooting process, converge
with the temporal fragments whose duration may be roughly determined during the shooting, but whose final duration is estab-

lished only on the editing table" (p. 4). As he conceives of the term, *découpage* includes three aspects which figure significantly in the construction of a film: "the spatiotemporal characteristics of the match, the relationships between screen space and off-screen space, and plastic interactions between shots" (p. 51).

Spatiotemporal Articulations

Burch calls the process of transitions between shots "the basic element" in the construction of structures in film (p. 12). He complains that not enough film makers are aware of the importance of "organizing the transitions . . . the articulations between shots as a function of the total composition of each shot—thereby creating a structural framework capable of incorporating the formal elements" we saw described in the previous section (pp. 35–36). Burch provides a most useful catalogue of articulations between shots which draws attention to the various ways we can be led from one shot to another.

Speaking of straight cutting which does not involve any use of transition devices like dissolves or fades, he lists five ways of moving *temporally* between two shots. First, with *absolute temporal continuity,* there is no loss of time between shots; a character starts to open a door and in the next shot continues to complete the specific action without any gap in time. Second, with a *temporal ellipsis* or *time abridgement,* a short, measurable period of time is missing between shots; a character puts his hands on a doorknob and in the next shot is seen closing the door inside the room he was entering. Such abridgements can eliminate superfluous footage. In contrast, the third temporal articulation involves an *indefinite time ellipsis:* "an hour or a year, the exact extent of the temporal omission being measurable only through the aid of something 'external'—a line of dialogue, a title, a clock, a calendar, a change in dress style, or the like" (p. 6). As an example of this, we could point to the puzzle montage sequence in *Citizen Kane* during which the various subjects of the puzzles worked by Susan as well as her changes in jewelry indicate the passage of time from shot to shot. The fourth and fifth articulations involve time reversal, forward or backward. Type four, a *short time reversal,* is definite and measurable, like type two, and occurs most commonly when parts of an action are repeated, as in Eisenstein's treatment of the bridge in *October* when the opening is seen several times from different angles. An *indefinite time reversal*, the fifth type, includes flashforwards and flashbacks suggesting a longer time gap than that in type four, a period of time not easily determinable merely through the articulation.

For every temporal articulation we see, there exists one of three kinds of *spatial* articulation between shots as well. First, there may be *absolute spatial continuity* between shots; we remain in shot B where we were in shot A. Second, we may find an *absence of spatial continuity* between shots. This discontinuity may be *proximate* or *radical*. That is, either shot B moves a short distance from the space in shot A, or else it moves into a totally different setting of space. An example of proximate discontinuity would be change of space from the interior of Susan's apartment in *Citizen Kane* to the stairway and exterior of her apartment building. An example of radical discontinuity would be the shift in space in the same film during the political montage, from Leland's speech on the streetcorner to Kane's speech in Madison Square Garden.

Thus, we have fifteen potential kinds of articulations between shots. For example, there can be indefinite time ellipsis with continuous space—the puzzle montage in *Citizen Kane;* indefinite time reversal with radical change of space—the flashbacks involving Joe Buck in *Midnight Cowboy;* absolute continuity with proximate spatial change—the entrance of the plague-ridden marchers in *The Seventh Seal.* The value of such a process of categorization for viewers arises partly from its convenience; one can avoid clumsy circumlocutions and even reduce the articulations to a code: T (for temporal articulations) 1 through 5, and S (for spatial articulations) 1 through 3. Even more valuable, I think, is its usefulness in making us examine the general pattern of articulations in a given film. By employing these categories, we are in a better position to describe the surface of a film and to assess the film maker's general method. For example, do we find a director new to us relying on a certain type of temporal articulation more than on another? Can we find a director utilizing a certain pattern of spatiotemporal articulations in films from one period to another?

Can we contrast the methods of two directors by examining the different spatiotemporal articulations of each? etc.

Screen and Off-Screen Space

Space itself constitutes the second subject included in *découpage*. Burch wants to determine the importance of the various "spatial segments . . . in the formal development of the film" (p. 18), and does so by isolating seven potential areas: first, the surface of the screen, the playing area; and second, all off-screen space which includes six areas—the area surrounding the four sides of the screen, behind the scene projected on the screen, and the camera. He uses an examination of Jean Renoir's *Nana* to define the ways available to a director to indicate off-screen space: entrances and exits from the frame; glances off-screen by characters; and partial framing of characters so that part of a character extends off-camera in a realm beyond immediate screen space, thus establishing the existence of off-screen space. A good example of the way a director defines the off-screen space in the area of the camera occurs in Tony Richardson's *Tom Jones* at the moment when Tom puts his hat in front of the camera to block our view of the nearly naked Mrs. Waters. It is a joke, of course, but nonetheless his action establishes the existence of a space beyond the surface of the screen.

We see that there will always be a dialectical relationship between screen and off-screen space. Burch points to an important implication following from this dialectic as he notes that an essentially empty frame which lacks human beings and shows only landscape or animals can bring attention to off-screen space: "it is thus principally the *empty frame* that focuses attention on what is occurring off screen, thereby making us aware of off-screen space, for with the screen empty, there is nothing as yet (or nothing any longer) to hold the eye's attention" (p. 19). Such an empty frame can even create a kind of tension, insofar as our attention is torn between what we do and do not see. Here we could cite Joseph Losey's *Accident*, a film in which the director very often lets his characters leave the frame and then lingers on with his camera. The effect he produces is quite ironical; since the world of *Accident* is peopled with some most unpleasant personalities, the empty frames of cheery landscapes function almost like relieving and soothing images in contrast to the unrelenting nastiness of the characters.

Static and Dynamic Articulations

There are two basic kinds of interactions between shots in respect to their plastic content. In a *static* cut, the shots linked together display inactive material; in a *dynamic* articulation, one or both shots pictures active material. Through his choice of articulations, a director can affect the given filmic space. Burch singles out Eisenstein's use of static articulations when shooting the same object from several angles and compares this method with Cubist art and its tendency to present an object as if glimpsed from multiple points of view. Eisenstein's practice proceeds from "his approach to editing as a function of the composition of each successive shot" (p. 36). From this overall sense of the interrelationship of shots the director "creates" space; that is, space is a product of the succession of shots. For example, in the scene in *Ivan the Terrible* in which the boyars wait for the tsar's death, Eisenstein connects three static shots of individuals, each with an object common to all three shots, an icon which is seen from different angles, depending on the placement of the camera: "Eisenstein has here managed to create a very unusual sort of cinematic space: It exists only in terms of the totality of shots included in the sequence; we no longer have any sense of surrounding space endowed with independent existence from which a sequence of shots has somehow been excerpted" (p. 39). Burch also praises Eisenstein's dynamic articulations in *Potemkin,* in particular during the Odessa Steps massacre when the director cuts from the descending motion of the soldiers to the motion of the townspeople ascending the stairs.

Throughout this discussion of static and dynamic articulations, Burch is careful to note how many of his examples involve violations of standard ideas about the correct kinds of "match." That is, traditionally cuts from one shot to another are supposed to hold to certain understood "rules": retain similarity of direction in camera angle; if of the same object, successive shots should

present a thirty-degree change of angle; size and eye-line should
also be consistent. The very fact that there exist so many exceptions to these "rules" is a good sign, for it indicates that film
makers see the potential effects to be gained by working inven-
tively with articulations between shots. But such practices are
valid aesthetically only when they provide an effect which contributes to the establishment of a formal structure, or dialectic, in
the film.

The Zero Point of Cinematic Style

Burch discusses this concept in the context of his discussion
of spatial matches and violation of the "rules." Essentially he
would say that a cinematic sequence displays the "zero point of
cinematic style" when the director has tried to *disguise* any sense
of discontinuity between shots. Burch notes that as film style became more sophisticated in the silent and early sound periods,
there arose an increasing tendency to stress the continuity between individual shots. Any radical shifts in what the spectator
viewed were to be avoided so that there would be no breaking up
of the apparent space captured on film. Cinematic junctures such
as Eisenstein presents in *October* and *Potemkin* went out of favor
since these drew attention to, rather than obscured the articulations between, shots: "'jump cuts' and 'bad' or 'unclear' matches
were to be avoided because they made the essentially *discontinu-
ous* nature of a shot transition or the *ambiguous* nature of
cinematic space too apparent" (p. 11). Eventually, as in Hitchcock's *Rope* (which has no breaks at all and is essentially one long
take of ninety minutes effected through tricky reel changes) and
in the films of some Italian neorealists, directors seemed to be
attempting to eliminate cutting altogether.

Burch does not support such a technique. He is thus mark-
edly different from Bazin, who favors as much as possible the
fluid movements of an unobtrusive camera and the long take.
Obviously the smoothing out of cutting to a minimum level
explicitly denies what Burch sees as the vital forces informing the
organization of a film—its spatiotemporal articulations; that is, to
deny through technique the movement from shot to shot is to
suppress the basic dialectic which controls all aspects of film.

In addition, this kind of illusionism, which goes with the zero point of cinematic style, is inimical to a sense of collective participation in the construction of a film. Citing a similar argument from Eisenstein, Burch says that the viewer's awareness of the artistic process, in this case the articulations between shots, constitutes a salutary experience because it puts one in touch with the creative activity that produced the work: "in Eisenstein's view—as in my own—a complete reading of the artistic process, including the conscious perception of form, is a liberating activity" (p. xix). He quotes with approval Eisenstein's comment that recognition of form "draws the spectator into a creative act in which his own personality is not dominated by that of the author, but fully develops in harmony with the author's conception, just as the personality of a great actor fuses with that of a great playwright in the process of creating a classical image on the stage" (p. xix: quoted in *Notes of a Film Director* [New York: Dover, 1970], p. 78). Consequently many of the techniques which we recognize from cinema's early history and which we now see in New Wave and avant-garde films—iris in and out, jumps, bad matching shots, disruptions of illusion—are acceptable to Burch by virtue of the fact that these draw attention to the craft of the artist and, as such, invite our identification with the creative act. Thus he welcomes such allusions to older movies for somewhat different reasons than we see in Kael and in Sarris.

A Simple History

Burch praises various films in *Theory of Film Practice*, but the one which receives probably his most enthusiastic commentary is *A Simple History* by Marcel Hanoun. A moving and powerful film, it depicts the events transpiring over a period of a few days as a destitute mother tries to find employment so that she can support herself and her daughter. Its most unique feature is its use of sound. Here we have the antithesis of the zero point of cinematic style, and something more like Eisenstein's call for the asynchronous use of sound, for Hanoun manipulates the soundtrack in ways quite at odds with any strict realism or illusionism. The mother who narrates almost all the film relates details of her activities and conversations, most of which are never quite synchronized with the filmic rendering. The relationship of her commentary "to both the visual images and the spoken dialogue is constantly shifting in an extraordinary and extremely complex way throughout the entire film, in accord with a principle of variation fully deserving the term *dialectical*" (p. 82). Burch explores the subtle effects gained by Hanoun through the absence of synchronization, and the structural integrity of the film itself, particularly aspects of time and the woman's progress to despair; it is a masterful discussion of a neglected masterpiece. Those fortunate enough to see it (it is available through an American distributor) will appreciate Burch's sensitive analysis.

CHRISTIAN METZ*

Possibly the most controversial theoretician in cinema studies today is Christian Metz (b. 1931), a French semiotician and structuralist. Roundly praised or condemned by his supporters or detractors, Metz has put forth various proposals for explaining the operation of a film, for understanding our experience of the medium, and for defining the nature of film and cinema. Two central influences are discernible: linguistic theory, especially as formulated by André Martinet, Louis Hjelmslev and Emile Benveniste; and psychoanalytical theory, as presented by Sigmund Freud and Jacques Lacan. (For the latter, see "The Imaginary Signifier," *Screen*, 16 [Summer 1975], 14–76.) Readers will be continually challenged by his works and will find much that is useful. Although all his writings deserve note, I want to concentrate on particular elements in *Film Language* and *Language and Cinema* that appear most readily applicable to explaining and to understanding the nature of film. I will consider how Metz explores film as a language and indicate how semiotics provides him an analytical tool, especially in his proposal for a *grand syntagmatique*, the system of organization in a film of its shots, scenes and sequences. I also want to note briefly his discussion of the way in which the concept of cinematic and non-cinematic codes can help us define what we mean by a genre.

---

*Key to Abbreviations:

F = *Film Language*, trans. Michael Taylor (New York: Oxford University Press, 1974). By permission of Oxford University Press.

L = *Language and Cinema*, trans. Donna Jean Umiker-Sebeok (The Hague: Mouton, 1974). By permission of Mouton Publishers.

Film as Language

As we noted at the beginning of the *Guide*, in 1915, during the dawn of film theory, Vachel Lindsay spoke of film as "Esperanto," a new language of picture-words and hieroglyphs. Fifty years later, Metz employs the same term, "Esperanto," but with a difference that reflects the increased complexity that attends film theory today. On the one hand, Metz rejects the earlier description of cinema as Esperanto because the latter is a self-contained "system that is totally conventional, specific, and organized" (F, p. 63). On the other hand, he grants provisionally the possible use of the term for cinema in a special sense, as the complete *opposite* of a linguistic Esperanto because, as a language, "cinema... has a dearth of linguisticity" (F, p. 64).

Dominating all Metz's writing is the argument that cinema must be considered a *language* rather than a *language system* like Esperanto, or the English or German or Italian language systems. He derives this distinction from Ferdinand De Saussure, the Swiss linguist who has exercised immeasurable influence on all structuralist thought since his lectures were collected by his students in *A Course in General Linguistics*. Besides calling for a study of language along synchronic rather than diachronic lines (that is, examining its existing structures rather than tracing its evolutionary developments), De Saussure distinguished three aspects of linguistic experience: language in general (*langage*)—the universal capacity for utterance or discourse; language system (*langue*)—a particular, organized and articulated system of communication like the French language; and speech itself (*parole*)— the individual's realization, through verbal activity, of the potential inherent in his particular language system.

Metz holds that cinema is not a language system, like the French tongue, but language or discourse which itself includes various systems, *langage* rather than *langue*. Unlike a language system, film lacks the *double articulation:* it has no *phonemes,* minimal units of sound (the second articulation) which combine into *morphemes* or *monemes,* minimal units of meaning (the first articulation). In other words, various units of sound do not combine to form words. In the English language system, /tay/ in combination with /gər/ yield /taygər/—the phonetic spelling of "tiger." Instead, in a film we see the image of a tiger. Second, a shot of a tiger can *not* be construed to be the cinematic equivalent of the word "tiger," as earlier theorists like Kuleshov and Pudovkin had suggested. There are no morphemes or monemes, minimal units of meaning; the shot always gives us more than a word, and is comparable, at least, to a sentence. A shot of a tiger says to Metz, "Here is a tiger" rather than simply "tiger." Third, the relation between the image of the tiger and the meaning we derive from the image is *motivated*. According to De Saussure, in language systems the relation between the linguistic signifier (the acoustical image) and the signified (the meaning of the image, the referent to which it points) is not motivated but arbitrary; that is, "tiger" means something (members of the cat family residing in certain parts of the world) by virtue of a *convention* which has established a connection between the acoustical image and the meaning. The sign which results from an English-speaking individual's apprehension of the signifier-signified is part of our language system. But there is no reason why another sign could not have arisen to designate tiger. In fact, the signifier-signified construct for tiger could as easily have been "lion"—and vice versa—because of the arbitrary nature of linguistic meaning and the way in which concepts are joined to sound images.

Metz thinks cinema is truly a universal language rather than an individualized language system because its images are *always* motivated. An image of a tiger on the screen actually resembles a tiger. We see an image on the screen, and, on the denotative level, immediately apprehend the tight relationship between the signifier, the image of the tiger, and the signified. Compare Bazin's suggestions about the relationship of the image with its object, as well as Wollen's comments about iconical and indexical signs to Metz's assertion that "the signifier is coextensive with the whole of the significate [signified], the spectacle its own signification" (F, p. 43); there is a "lack of distance between the significate and the signifier" (F, p. 59); "the signifier is an image, the significate is what the image represents" (F, p. 62). Ordinary language systems are comprised of signs used for intercommunication. But cinema is *one*-way communication. It is not a system because it lacks the double articulation which constitutes the arbitrary signs. And the image does not stand in an arbitrary relation

to its object: "the image is first and always an image. In its perceptual literalness it reproduces the signified spectacle whose signifier it is; and thus it becomes what it shows" and "from the very
first an image is not the indication of something other than itself
[as the acoustical image "tiger" is] but the pseudopresence of the
thing it contains." Films can present all sorts of subjects, and be
either realistic or naturalistic, "but whatever the case, the film
itself only shows whatever it shows" (F, p. 76). As a result, since
visual perception is a common activity which admits of virtually
no variation throughout the world—a tiger is recognized as a tiger
by people who speak different languages—the image is always
translatable. There are no phonemes or morphemes; discourse
occurs primarily through images: "image discourse needs no
translation . . . because, having no second articulation, it is already
translated into all languages: The heighth of the translatable is the
universal" (F, p. 64).

Cinematic Meaning and Discourse

One speaks more properly of cinema as language when images are put together to form a narrative. Throughout *Film Language* and *Language and Cinema,* Metz deals primarily with
filmed narratives having plots, themes, characters, etc. As he
conceives it, " 'cinematographic language' is first of all the literalness of a plot" (F, p. 99). Although the images we see convey
reality to such an extent that there is virtually no distance between the signifier and the signified, these images are nonetheless distinct from the external reality to which they point; that is,
mere reality itself does not give us a narrative—only a work of art
can do that. In this sense cinema is language "to the extent that it
orders signifying elements within ordered arrangements different
from those of spoken idioms—and to the extent that these elements are not traced on the perceptual configurations of reality
itself (which does not tell stories). Filmic manipulation transforms
what might have been a mere visual transfer of reality into discourse" (F, p. 105).

Within this discourse, he identifies five cinematographic
codes which convey messages to the viewer: "cinematic discourse
depends on five different sensory orders: the visual image, the

musical sound, the verbal sounds of speech, sound effects, and the graphic form of credits" (L, p. 16). The total semiotic study of a film would operate on two levels: one analyzing everything the signifying codes embody in respect to psychological, sociological, cultural and aesthetic meaning; and one examining the cinematic manner by which the codes are presented to us. Although Metz has some examples in *Language and Cinema* of what he would do in regard to the first level of analysis, thus far he has devoted most of his criticism to the second aspect and has engaged in complex semiotic studies of the way in which the medium allows for signification. It is this second level, the study of cinematic language and signification, that we shall pursue here.

He believes that, historically speaking, all the "specific signifying procedures" were established or codified for cinema by 1915. The semiotician can thus point to such aspects of cinematic language as camera movements, double exposures, optical effects, dissolves, fades, pans, close-ups, tracking shots, parallel and alternate montage, and can raise diachronic or evolutionary considerations—that is, who uses which of these for the first time; or the semiotician can discuss these in synchronic terms, and analyze a film or group of films to understand how these aspects of cinematic language are used to present the *diegesis*, Metz's term for the sum of all narrative elements or "a film's denotation" (F, p. 98).

Essentially the semiotician explores the nature of the image as sign and the way images are ordered in the narrative as a whole. To understand how Metz approaches the first of these activities, observe his discussion of a common setting in gangster films, in which the represented image shows a waterfront area at night, with such aspects as docks, wet pavements, etc. Using a model proposed by Roland Barthes, Metz suggests that here the actual image we see—the material on the screen—be considered the *signifier of denotation*. The *signified*, or meaning of the image, would be "the scene represented (dimly lit, deserted wharves, with stacks of crates and overhead cranes...)" (F, p. 97). The product of this signifier/signified relationship is a *sign*. Now this *sign* becomes in turn the *signifier* of a *connotative* relationship; that is, the image and its denotative meaning (docks and wharves presented in a particular way) constitute the "signifier of connotation" that has as *its* signified "an impression of anxiety

and hardness." In other words, he posits a two-stage process
viewers go through when watching: first reading the image for its
denotative content; and then considering what the image suggests
connotatively.

This two-stage process, as he presents it, has potential value
for viewers who wish to analyze the distinction between denotation and connotation in given images. Let us take an image from
Citizen Kane—the scene in the Thatcher Library where
Thompson sits at the desk about to read Thatcher's memoirs. The
signified of denotation is the scene represented: certain lighting
effects and interiors which are read on the level of the signified as
meaning cavernous room, high ceilings, a beam of light falling on
the table, the clanging of a door as Thompson is left alone. The
denotative construct signifier/signified acting as a sign becomes
the signifier of a larger connotative meaning in this way. The
scene represented suggests the mystery (the lighting and the
strange room) and foreboding (the ominous clang of the door) that
we could without much distortion associate with a tomb. In terms
of the diegesis, this connotative meaning is not inappropriate,
since in fact Thompson is trying to unearth a mystery buried in
the past.

Metz points out that if any aspect of the dock scene were
changed in respect to its manner of filming, the whole process of
signification would be altered. The scene photographed in bright
light rather than at night would take away from the eeriness.
Similarly, in our example from *Kane*, consider how the connotation of the scene would be changed if the library were brightly
lighted. In other words, in both cases the setting would still be
the same—denotatively a dock area or a library room; but the
connotation would be different—elimination of frightening suggestions and associations. That is, the way the image is delivered to
us through the photographic medium affects its meaning, its signification.

The Ordering of the Images

Turning to consideration of the ways in which images are
assembled in the diegesis, we encounter a distinction borrowed
from linguistic theory between a *paradigm* and a *syntagm*. As

Metz uses these terms, paradigm refers to "a class of elements,
only one of which figures in the text"; and syntagm to "a set of
elements which are comanifest in the same fragments of texts,
which are already *next* to one another before any analysis" (L,
pp. 164–165). Perhaps a linguistic example will explain his meaning here. In linguistics we can speak of a paradigm or class containing all the possible forms of a particular word, "love" for
example: "love," "loves," "loved," "loving," "lover," "lovable."
Looking at a line of prose or verse with the word in it, such as
"He loves good weather," we would say that we discover the verb
"loves" in a syntagmatic relationship with the pronoun "he" and
the phrase "good weather" used as direct object. If another form
of "love" had been drawn from the paradigm, the meaning of the
utterance could be different; if the line read, "He loved good
weather," the inference we draw might be that he no longer does
so. The point is that the speaker draws out of the paradigm the
form of the word which best suits the particular communication
he desires to make. Once the word has been taken from the
paradigm and entered into communication, we speak of it as a
syntagm.

In general, Metz denies that there are paradigms of images
as such, in the way that there are paradigms of the forms of a
given word like "love." Instead, there are paradigms of cinematic
signifying codes which we can consider when examining how images are ordered in the films. For example, he discusses transitions between scenes in a film and says that the alternatives
"fade" and "dissolve" constitute a paradigm. I see no reason why
we cannot also add the possibility of "straight cut" as well. Thus
the paradigmatic category for "conjunction of two sequences"
would include three possibilities: cut, dissolve, fade. When any
one of these occurs as a link between sequences, we call it a
syntagm—an element from a paradigmatic category observed in
active relation to another element.

As I mentioned earlier, Roman Polanski uses the syntagm
"straight cut" almost exculsively in *Chinatown*, varying only to
the syntagm "fade" when the hero is knocked unconscious. Recall
the comment of Balázs in regard to the distinction between fades
and dissolves here, and see how it is adaptable to Metz's point;
that is, the director chooses either a fade or dissolve when he

wishes to communicate to the viewer the sense of a particular passage of time. The signifier carries with it a particular signified: fade—long passage of time; dissolve—interrelationship of scenes thus joined, brief passage of time. Obviously any of the syntagms from the paradigm of transitions can be used for other purposes as well. Thus a straight cut in *Last Year at Marienbad* is sometimes used to join scenes that may be one year apart in time; the fades and dissolves in *Cries and Whispers* sometimes function in relation to time (flashbacks) and, at other times in relation to a symbolic realm of timelessess as Bergman fades in and out to the color red.

The "Grand Syntagmatique"

By far the most important aspect of *Film Language* is Metz's attempt to define the very nature of narrative units in film, what he calls his "grand syntagmatique"—or the large syntagmatic system. Essentially he proposes to describe narrative discourse in terms of cinematic language; that is, each type of image, scene, and sequence can be defined and assigned a particular name. Here he suggests that there exist eight syntagms in the major paradigm of elements which permit the structuring of denotation. When making a film, a director must decide how all the shots and scenes will be assembled, what Pudovkin was talking about with his terms "differentiation" and "integration." Metz is after the same thing, basically, only he uses a linguistic model to conceive of the process by which the director utilizes a particular kind of cinematic discourse. As in the operation of language, an individual who wishes to communicate draws his utterance from the potentialities, the "deep structures" of possible utterances and constructions open to him as a speaker of a given language. Similarly, Metz says that that director draws from a paradigm of eight syntagmatic categories available to him, an "outline of the *deep structure* of the choices that confront the film-maker for each one of the 'sequences' of his film" (F, p. 123).

The first type, from the paradigm of denotative structures, is the *automonous segment*, which is constituted by *one shot*. This can be extended, as in the long take or sequence shot encountered in Italian neorealist films and in *Citizen Kane* (the scene in

the boardinghouse when Mrs. Kane signs over Charles to Thatcher);
or it can be short, even subliminal, as in one-shot interpolations
and inserts. Metz lists four such inserts: the *nondiegetic* insert,
which shows something external to the action directly represented; the *subjective* insert, which presents an image conceived
of in relation to a character—a dream or memory; a *displaced
diegetic* insert, which is an image related to the main action but
not made dominant (showing only one image of the pursued in a
sequence covering the activities of the pursuers); and the *explan-
atory* insert, which uses a close-up or camera movement to give
viewers a better sight of a detail.

The remaining seven types of narrative syntagms are autonomous segments made up of *more than one shot:* "autonomous
segments having more than one minimum segment" (F, p. 124).
Note carefully that a single autonomous shot can constitute a
segment (type one), but more typically autonomous shots are
combined to form segments having more than one shot.

Types two and three are *nonchronological* and do not posit
any temporal relationship between their units. In type two, we
see *parallel montage,* or syntagms in which "montage brings together and interweaves two or more alternating 'motifs,' but no
precise relationship (whether temporal or spatial) is assigned to
them—at least on the level of denotation" (F, p. 125). For example, recall Pudovkin's description of the sequence contrasting the
rich, well-fed man with the poor, hungry man; the images are
interwoven with no reference to time or place or interrelation.
The third type, or *bracket syntagm* (previously called frequenta-
tive syntagm by Metz), includes sequences in which a particular
activity is described: "a series of very brief scenes representing
occurrences that the film gives as typical samples of a same order
of reality, without in any way chronologicallly locating them in
relation to each other" (F, p. 126). There is no alternation of images, as in type two, but rather a series of actions depicting related facts. For example, in *The Godfather, Part I* we could cite
the series of shots indicating the activities of the Corleone "family" when the members have gone underground. The viewer
senses that the events are happening at the same general time,
but has no way of knowing precisely the exact order in which the
events occur; for example, one cannot tell precisely when the
spaghetti meal takes place in diegetic time.

The remaining five syntagms are all chronological: "the temporal relationships between the facts that successive images show us are defined on the level of denotation (i.e., literal temporality of the plot, and not just some symbolic, 'profound' time)" (F, p. 127). In type four, the *descriptive syntagm*, the chronological element is construed as being simultaneous, as when in an establishing sequence the camera shows us in various shots *spatially* related elements coexisting at the same moment. Metz's example is of a landscape in which we see separate shots of a tree, a stream near the tree, and a hill beyond. We could also mention the opening of *Citizen Kane* which presents the descriptive syntagm; the shots of the link fence, "Xanadu," the lighted window, etc., combine to give us a single moment of reality as the camera picks out details which establish and locate the estate and property as belonging to a common space.

Types five through eight are *narrative syntagms* in which there occurs an actual passage of time, consecutiveness. In type five, the *alternate narrative syntagm*, the director switches from scene A to Scene B to scene A, etc., as in a sequence where we watch the pursuer and the pursued alternately. In each diegetic element (A or B) time is consecutive; but we are to understand that A and B occur simultaneously, as in the old-time thriller device of switching from shots of a hapless woman tied to the railroad tracks and the approaching train.

Metz conceives of the sixth syntagm as the *scene*, most typically appearing in conversations in which time flows consecutively and in which there are *no temporal breaks*. A common example is dialogue between two characters using the shot/reverse shot/shot pattern as the camera shows us the speaker, the listener, the speaker, etc. But we could include any scene as long as there is no break in time and as long as it is constituted by *more than one shot:* for example, the point at which we pick up Kane's speech in Madison Square Garden with the cuts from Kane to his son, to Leland and to Gettys—one scene in which time passes consecutively and in which we have more than one shot.

The remaining two syntagms are more complex, and are called "sequences proper." Type seven, the *episodic sequence*, "strings together a number of very brief scenes, which are usually separated from each other by optical devices (dissolves, etc.) and which succeed each other in chronological order" (F, p. 130). He offers the famous breakfast table sequence in *Citizen Kane* as an example. The six scenes there are linked by swing dissolves and, with amazing economy, create a sequence which indicates the deterioration of Kane's marriage. We could also mention from the same picture the episodic sequence in which Thatcher follows the career of Kane by reading the headlines of various newspapers.

The last type of syntagm, the *ordinary sequence*, covers a single action but does so with spatial and temporal breaks. What we see are the elements in the particular action that have *not* been omitted: "the sequence is based on the unity of a more complex action . . . that 'skips' those portions of itself that it intends to leave out and that is therefore apt to unfold in several different location (unlike the scene)" (F, p. 132). Metz's example is that of an escape sequence in which our real time does not coincide with the diegetic time, as it does in a scene. Instead, we might watch a sequence lasting ten minutes in which an action understood to be lasting two hours takes place; for example, the two hours time it takes for men to tunnel out from a prison. The omission in no way interferes with the unity of the action: "one encounters diegetic breaks within the sequence . . . but these hiatuses are considered insignificant—at least on the level of denotation—and are to be distinguished from those indicated by the fades or by any other optical device between two autonomous segments" (F, p. 132). Some other examples we could mention here include the orgy sequence in *Midnight Cowboy;* this lasts about ten minutes in real time, but is supposed to be taking hours of diegetic time. Similarly, the Odessa Steps massacre in *Potemkin* is over in a matter of seven minutes at the most of our time, but the implication is that a much longer diegetic time is involved.

Metz applies his syntagmatic categories directly to a relatively unknown film by Jacques Rozier, *Adieu Philippine*, which is available now in the United States. Ideally, readers of Metz should be able to view the film in order to see and understand how he makes practical use of his categories to analyze a film completely. My own reaction after seeing the film four times is that some of his assignments of segments to various syntagmatic categories are highly debatable. There are times when the deci-

sions seem somewhat arbitrary, and others when they seem in-
correct by his own standards. Nonetheless, the method of examining a film on this basis does have the potential merit of helping us
talk about the construction and pattern of the film's structure in
objective terms. For example, Metz shows how two events represented in the film have the same syntagmatic pattern: 1) hero has
liaison with girl A who later returns secretively to her companion,
girl B; 2) hero has liaison with girl B who later returns secretively
to her companion, girl A. It helps to be able to say that both are
episodic sequences, and, as such, underline in their parallel
structure the parallel activities of the characters. When we have
such terms at our fingertips, we are able to facilitate our discussion of film considerably, just as we can by using Burch's
spatiotemporal articulations.

In addition, as Metz suggests, one using the syntagmatic
categories can determine whether films of a given period display
a certain tendency to use particular syntagms more than those of
other periods. Such historical analysis need not be limited to con-
firming the obvious—the frequency of alternate narrative syntagms in the silent period, the reliance on sequence shots using
deep focus in the 1940s, etc. In fact, the application of the
categories might be an effective way to *test* the validity of exactly
such assertions about what kind of structural tendencies dominate
film making at a given period. Used intelligently, this or a similar
codification of syntagmatic categories could provide a means to
distinguish structures between genres, or within the works of a
given director. In this connection, it becomes not only a historical
tool, but an important means of bringing precision to that most
elusive topic, directorial style.

Cinema, Genre and Codes

In *Language and Cinema* Metz attempts to bring a degree of
precision to the way in which we discuss genre by discussing
codes. A code is "a generally coherent system" (L, p. 61). In
cinema we speak of "*general cinematic codes*" which can appear
in any kind of film; "*particular cinematic codes* include those
elements of signification which appear only in certain types of
films" (L, p. 62). Thus we might say that vast panning shots are

general, since they can and do appear in any film, but that "certain types of long shots are common only to the Western, certain types of camera movements only to the German expressionist school, etc." (L, p. 62). In addition to general and particular cinematic codes, Metz also identifies *non*-cinematic codes in a film; these can appear in any cultural manifestation: in the western, for example, there may be "a certain code of honor and friendship, of restrictive rituals concerning gun duels, etc." When we come to define a particular genre, what we do essentially is say what particular cinematic and non-cinematic codes figure most prominently. Again, his example is the western: "What characterizes the classic film of the West, and it alone, is a certain number of selections that are made from among these codes, and the arrangement of those elements into a quite definite overall configuration resulting from interaction between the cinematic and extra-cinematic options. This configuration is thus a textual system" (L, p. 121).

Observe how this model can be adapted to other genres. For example, the cinematic codes particular to the gangster films might include tight framing, certain kinds of lighting, reliance on certain syntagmatic relationships (the scene rather than the episodic sequence), etc. Non-cinematic codes belonging to the culture in general might include ritual codes of honor (the taboo against squealing), the association of gangsters with cities, etc. It follows from Metz's discussion that when we say a film belongs to a genre, such as that of the gangster film, we are claiming that it displays a number of codes exclusively bound up in that configuration we have seen previously in films of that nature.

PETER WOLLEN*

The *Guide* concludes with a discussion of Peter Wollen (b. 1938), the noted British film theorist, teacher, film maker and writer (he co-authored Michelangelo Antonioni's *The Passenger*). In *Signs and Meaning in the Cinema*, Wollen provides extensive analysis of Eisenstein, the *auteur* theory and semiology. The first of these should be consulted by those interested in a detailed examination of Eisenstein's souces and influences. Wollen offers a sympathetic and thorough evaluation of the Russian who, in his view, was unable to integrate and synthesize political and aesthetic concepts satisfactorily. In this section our attention will be directed to Wollen's discussion of the *auteur* theory and semiology: to the former he applies a structuralist model derived from anthropological studies; to the latter a triadic model of the sign formulated by C. S. Peirce. Notice how Wollen attempts to synthesize various current approaches to the understanding and evaluation of film.

The "Auteur" Theory and Structural Analysis

In the first edition of *Signs and Meaning in the Cinema,* Wollen offers his Pantheon of Directors just as Andrew Sarris does in *The American Cinema*. Even though Wollen counts himself an *auteur* critic, one influenced by Sarris, there is an important distinction to be made between the two. As we saw, Sarris rejects structuralism as a critical tool. In contrast, Wollen argues that this approach permits us to investigate a director's work effectively while preventing anything like the cult of personality

---

*Unless noted, all quotations are from *Signs and Meaning in the Cinema*, 3rd ed. (Bloomington: Indiana University Press, 1973). By permission of Indiana University Press and of Martin Secker & Warburg Ltd. (reprinted from their Cinema One series).

worship that so worried Bazin. Specifically, Wollen adapts the model presented by structural anthropology to the *auteur*. As he explains it: "I was reading Lévi-Strauss and began to wonder whether his work on myths could not be applied to films too. I wanted a theory which recognized the concept of the individual (I had been convinced of the *politique des auteurs* by reading *Cahiers*... and by friends such as Eugene Archer and Andrew Sarris). But I was hostile to ideas of subjective creation, personal expression and so on. I thought a nongeneric structuralism might solve this problem" ("Structuralism Implies a Certain Methodology... ," interview with Peter Wollen in *Film Heritage*, 9 [1974], 25).*

From Lévi-Strauss and his anthropological studies, Wollen takes the following concepts. First, one examines myth for its basic features which, upon analysis, are seen to resolve into basic antinomies, or categories of binary oppositions. For example, the Oedipus myth as Lévi-Strauss conceives of it posits two basic constructs: a view of man as emerging from the earth (autochthonous) as opposed to a conception of man as self-generated through sexual relations. The "meaning" of the Oedipus story is explained in terms of the tension between the two antinomies: "the myth has to do with the inability, for a culture which holds the belief that mankind is autochthonous... to find a satisfactory transition between this theory and the knowledge that human beings are actually born from the union of man and woman. Although the problem obviously cannot be solved, the Oedipus myth provides a kind of logical tool which, to phrase it coarsely, replaces the original problem: born from one or born from two; born from different or born from same?" (Claude Lévi-Strauss, "The Structural Study of Myth,"** in *The Structuralists from Marx to Lévi-Strauss*, ed. Richard and Fernande DeGeorge [New York: Anchor Books, 1972], p. 180). Second, the structural anthropologist considers a myth in relation to all its forms, and studies the presence or absence of elements in the various manifestations of the myth. Often the apparent absence of one feature (like a particular

---

*Quoted by permission of *Film Heritage*.
**Reproduced by permission of the American Folklore Society from the *Journal of American Folklore* 68:270, 1955, where this essay originally appeared.

character or conflict) will appear, upon analysis, to be present in
another form, or transformation—rather like what we said earlier
about the various transformations of the vamp figure in movies
since the time of Theda Bara. Lévi-Strauss studies four versions
of the same Winnebago myth, noting how the fourth and apparently most divergent form can be seen as a transformation, still
belonging to the basic group which, as do all myths, tries to solve
a problem. He discovers that the variants maintain with different
details the same basic properties of the myth and concludes: "a
plot and its component parts should neither be interpreted by
themselves nor relative to something outside the realm of the
myth proper, but as *substitutions* given in, and understandable
only with reference to *the group made up of all the myths of the
same series*"* ("Four Winnebago Myths," DeGeorge, p. 205).

The influence of structuralist thinking appears prominently in
Wollen's examination of Howard Hawks and John Ford. He explains that "what the *auteur* theory does is to take a group of
films—the work of one director—and analyse their structure" (p.
104). In his hands, the structural approach is used to arrive at a
"definition of a core of repeated motifs" and, thus, "has evident
affinities with methods which have been developed for the study
of folklore and mythology" (p. 93). Like Lévi-Strauss, he wants to
identify the basic resemblances as well as the distinguishing variants within the context of a director's work.

The films of Hawks, who has worked in virtually all the
genres (western, detective, epic, comedy, etc.), can be seen to
group into the basic categories of adventure drama and crazy
comedy. In all, Wollen finds "the same thematic preoccupations,
the same recurring motifs and incidents, the same visual style and
tempo" (p. 81). In the adventure film, the Hawks hero attempts
to find transcendent values by establishing solidarity within a
group. The camaraderie which the director presents again and
again occurs in basically male communities whose constituents
face either natural or human crises, demand new members to
pass ritual tests, and ask loyalty of each man. The comedies provide an antithesis to the adventure dramas. The two major
themes in the comedies are infantilism (*Monkey Business*) and sex

---

*Reproduced by permission of Columbia University Press.

or role reversal (*I Was a Male War Bride*); "whereas the dramas show the mastery of man over nature, over woman, over the animal and childish; the comedies show his humiliation, his regression. The heroes become victims; society, instead of being excluded and despised, breaks in with irruptions of monstrous farce" (p. 91). Thus Wollen sees "a systematic series of oppositions" in the canon of the director's films (p. 93).

The works of John Ford present more complicated problems for structural analysis, since in his films Wollen detects a number of antinomic structures: "garden versus wilderness, ploughshare versus sabre, settler versus nomad, European versus Indian, civilised versus savage, book versus gun, married versus unmarried, East versus West" (p. 94). What makes Ford so significant is that the various antinomies shift from film to film; that is, the *basic* oppositions may remain, but their forms vary: "the relevant pairs of opposites overlap; different pairs are foregrounded in different movies" (p. 94).

Wollen identifies the chief antinomy in the films as the same dialectic argued by Henry Nash Smith in his study of the United States frontier, *Virgin Land*—the contrast between the wilderness and the garden. The heroes of *My Darling Clementine* (Wyatt Earp), *The Searchers* (Ethan Edwards), and *The Man Who Shot Liberty Valance* (Tom Doniphon) evince different conceptions when considered in relation to this antinomy. Earp passes from the natural to the civilized; Edwards goes back and forth between the antinomies while embodying related antinomies (European versus savage, wanderer versus settler); like Edwards, Doniphon finds that "the wilderness becomes a garden," but, unlike him, is cut off from the garden (p. 97).

Wollen also explains the motif of the quest or search, so common in myth, and finds it figuring prominently in Ford's work: "a number of Ford films are built around the theme of the quest for the Promised Land, an American re-enactment of the Biblical exodus, the journey through the desert to the land of milk and honey, the New Jerusalem. This theme is built on the combination of two pairs: wilderness versus garden and nomad versus settler. . . . Thus, in *Wagonmaster,* the Mormons cross the desert in search of their future home; in *How Green Was My*

Valley and *The Informer*, the protagonists want to cross the Atlantic to a future home in the United States. But, during Ford's
career, the situation of home is reversed in time. In *Cheyenne
Autumn*, the Indians journey in search of the home they once had
in the past; in *The Quiet Man*, the American Sean Thornton returns to his ancestral home in Ireland" (p. 97).

It is in part because of this changing use of the quest motif
and his varying of the wilderness-garden antinomy that Wollen
finds Ford ultimately a more rewarding director than Hawks. The
structuralist method as employed here on an *auteur* becomes a
tool for Wollen to identify antinomies and also to evaluate the
director: "it is the richness of the shifting relations between antinomies in Ford's work that makes him a great artist" (p. 102). In
other words, the methodology which identifies and isolates basic
patterns and motifs can also be used as an evaluative element
insofar as it reveals not only a fullness in the observed structures
but also a complexity and variation in these as they are considered in relation to the complete works of a director.

Wollen thinks his structuralist-*auteur* criticism can also help
viewers by making them examine a given film more closely in
relation to a director's work. Of course this is possible without the
structuralist model, which he uses to emphasize mythic patterns.
Nonetheless, he defends this claim by noting how what seems to
be just a routine film by Ford, *Donovan's Reef*, is seen "to reveal
a whole complex of meaning" when taken in the context of Ford's
interests. In addition, *Wings of Eagles* should be seen in relation
to *The Searchers;* both employ the "vagrancy versus home antinomy, with the difference that when the hero does come home,
after flying round the world, he trips over a child's toy, falls down
the stairs and is completely paralysed so that he cannot move at
all. . . . This is the macabre *reductio ad absurdum* of the settled"
(p. 102).

Wollen maintains that his application of structuralism in the
way we have discussed is suited to *auteur* criticism which is *not*
personal or subjective. Such structuralist criticism engages in a
process of "decipherment" and "does not limit itself to acclaiming
the director as the main author of a film" (p. 77). When examining an *auteur*, he works a posteriori to reconstruct his meaning

(p. 78). He is interested in this meaning as a structure of oppositions rather than as personal vision. An *auteur* is a director
whose works permit the critic to identify and abstract a discernible core of meaning and recurring patterns and motifs: "the structure is associated with a single director, an individual, not because he has played the role of artist, expressing himself or his
own vision in the film, but because it is through the force of his
preoccupations that an unconscious, unintended meaning can be
decoded in the film" (pp. 167–168). The *auteur* is "an unconscious catalyst" whose presence effects the realization of all the
elements in the film. *Auteur* criticism "consists of tracing a structure (not a message) within the work, which can then *post factum*
be assigned to an individual, the director, on empirical grounds"
(p. 168).

　　He distinguishes between a "structure" and a "message" in
the following way. First, "the film is not a communication, but an
artefact which is unconsciously structured in a certain way" (p.
168). As such, critics must "read" the text to discover the various
structures and patterns inhering there. Wollen contrasts the kind
of critical reading he demands with earlier theories of interpretation. In the past, the work of art has been conceived of as a
construct which stands *between* the audience and meaning; as
such, one analyzes the work to get at the truth which it shrouds.
Thus the work becomes a means to an end outside itself—a pre-
sumed truth. But the modern age has no such confidence in
"truth." Wollen rejects the kind of theory which we saw in
Kracauer, who praises film for its ability to give us at least surface
reality; Wollen calls this type of thesis "sleight-of-hand": "this
aesthetic rests on a monstrous delusion: the idea that truth resides in the real world and can be picked out by a camera" (p.
166). The only truth for Wollen lies in the structures to be found,
and the aesthetic experience in which we are engaged. Like many
other modern critics, he argues that the work of art need not
point to anything but itself. In addition, sounding very much like
literary theorists interested in hermeneutics, Wollen suggests that
the audience stands in a most intimate relationship to the work of
art, and does not use it to abstract eternal verities, but to grasp
its inner pattern of coherence: "the consciousness of the reader or
spectator [is] no longer outside the work as receiver, consumer
and judge." Instead of using the work as a passageway to an ex-

ternal truth, critics must explain the codes inside: "a text is a
material object whose significance is determined not by a code
external to it, mechanically, nor organically as a symbolic whole,
but through its own interrogation of its own code" (p. 162). Reading in this way forces the spectator to "put his consciousness at
risk within the text itself, so that he is forced to interrogate his
own codes, his own method of interpretation, in the course of
reading, and thus to produce fissures and gaps in the space of his
own consciousness (fissures and gaps which exist in reality but
which are repressed by an ideology, characteristic of bourgeois
society, which insists on the 'wholeness' and integrity of each individual consciousness)" (p. 162).

Index, Sign, Symbol

The full interrogation of the text includes not only examination of motifs, but also analysis of its semiological nature. Following the model of the American philosopher C. S. Peirce, Wollen
distinguishes between three types of signs. First, the *icon* "represents its object mainly by its similarity to it; the relationship between signifier and signified is not arbitrary but is one of resemblance or likeness" (p. 122). Thus a photograph or a painting of a
man would constitute an iconic sign, since it resembles and is
motivated. Second, the *index* "is a sign by virtue of an existential bond between itself and its object" (p. 122). Wollen cites
Peirce's examples of a sailor's "rolling gait," the appearance of
a jockey, "a bowlegged man in corduroys, gaiters and a jacket,"
and the action of a weathercock, "a sign of the direction of the
wind which physically moves it" (pp. 122–123). In all these examples of indexical signs, the thing itself, the signifier, is bound up
existentially with the thing signified, the meaning to which it
points. Unlike the icon and the index, the *symbol* is an arbitrary
rather than a motivated sign: it "demands neither resemblance to
its object nor any existential bond with it. It is conventional and
has the force of a law"—as Wollen notes, exactly like De Saussure's concept of the arbitrary nature of words (p. 123).

Cinema employs all three signs; thus it is pointless to attempt to base an aesthetic theory on any of these alone. Wollen
thinks Bazin's view of the ontological identity of the photographic

image and the object puts too much importance on the indexical aspect of signs; as a result, Bazin does not welcome expressionism or montage. In place of such an emphasis on realism and the indexical sign, Wollen suggests Josef Von Sternberg's general emphasis on the importance of basic resemblances, "the iconic aspect of the sign . . . detached from the indexical in order to conjure up a world, comprehensible by virtue of resemblances to the natural world, yet other than it, a kind of dream world, a heterocosm" (p. 137).

The semiologist examines the entire range of signs on the screen, acknowledging the dominance of iconic and indexical signs as well as the presence of symbols (p. 141). Since Wollen praises John Ford for the richness of his films resulting from the complex antinomic structures, we are not surprised when he lauds Jean-Luc Godard for making use of cinema's potential to employ all three kinds of signs. Godard is "unafraid to mix Hollywood with Kant and Hegel, Eisensteinian montage with Rossellinian Realism, words with images, professional actors with real people, Lumière with Méliès, the documentary with the iconographic. More than anybody else Godard has realised the fantastic possibilities of the cinema as a medium of communication and expression. In his hands, as in Peirce's perfect sign, the cinema has become an almost equal amalgam of the symbolic, the iconic and the indexical" (pp. 153–154).

Proppian Analysis

A recent development in Wollen's structuralist criticism has been his application of model from Vladimir Propp's *Morphology of the Folktale*. Propp examines various Russian fairy tales and isolates their basic features such as hero, villain, lack, reward, noting similarities and omissions of elements in related narratives, with the ultimate aim of classifying the essential structures which inform the works. Wollen uses the Proppian method with its identification of particular "functions" on Hitchcock's *North by Northwest* to see how applicable the method is beyond the confines of the folktale; to determine whether there are relationships between oral and mass culture; to examine the film in relation to others in Hitchcock's canon; to find out if the Proppian analysis can be integrated with Metz's semiotics; and to test its possible use in connection with psychoanalytic approaches. His implementation of the method is fascinating, and suggests that there is more to be done. He is "surprised how easily Propp's functions and method of analysis in general could be applied. . . . The basic structure described by Propp is present in *North by Northwest*. This can be expressed as follows: a task is set the hero (by the dispatcher). If he performs it successfully, he will be rewarded (gift of the princess, by her father = the dispatcher). The task involves finding and bringing an object of desire, to liquidate a lack. This object may be the princess, or some other object. It may simply be lacking, or it may have been taken by a villain, from whom it must be taken in turn, by combat or by trickery. To retrieve the object the hero will need help and to receive this, he must perform a subsidiary task for a donor. At first he may fail and receive hindrance or harm instead of help (delaying mechanism). After retrieving the object of desire, he may still have to perform a further task or tasks before claiming his reward. This may be because an imposter has claimed the reward and concomitantly the hero is not recognised" ("*North by Northwest:* A Morphological Analysis," *Film Form,* 1 [Spring 1976], 32).*

---

*Quoted by permission of *Film Form.*

BIBLIOGRAPHY

I. Works by Writers Included in the Guide

Agee, James. *Agee on Film.* Vol. 1. New York: Grosset & Dunlap, 1969.

Arnheim, Rudolf. *Art and Visual Perception.* Berkeley: University of California Press, 1974.

————. "Art Today and the Film." *Art Journal,* 25 (Spring 1966), 242–244.

————. *Entropy and Art: An Essay on Disorder and Order.* Berkeley: University of California Press, 1971.

————. *Film as Art.* Berkeley: University of California Press, 1971.

————. "Melancholy Unshaped." In *Toward a Psychology of Art.* Berkeley: University of California Press, 1971.

————. "Portrait of an Artist" [Erich von Stroheim]. In *Film Culture Reader,* edited by P. Adams Sitney. New York: Praeger, 1970.

————. "To Maya Deren." In *Film Culture Reader,* edited by P. Adams Sitney. New York: Praeger, 1970.

————. *Visual Thinking.* Berkeley: University of California Press, 1969.

Balázs, Béla. *Theory of the Film: Character and Growth of a New Art.* Translated by Edith Bone. New York: Dover Books, 1976.

Bazin, André. *Jean Renoir.* Edited by François Truffaut. Translated by W. W. Halsey II and William H. Simon. New York: Delta Books, 1974.

————. "The Originality of Orson Welles as a Director." Translated by Mark Bernheim and Ronald Gottesman. In *Focus on "Citizen Kane,"* edited by Ronald Gottesman. Englewood Cliffs, N.J.: Prentice-Hall, 1971.

————. *Orson Welles: A Critical View.* Translated by Jonathan Rosenbaum. New York: Harper & Row, 1978.

————. "Othello." Translated by Charles Eckert. In *Film Theory and Criticism: Introductory Readings,* edited by Gerald Mast and Marshall Cohen. New York: Oxford University Press, 1974.

————. *What Is Cinema?* Edited and translated by Hugh Gray. 2 vols. Berkeley: University of California Press, 1971–72.

Burch, Noël. "Avant-Garde or Vanguard." *Afterimage,* no. 6 (Summer 1976), pp. 52–63.

————. "Beyond Theory of Film Practice: An Interview with Noël Burch." *Women and Film,* 1, nos. 5–6 (June 1974), 20–31.

————. *Theory of Film Practice.* Translated by Helen R. Lane. New York: Praeger, 1973.

Eisenstein, S. M. *Film Essays and a Lecture.* Edited and translated by Jay Leyda. New York: Praeger, 1970.

————. *Film Form: Essays in Film Theory.* Edited and translated by Jay Leyda. New York: Harcourt, Brace & World, 1949.

————. *The Film Sense.* Edited and translated by Jay Leyda. New York: Harcourt, Brace & World, 1947.

————. *Notes of a Film Director.* Translated by X. Danko. New York: Dover Books, 1970.

Haskell, Molly. *From Reverence to Rape: The Treatment of Women in the Movies.* Baltimore: Penguin Books, 1974.

————. "I'm a Film Critic First and a Feminist Second" [Interview with Molly Haskell]. *Film Heritage,* 11 (Winter 1975–76), 13–33.

Kael, Pauline. *The Citizen Kane Book.* New York: Bantam Books, 1974.

_____. *Deeper into Movies*. New York: Bantam Books, 1974.

_____. *Going Steady*. New York: Bantam Books, 1971.

_____. *Kiss Kiss Bang Bang*. New York: Bantam Books, 1969.

_____. *I Lost It at the Movies*. Boston: Atlantic Monthly Press, 1965.

_____. *Reeling*. Boston: Atlantic Monthly Press, 1976.

Kauffmann, Stanley. *Figures of Light: Film Criticism and Comment*. New York: Harper & Row, 1971.

_____. *Living Images: Film Comment and Criticism*. New York: Harper & Row, 1975.

_____. Review of *The Passenger*. *New Republic*, 19 April 1975, p. 22.

_____. *A World on Film: Criticism and Comment*. New York: Delta Books, 1966.

Kracauer, Siegfried. *From Caligari to Hitler: A Psychological History of the German Film*. Princeton: Princeton University Press, 1974.

_____. *Theory of Film: The Redemption of Physical Reality*. New York: Oxford University Press, 1971.

Kuleshov, Lev. *Kuleshov on Film*. Edited and translated by Ronald Levaco. Berkeley: University of California Press, 1974.

Lindsay, Vachel, *The Art of the Moving Picture*. Rev. ed. 1922. Reprint. New York: Liveright, 1970.

Mellen, Joan. *Big Bad Wolves: Masculinity in American Film*. New York: Pantheon Books, 1978.

_____. *Filmguide to "The Battle of Algiers."* Bloomington: Indiana University Press, 1973.

_____. *Marilyn Monroe*. New York: Pyramid Publications, 1973.

_____. *Voices from the Japanese Cinema*. New York: Liveright, 1975.

_____. *The Waves at Genji's Door: Japan Through Its Cinema*. New York: Pantheon Books, 1976.

————. *Women and Their Sexuality in the New Film.* New York: Horizon Books, 1973.

Metz, Christian. "Current Problems of Film Theory: Review of Jean Mitry's *L'Esthétique et psychologie du cinéma,* Vol. II." Translated by Diana Matias. *Screen,* 14, nos. 1-2 (Spring/ Summer 1972), 40-87.

————. *Film Language: A Semiotics of the Cinema.* Translated by Michael Taylor. New York: Oxford University Press, 1974.
————. "History/Discourse: Note on Two Voyeurisms." *Edinburgh '76 Magazine,* no. 1 (1976), pp. 21-25.
————. "The Imaginary Signifier." Translated by Ben Brewster. *Screen,* 16, no. 2 (Summer 1975), 14-76.
————. *Language and Cinema.* Translated by Donna Jean Umiker-Sebeok. The Hague: Mouton, 1974.
————. "Methodological Propositions for the Analysis of Film." Translated by Diana Matias. *Screen,* 14, nos. 1-2 (Spring/ Summer 1972), 89-101.
————. "*Trucage* and the Film." *Critical Inquiry,* 3, no. 4 (Summer 1977), 657-675.

Münsterberg, Hugo. *The Film: A Psychological Study.* 1916. Reprint. New York: Dover Publications, 1970.

Pudovkin, V. I. *Film Technique and Film Acting.* Edited and translated by Ivor Montagu. New York: Grove Press, 1970.

Rosen, Marjorie. *Popcorn Venus: Women, Movies and the American Dream.* New York: Avon Books, 1974.

Sarris, Andrew. "The Actor as Auteur." *American Film,* 2, no. 7 (1977), 16-19.

————. *The American Cinema: Directors and Directions 1929-1968.* New York: E. P. Dutton, 1969.
————. "The Auteur Theory Revisited." *American Film,* 2, no. 9 (1977), 49-53.
————. "*Citizen Kane:* The American Baroque." In *Film Culture Reader,* edited by P. Adams Sitney. New York: Praeger, 1970.

————. *Confessions of a Cultist: On the Cinema, 1955–1969.*
New York: Simon & Schuster, 1970.
————. "Film Books in Focus." *Village Voice,* 19 December
1977, pp. 96–98.
————. "Films in Focus." *Village Voice,* 25 April 1974, pp.
75–76.
————. "Films in Focus." *Village Voice,* 11 August 1975, pp. 1,
63–64, 66.
————. *The Films of Josef von Sternberg.* New York: Museum of
Modern Art, 1966.
————. *The John Ford Movie Mystery.* Bloomington: Indiana
University Press, 1975.
————. "A Movie Is a Movie Is a Movie Is a." In *The Emergence
of Film Art.* Edited by Lewis Jacobs. New York: Hopkinson
& Blake, 1969.
————. *Politics and Cinema.* New York: Columbia University
Press, 1978.
————. *The Primal Screen: Essays on Film and Related Subjects.*
New York: Simon & Schuster, 1973.
————, ed. *Interviews with Film Directors.* New York: Avon
Books, 1969.

Warshow, Robert. *The Immediate Experience: Movies, Comics,
Theatre and Other Aspects of Popular Culture.* New York:
Atheneum, 1971.

Wollen, Peter. "Counter Cinema: Vent d'Est." *Afterimage,* no. 4
(Autumn 1972), 6–16.

————. "*North by Northwest:* A Morphological Analysis." *Film
Form,* 1 (1976), 19–34.
————. "'Ontology' and 'Materialism' in Film." *Screen,* 17
(Spring 1976), 7–23.
————. "Semiotics and *Citizen Kane.*" *Film Reader,* 1 (1976),
9–54.
————. *Signs and Meaning in Cinema.* 3rd ed. Bloomington: In-
diana University Press, 1973.
————. *Sociology and Semiology.* London: British Film Institute,
1969.
————. "Structuralism Implies a Certain Kind of Methodology"
[Interview]. *Film Heritage,* 9 (Summer 1974), 21–29.

――――. "The Two Avant-Gardes." Reprinted in *Edinburgh '76 Magazine*, no. 1, 77–86.

II. Related Studies, Criticism and Theory

Altman, Charles F. "Psychoanalysis and Cinema: The Imaginary Discourse." *Quarterly Review of Film Studies*, 2 (August 1977), 257–272.

Andrew, J. Dudley. *André Bazin*. New York: Oxford University Press, 1978.

Barna, Yon. *Eisenstein*. Bloomington: Indiana University Press, 1973.

Baudry, Jean-Louis. "Ideological Effects of the Basic Cinematographic Apparatus." *Film Quarterly*, 28, no. 2 (Winter 1974–75), 39–47.

Benjamin, Walter. "The Work of Art in the Age of Mechanical Reproduction." In *Illuminations*, edited by Hannah Arendt. New York: Harcourt Brace Jovanovich, 1968.

Bettetini, Gianfranco. *The Language and Technique of the Film*. Translated by David Osmond-Smith. The Hague: Mouton, 1972.

Bogdanovich, Peter. "The Kane Mutiny." *Esquire*, 78, no. 4 (October 1972), 99–105, 180–190.

Braudy, Leo. *The World in a Frame: What We See in Films*. Garden City: Doubleday, 1976.

Cahiers du Cinéma, Editors. "John Ford's *Young Mr. Lincoln*. In *Movies and Methods*, edited by Bill Nichols. Berkeley: University of California Press, 1976.

Cavell, Stanley. *The World Viewed: Reflections on the Ontology of Film*. New York: Viking Press, 1971.

Cawelti, John. *The Six-Gun Mystique*. Bowling Green: Bowling Green University Press, 1971.

Cegarra, Michel. "Cinema and Semiology." *Screen*, 14, nos. 1–2 (Spring-Summer 1973), 129–187.

Corliss, Richard. *Talking Pictures: Screenwriters in the American Cinema*. New York: Penguin Books, 1974.

————, ed. *The Hollywood Screenwriter*. New York: Avon Books, 1972.

Dayan, Daniel. "The Tutor-Code of Classical Cinema." *Film Quarterly*, 28, no. 1 (1974), 22–31.

Dovzhenko, Alexander. *Alexander Dovzhenko: The Poet as Film Maker. Selected Writings*. Edited and translated by Marco Carynnyk. Cambridge, Mass.: MIT Press, 1973.

Eberwein, Robert T. "Spectator-Viewer." *Wide Angle*, 2, no. 2 (1978), 4–9.

Eckert, Charles W. "The English Ciné-Structuralists." *Film Comment*, 9 (May–June 1973), 46–51.

Eco, Umberto. "Articulations of the Cinematic Code." In *Movies and Methods*, edited by Bill Nichols. Berkeley: University of California Press, 1976.

Farber, Manny. *Movies* [original title: *Negative Space*]. New York: Hillstone, 1971.

Ferguson, Otis. *The Film Criticism of Otis Ferguson*. Edited by Robert Wilson. Philadelphia: Temple University Press, 1972.

Geduld, Harry M., and Gottesman, Ronald, eds. *Sergei Eisenstein and Upton Sinclair: The Making and Unmaking of "Que Viva Mexico!"* Bloomington: Indiana University Press, 1970.

Godard, Jean-Luc. *Godard on Godard*. Edited by Jean Narboni and Tom Milne. Translated by Tom Milne. New York: Viking Press, 1972.

Grant, Barry K., ed. *Film Genre: Theory and Criticism.*
Metuchen, N.J.: Scarecrow Press, 1977.

Grierson, John. *Grierson on Documentary.* Edited by Forsyth
Hardy. New York: Praeger, 1971.

Hanhardt, John G., and Harpole, Charles H. "Linguistics, Structuralism, and Semiology: Approaches to Cinema, with a Bibliography." *Film Comment,* 9 (May-June 1973), 52-59.

Heath, Stephen. "Cinema and Suture." *Screen,* 18, no. 4 (Winter
1977-78), 35-47.

_____. "Film and System, Part 1." *Screen,* 16, no. 1 (Spring
1975), 7-77. "Film and System, Part 2." *Screen,* 16, no. 2
(Summer 1975), 91-113.
_____. "Film/Cinetext/Text." *Screen,* 14, nos. 1-2 (Spring-
Summer 1973), 102-127.
_____. "Narrative Space." *Screen,* 17, no. 3 (1976), 68-112.
_____. "Notes on Suture." *Screen,* 18, no. 4 (1977-78), 48-76.
_____. "On Screen, In Frame." *Quarterly Review of Film
Studies,* 1 (1976), 251-265.

Henderson, Brian. "Critique of Ciné-Structuralism, Part 1."
Film Quarterly, 26 (Fall 1973), 25-34. "Critique of Ciné-
Structuralism, Part 2." *Film Quarterly,* 26 (Winter 1973-74),
37-46.

_____. "Metz: *Essais I* and Film Theory." *Film Quarterly,* 28,
no. 3 (Spring 1975), 18-33.
_____. "Segmentation." *Film Quarterly,* 31, no. 1 (Fall 1977),
57-65.
_____. "The Structure of André Bazin's Thought." *Film Quar-
terly,* 25, no. 4 (Summer 1972), 15-27.

Hess, John. "La Politique des Auteurs: Part One, World View as
Aesthetic." *Jumpcut,* no. 1 (May-June 1974), 19-22.
_____. "La Politique des Auteurs: Part Two, Truffaut's Man-
ifesto." *Jumpcut,* no. 2 (July-August 1974), 20-22.

Kaminsky, Stuart M. *American Film Genres: Approaches to a Critical Theory of Popular Film.* Dayton: Pflaum Publications, 1974.

Kawin, Bruce F. *Mindscreen: Bergman, Godard, and First-Person Film.* Princeton: Princeton University Press, 1978.

Kitses, Jim. *Horizons West: Studies in Authorship in the Western.* Bloomington: Indiana University Press, 1970.

Lorentz, Pare. *Lorentz on Film.* New York: Hopkinson & Blake, 1975.

Lotman, Jurij. *Semiotics of Cinema.* Translated by Mark E. Suino. Ann Arbor: University of Michigan Press, 1976.

Luhr, William, and Lehman, Peter. *Authorship and Narrative in the Cinema: Issues in Contemporary Aesthetics and Criticism.* New York: G. P. Putnam's Sons, 1977.

MacBean, James Roy. *Film and Revolution.* Bloomington: Indiana University Press, 1975.

McConnell, Frank D. *The Spoken Seen: Film and the Romantic Imagination.* Baltimore: Johns Hopkins University Press, 1975.

McCormick, Ruth. "Christian Metz and the Semiology Fad." *Cinéaste,* 6, no. 4 (1975), 23–25.

Macdonald, Dwight. *Dwight Macdonald on Movies.* Englewood Cliffs, N.J.: Prentice-Hall, 1969.

Mast, Gerald. *The Comic Mind: Comedy and the Movies.* Indianapolis: Bobbs-Merrill, 1973.

————. *Film/Cinema/Movie.* New York: Harper & Row, 1977.

Mekas, Jonas. *Movie Journal: The Rise of the New American Cinema.* New York: Collier Books, 1972.

Mitry, Jean. *Esthétique et psychologie du cinéma.* Vol. 1: *Les Structures* (1963). Vol. 2: *Les Formes* (1965). Paris: Editions Universitaires.

Montagu, Ivor. *With Eisenstein in Hollywood, a Chapter of Autobiography.* New York: International Publications, 1967.

Moussinac, Léon. *Sergei Eisenstein.* Translated by D. S. Petrey. New York: Crown Publishers, 1970.

Nichols, Bill. "Style, Grammar, and the Movies." *Film Quarterly,* 28, no. 3 (Spring 1975), 33–49.

Nilsen, Vladimir. *The Cinema as a Graphic Art.* Translated by Stephen Garry. New York: Hill & Wang, [1959].

Nizhny, Vladimir. *Lessons with Eisenstein.* Edited and translated by Ivor Montagu and Jay Leyda. New York: Hill & Wang, 1969.

Oudart, Jean-Pierre. "Cinema and Suture." *Screen,* 18, no. 4 (1977–78), 35–47.

Panofsky, Erwin. "Style and Medium in the Motion Pictures." In *Film Theory and Criticism,* edited by Gerald Mast and Marshall Cohen. New York: Oxford University Press, 1974.

Pasolini, Pier Paolo. "The Cinema of Poetry." *Cahiers du Cinéma in English,* 6 (December 1966), 34–43.

———. *Pasolini on Pasolini.* Edited by Oswald Stack. Bloomington: Indiana University Press, 1970.
———. "The Pesaro Papers." *Cinim,* 3 (Spring 1969), 6–11.

Potamkin, Harry Alan. *The Compound Cinema: The Film Writings of Harry Alan Potamkin.* Edited by Lewis Jacobs. New York: Teachers College Press, 1977.

Powdermaker, Hortense. *Hollywood: The Dream Factory. An Anthropologist Looks at Movie-Makers.* Boston: Little, Brown & Co., 1950.

Rohdie, Sam. "Metz and Film Semiotics: Opening the Field." *Jumpcut*, no. 7 (May–July 1975), 22–24.

Rothman, William. "Against the System of the Suture." *Film Quarterly*, 29, no. 1 (Fall 1975), 45–50.

Sitney, P. Adams. *Visionary Film: The American Avant-Garde*. New York: Oxford University Press, 1974.

Thomson, David. *Movie Man*. New York: Stein & Day, 1969.

Truffaut, François. *The Films in My Life*. Translated by Leonard Mayhew. New York: Simon & Schuster, 1978.

Wright, Will. *Sixguns and Society: A Structural Study of the Western*. Berkeley: University of California Press, 1975.

Young, Vernon. *On Film: Unpopular Essays on a Popular Art*. New York: Times Books, 1972.

Youngblood, Gene. *Expanded Cinema*. New York: E. P. Dutton, 1970.

III. *Books on Film Theory and Criticism*

Andrew, J. Dudley. *The Major Film Theories*. New York: Oxford University Press, 1976.

Murray, Edward. *Nine American Film Critics*. New York: Frederick Ungar, 1975.

Tudor, Andrew, *Theories of Film*. New York: Viking Press, 1973.

IV. *Anthologies of Film Criticism*

Battock, Gregory, ed. *The New American Cinema*. New York: E. P. Dutton, 1967.

Bellone, Julius, ed. *Renaissance of the Film*. New York: Collier Books, 1970.

Cameron, Ian, ed. *Movie Reader*. New York: Praeger, 1972.

————, ed. *Second Wave*. New York: Praeger, 1971.

Cooke, Alistair, ed. *Garbo and the Night Watchmen*. New York: McGraw Hill, 1971.

Graham, Peter, ed. *The New Wave*. Garden City: Doubleday, 1968.

Hochman, Stanley, ed. *A Library of Film Criticism*. New York: Frederick Ungar, 1974.

Jacobs, Lewis, ed. *The Documentary Tradition: From Nanook to Woodstock*. New York: Hopkinson & Blake, 1971.

————, ed. *The Emergence of Film Art*. New York: Hopkinson & Blake, 1969.

————, ed. *Introduction to the Art of the Movies*. New York: Noonday Press, Farrar, Straus & Giroux, 1960.

————, ed. *The Movies as Medium*. New York: Noonday Press, Farrar, Straus & Giroux, 1970.

Kauffmann, Stanley, and Henstell, Bruce, eds. *American Film Criticism: From the Beginnings to "Citizen Kane."* New York: Liveright, 1972.

MacCann, Richard Dyer, ed. *Film: A Montage of Theories*. New York: E. P. Dutton, 1966.

McCarthy, Todd, and Flynn, Charles, eds. *Kings of the B's: Working within the Hollywood System*. New York: E. P. Dutton, 1975.

Mast, Gerald, and Cohen, Marshall, eds. *Film Theory and Criticism: Introductory Readings*. New York: Oxford University Press, 1974.

Nachbar, Jack, ed. *Focus on the Western*. Englewood Cliffs, N.J.: Prentice-Hall, 1974.

Nichols, Bill, ed. *Movies and Methods*. Berkeley: University of California Press, 1976.

Robinson, W. R., ed. *Man and the Movies*. Baltimore: Penguin Books, 1969.

Sitney, P. Adams, ed. *The Avant-Garde Film: A Reader of Theory and Criticism*. New York: New York University Press, 1978.

————, ed. *Film Culture Reader*. New York: Praeger, 1970.

Solomon, Stanley J. *The Classic Cinema: Essays in Criticism*. New York: Harcourt Brace Jovanovich, 1973.

Talbot, Daniel, ed. *Film: An Anthology*. Berkeley: University of California Press, 1969.

V. *Film and the Other Arts*

Bluestone, George. *Novels into Film*. Berkeley: University of California Press, 1971.

Eckert, Charles, ed. *Focus on Shakespearean Films*. Englewood Cliffs, N.J.: Prentice-Hall, 1972.

Fell, John. *Film and the Narrative Tradition*. Norman: University of Oklahoma Press, 1974.

Hurt, James, ed. *Focus on Film and Theatre*. Englewood Cliffs, N.J.: Prentice-Hall, 1974.

Jorgens, Jack. *Shakespeare on Film*. Bloomington: Indiana University Press, 1977.

Nicoll, Allardyce. *Film and Theatre*. New York: Thomas Y. Crowell, 1937.

Richardson, Robert. *Literature and Film*. Bloomington: Indiana University Press, 1969.

Scharf, Aaron. *Art and Photography*. Baltimore: Penguin Books, 1974.

Spiegel, Alan. *Fiction and the Camera Eye: Visual Consciousness in Film and the Modern Novel*. Charlottesville: University Press of Virginia, 1975.

Vardac, A. Nicholas. *Stage to Screen: Theatrical Method from Garrick to Griffith*. New York: B. Blom, 1968.

Wagner, Geoffrey. *The Novel and the Cinema*. Rutherford, N.J.: Fairleigh Dickinson University Press, 1975.

VI. *Additional Reading*

Barthes, Roland. *Mythologies*. Translated by Annette Lavers. New York: Hill & Wang, n.d.

————. "The Third Meaning." In *Image-Music-Text*. Translated by Stephen Heath. New York: Hill & Wang, 1977.
————. *Writing Degree Zero* and *Elements of Semiology*. Translated by Annette Lavers and Colin Smith. Boston: Beacon Press, 1970.

De George, Richard, and De George, Fernande, eds. *The Structuralists from Marx to Lévi-Strauss*. Garden City: Anchor Books, 1972.

Eco, Umberto. *A Theory of Semiotics*. Bloomington: Indiana University Press, 1976.

Ehrmann, Jacques, ed. *Structuralism*. Garden City: Anchor Books, 1970.

Jakobson, Roman. "Linguistics and Poetics." In *The Structuralists from Marx to Lévi-Strauss*, edited by Richard and Fernande De George. Garden City: Anchor Books, 1972.

————. "Two Aspects of Language and Two Types of Aphasic Disturbances." In *Selected Writings*, vol. 2. The Hague: Mouton, 1971.

Jameson, Fredric. *The Prison House of Language: A Critical Account of Structuralism and Russian Formalism.* Princeton: Princeton University Press, 1972.

Lacan, Jacques. *Ecrits: A Selection.* Translated by Alan Sheridan. New York: W. W. Norton, 1977.

_____. *The Four Fundamental Concepts of Psycho-Analysis.* Edited by Jacques-Alain Miller. Translated by Alan Sheridan. New York: W. W. Norton, 1978.

_____. *The Language of the Self: The Function of Language in Psychoanalysis.* Edited and translated by Anthony Wilden. New York: Delta Books, 1968.

Lane, Michael, ed. *Introduction to Structuralism.* New York: Basic Books, 1970.

Lévi-Strauss, Claude. "Four Winnebago Myths." In *Culture in History: Essays in Honor of Paul Radin.* Edited by Stanley Diamond. New York: Columbia University Press, 1960.

_____. "The Structural Study of Myth." *Journal of American Folklore,* 78 (October-December 1955), 428–444.

Macksey, Richard, and Donato, Eugenio, eds. *The Structuralist Controversy: The Languages of Criticism and the Sciences of Man.* Baltimore: Johns Hopkins University Press, 1972.

VII. *Bibliographies*

Ellis, Jack C.; Derry, Charles; and Kern, Sharon. *The Film Book Bibliography 1940–1975.* Metuchen, N.J.: Scarecrow Press, 1978.

Gerlach, John, and Gerlach, Lana. *The Critical Index: A Bibliography of Articles on Film in English, 1946–1973, Arranged by Names and Topics.* New York: Teachers College Press, 1974.

Heinzkill, Richard. *Film Criticism: An Index to Critics' Anthologies.* Metuchen, N.J.: Scarecrow Press, 1975.

Kay, Karyn, and Perry, Gerald. *Women and the Cinema: A Critical Anthology.* New York: E. P. Dutton, 1977.

Kowalski, Rosemary. *Women and Film: A Bibliography.* Metuchen, N.J.: Scarecrow Press, 1976.

MacCann, Richard Dyer, and Perry, Edward S. *The New Film Index: A Bibliography of Magazine Articles in English, 1930–1970.* New York: E. P. Dutton, 1975.

Powers, Anne. *Blacks in American Movies: A Selected Bibliography.* Metuchen, N.J.: Scarecrow Press, 1974.

GENERAL INDEX

FILM INDEX